AF412628

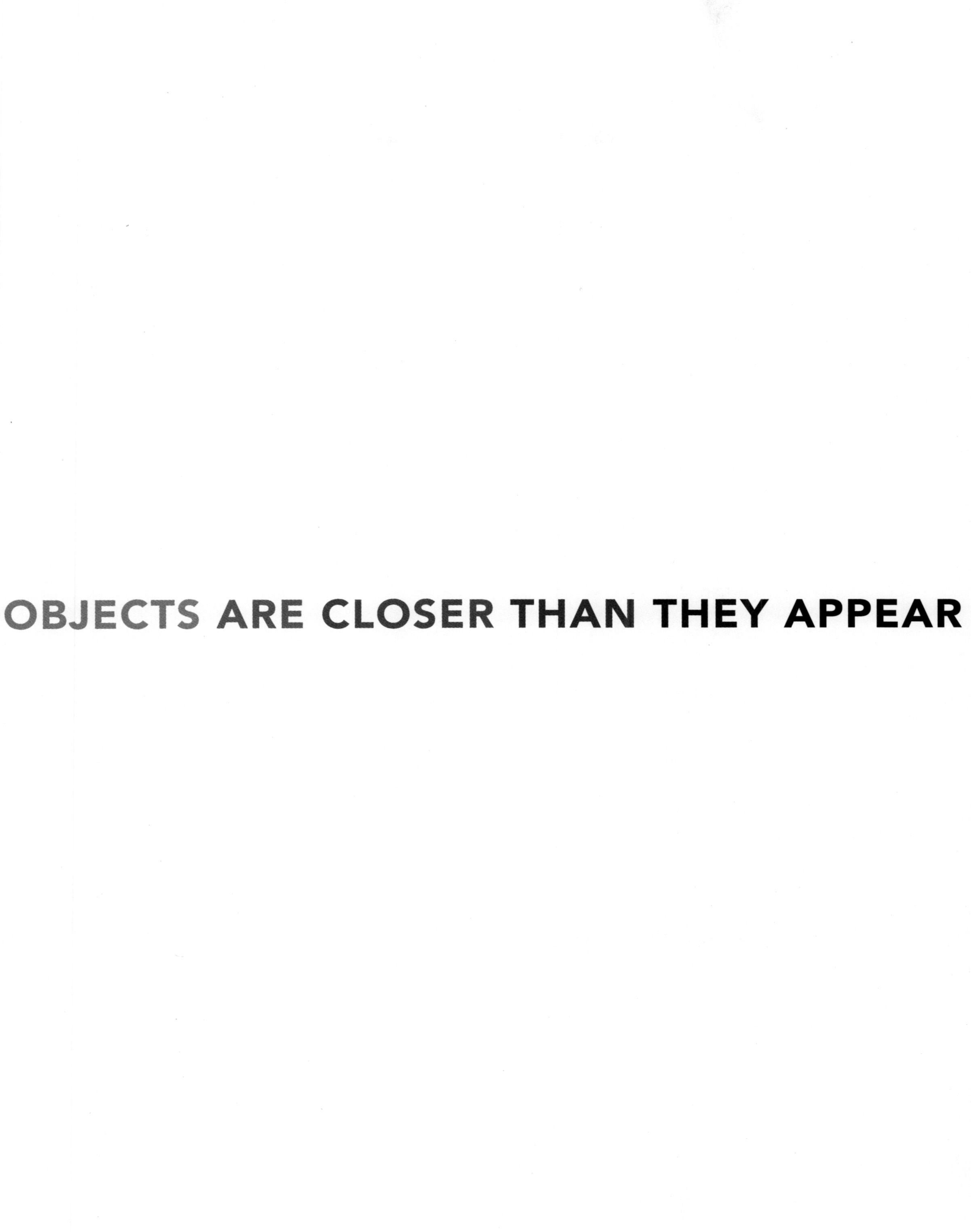
OBJECTS ARE CLOSER THAN THEY APPEAR

OBJECTS ARE CLOSE

MANFRED MÜLLER
THAN THEY APPEAR

ESSAYS BY

CLAUDIA BOHN-SPECTOR
HOWARD N. FOX

MARQUAND BOOKS, Seattle

AGAIN ROSE

CONTENTS

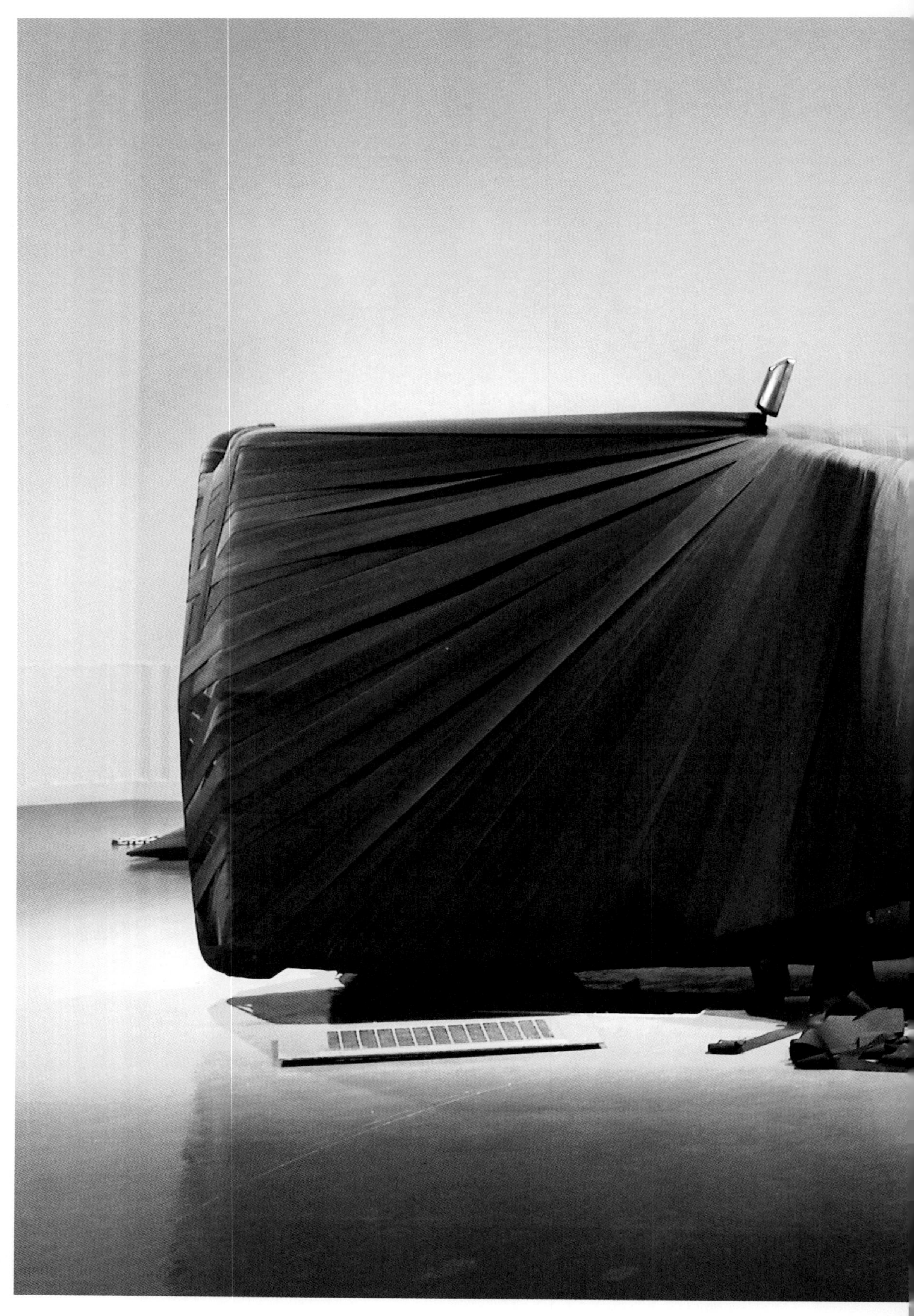

Body Shop, 2003

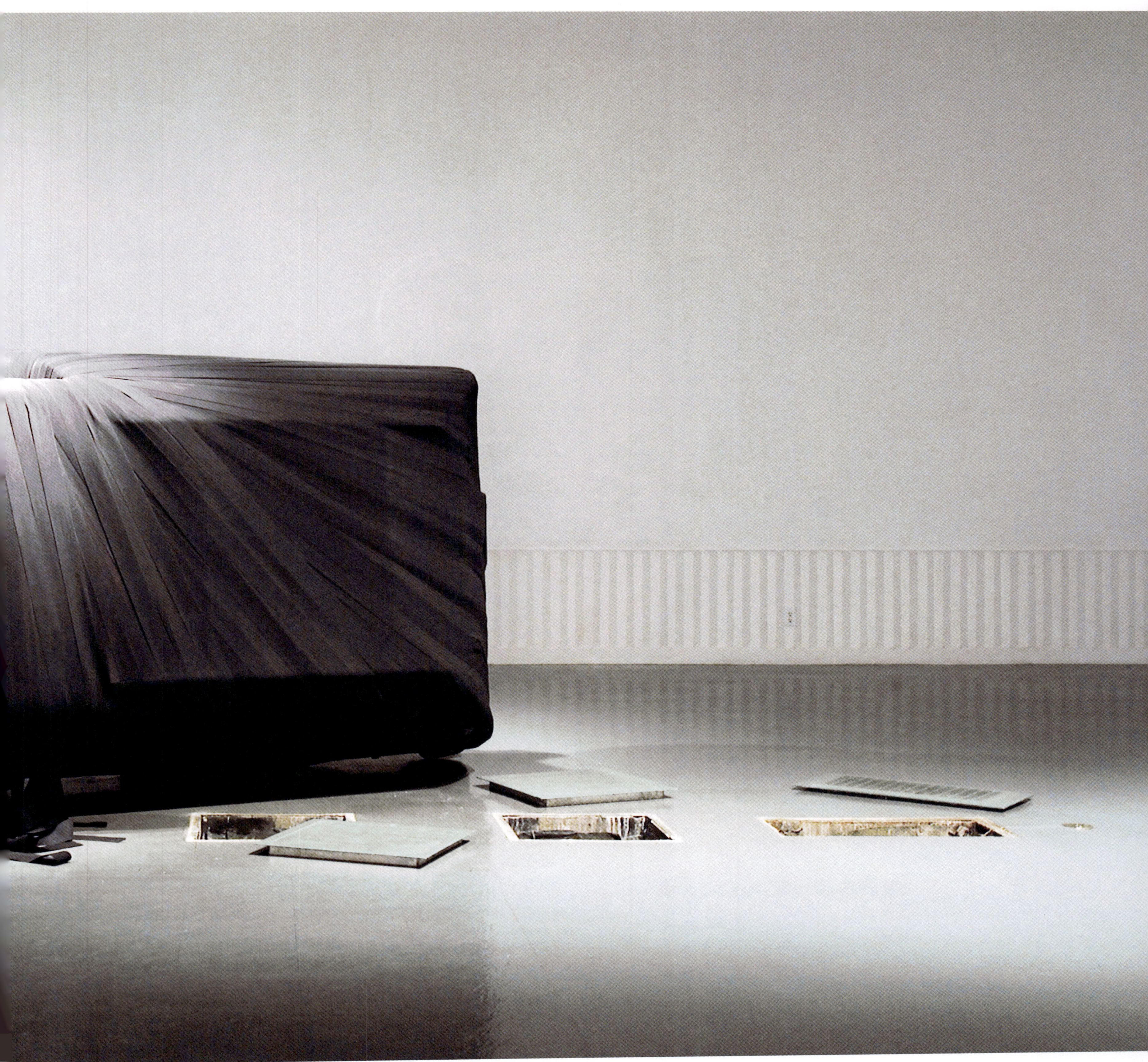

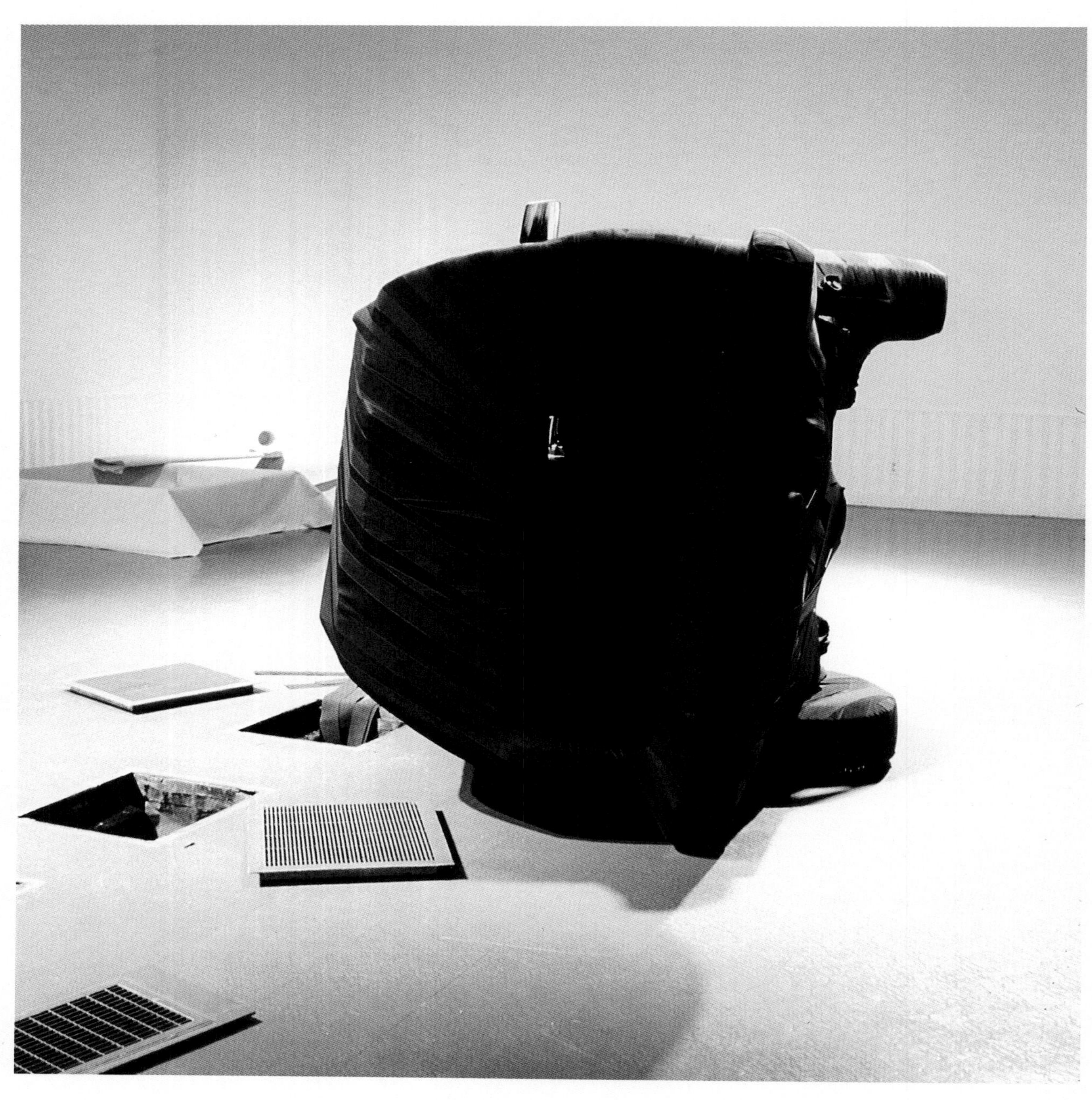

Body Shop, 2003

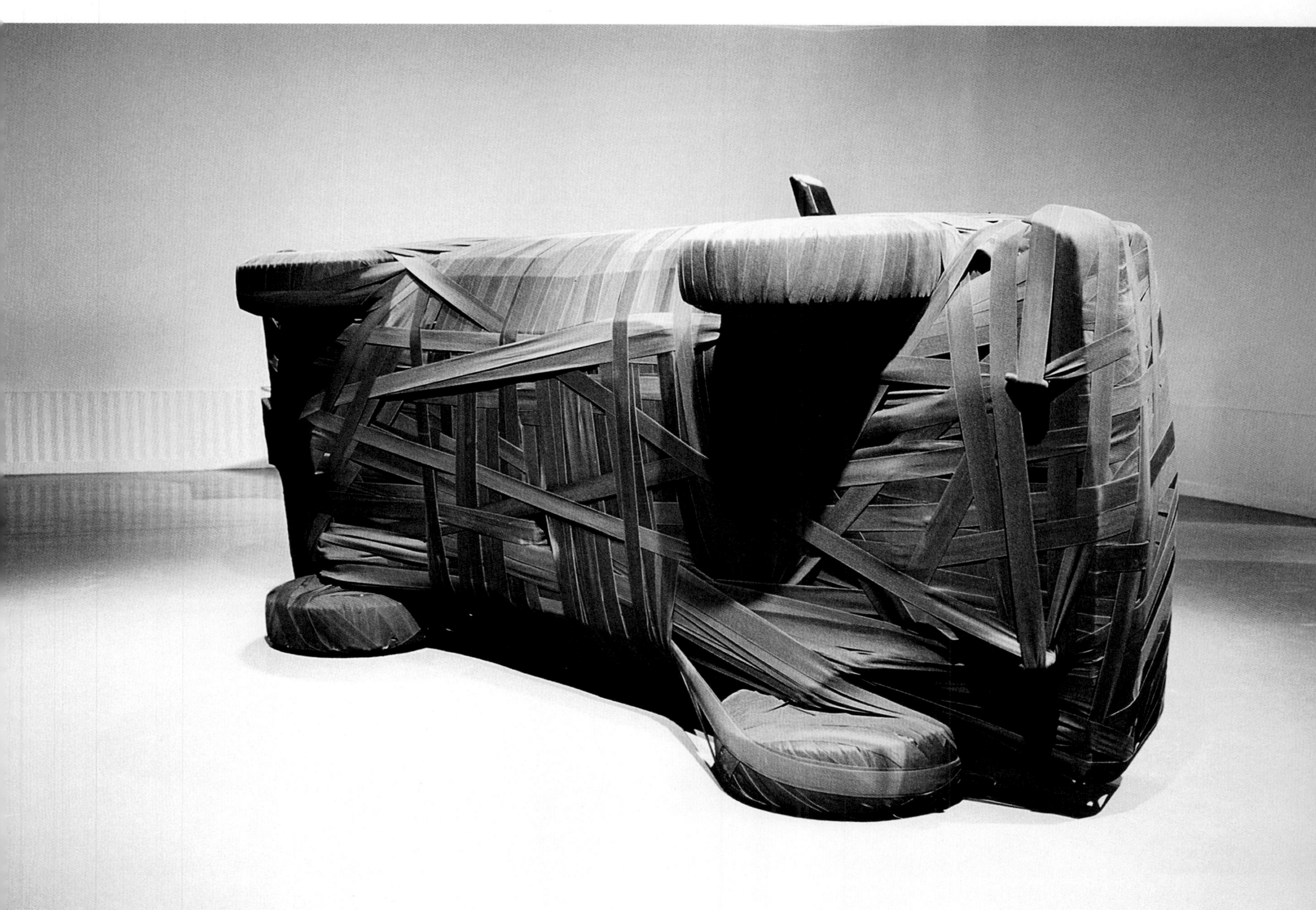

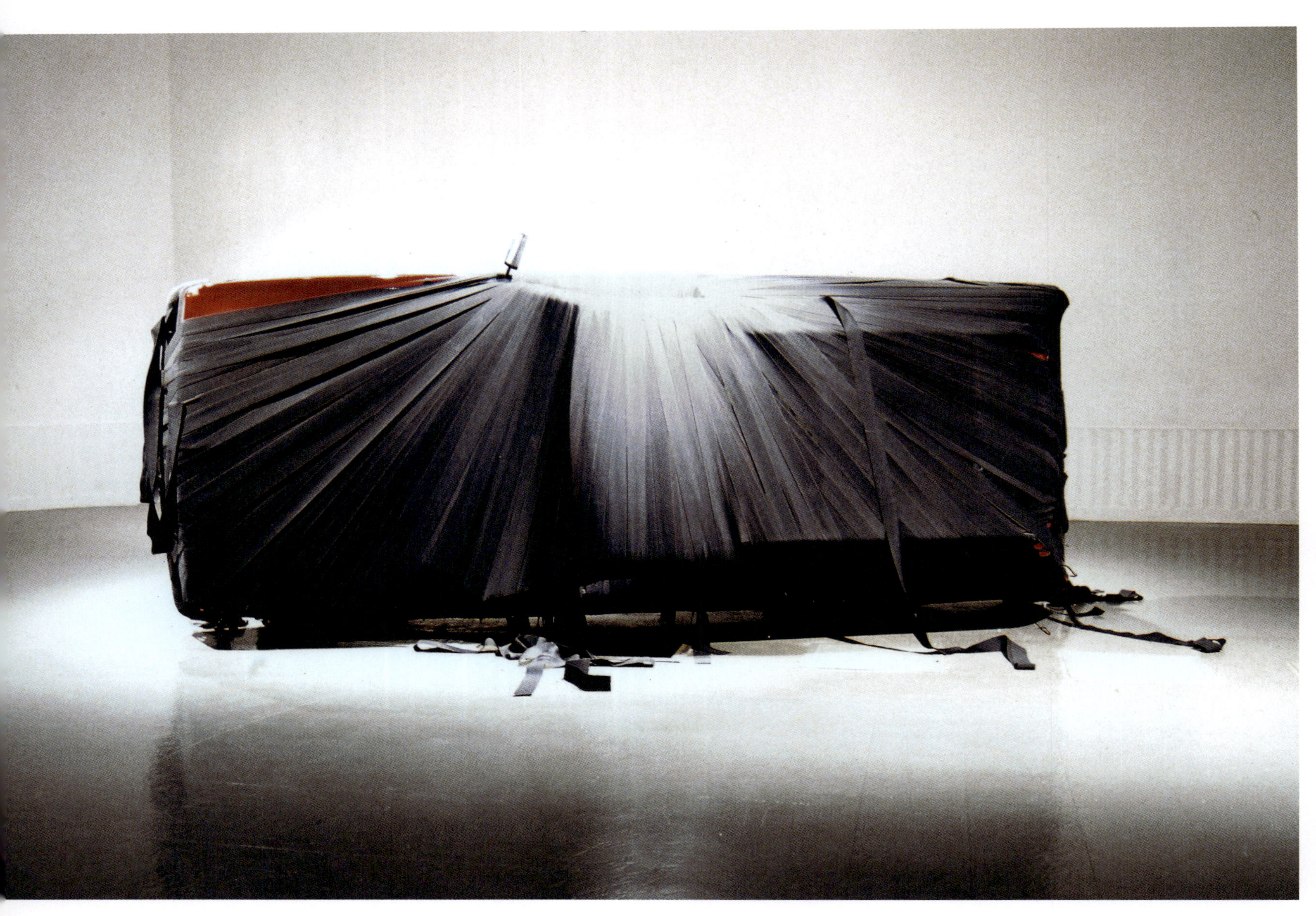

Body Shop, downstage sequenced perfomance, 2003

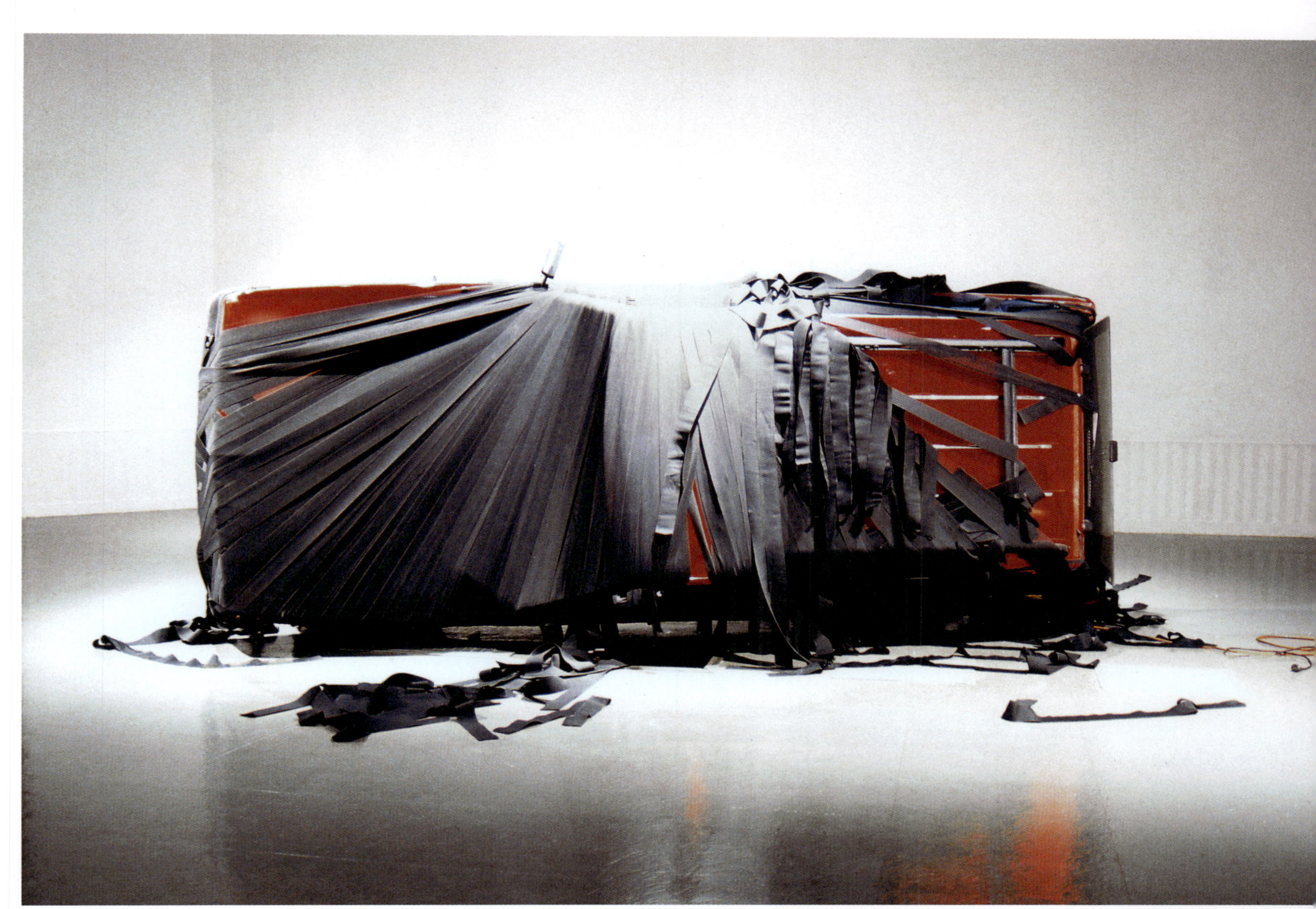

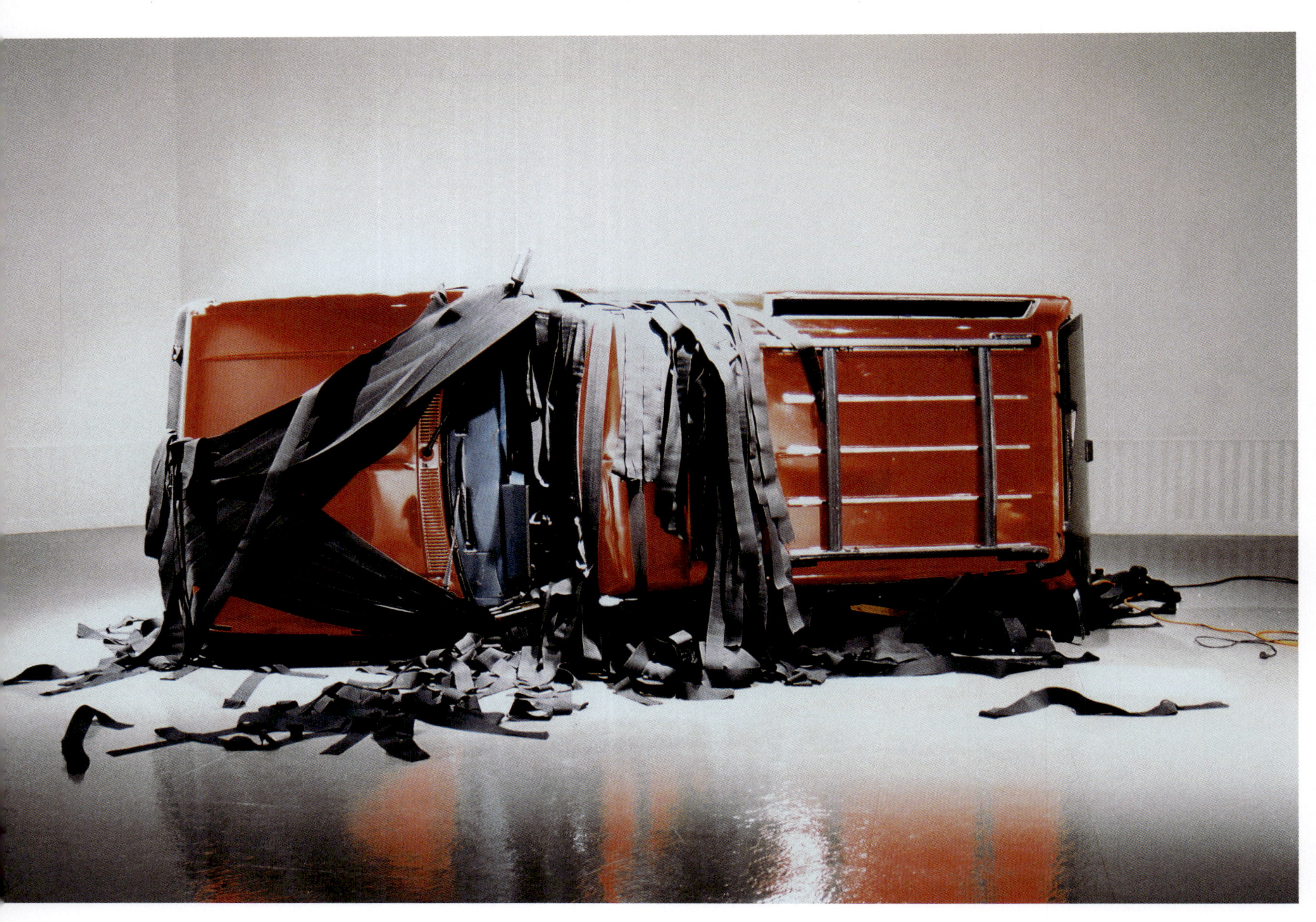

Body Shop, downstage sequenced performance, 2003

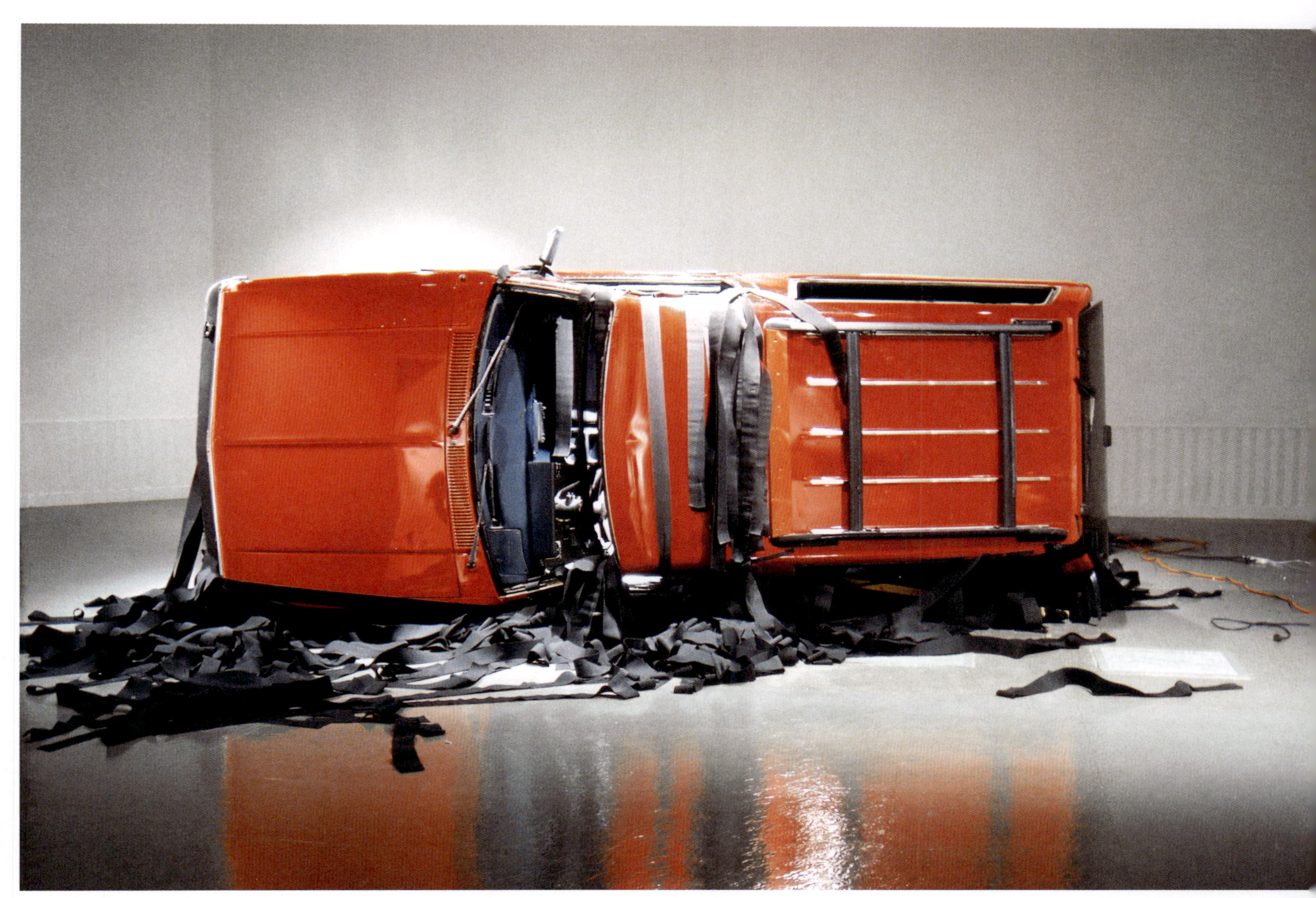

MANFRED MÜLLER: THINGS TO REMEMBER

CLAUDIA BOHN-SPECTOR

It was mid-October 1999. Manfred Müller worked all night in his studio at the Santa Monica Airport and then took to the road at four o'clock in the morning to deliver an artwork to a corporate client in San Francisco. A native of Düsseldorf, Germany, who relocated to Los Angeles ten years earlier, he stood at the height of his career as a visual artist, prolifically creating, exhibiting, and selling work in the United States and in Europe. But hurtling along Interstate 5 that night, tired and overworked, Müller, and his fast-paced cosmopolitan life, would come to a sudden standstill. Startled by a passing car that appeared to be cutting him off, he slammed on the brakes of his Ford Explorer and spun out of control. As the SUV overturned, a box flew forward from the back and knocked him unconscious. The Explorer landed upside down in a field by the side of the highway. Help arrived within minutes and Müller was airlifted to a nearby hospital. Severely injured, he didn't regain consciousness until days after the accident, confronted with the realization that his art and his life would never be quite the same.

Up until that moment, Müller's near-twenty-year career as an artist had unfolded along paths equally predictable and unexpected. Born on April 8, 1950, in Düsseldorf, in the heart of the industrial Rhine-Ruhr region of northwestern Germany, Müller had grown up very much a product of his time. Hardworking, disciplined, and resourceful, with a talent for technical proficiency and creative ideas, he had weathered all the trials and tribulations of a post–World War II German upbringing. His parents, Valentin and Annemarie, were busy rebuilding their war-torn lives when they met in Düsseldorf in 1947. Orphaned at age four, Müller's father was a child of the streets, a radical survivor, who joined gangs of small kids to stay alive. Lacking a formal education, he eventually became a house painter and a "black-market kind of guy," an ardent social democrat, atheist, and opponent of the Nazi regime, who avoided military service by hiding in basements and moving around the country.[1] Müller's mother had a softer edge. Well educated and devoutly Catholic, she had arrived in West Germany as a war refugee from East Prussia with just a suitcase of belongings. Despite their parents' early challenges, Manfred and his younger brother, Wolfgang, grew up in a loving and supportive home. Conversations around the kitchen table often revolved around leftist politics and the pros and cons of organized religion, subjects on which their father held strong opinions. Education, too, was important to Valentin, and he encouraged his sons to excel in school and seek out solid professional careers.

The younger Müller, however, hardly seemed cut out for the rigors of
academic life. Athletic, musical, and artistically gifted, he tired of school
as a teenager and apprenticed as a technical draftsman, a career choice
that was based on a misunderstanding. "Being a technical draftsman," he
recalled, "had nothing to do with *drawing*, which is what I had in mind. I
wanted to do artistic drawings, more like an illustrator." He nevertheless
completed his apprenticeship, maturing on the job and acquiring a lasting
appreciation for technical precision, architecture, and the intricacies of
mechanical engineering, which would serve him well later in life. Shaped
by his family's leftist politics, he also became an avid union organizer,
stirring his fellow apprentices into political action. In 1970, at the age of
twenty, he switched his focus to graphic design, a passion that may have
been fueled by his father's work as a poster of billboards. "He was out
and about even in the coldest winter, working with water and glue," notes
Müller. "He always came home with ads and posters that he liked, and
he collected them. . . . Maybe this was why I became involved in graphic
design." Encouraged by a friend, he enrolled at the Fachhochschule
Düsseldorf, a school of applied science, and began his studies in visual
communication, including all aspects of product design, art history,
photography, and illustration. One of his favorite professors, the artist
and illustrator Rudi Assmann, introduced him to nineteenth-century
Russian Realism, Expressionism, and the art of David Hockney. Müller
started to live alone at this time, renting a small room on Drakestrasse in
Oberkassel, on the left bank of the Rhine. In a remarkable coincidence
and foreshadowing, his neighbor down the street was none other than
Joseph Beuys (1921–1986), the embattled professor and art shaman at the
Kunstakademie Düsseldorf, a man that Müller was very eager to meet.

> I had friends who were part of the academy. They always gave me
> some kind of echo of what was happening there. . . . I didn't know
> [Beuys] then, but I knew that something very interesting was going
> on behind that gate. . . . One day I asked Beuys if I could visit him,
> and he very harshly said: "No way, I have no time." I met him later
> [at the Kunstakademie], and he was a big influence on me.

When Müller arrived at the Kunstakademie in 1976, his career as a
fine artist began in earnest. Founded in 1773, the academy is one of
the premier art schools in Europe, and its impact on Müller's work can
hardly be overstated. The abstract sculptor Norbert Kricke was the
director of the school, and Müller's fellow students included some of the

best-known German artists working today: Katharina Fritsch, Andreas Gursky, Candida Höfer, Axel Hütte, Markus Oehlen, and Thomas Ruff, to name just a few. In a remarkable stroke of good fortune, Müller avoided introductory course work when the pioneering photography and performance artist Klaus Rinke (born 1939) invited him to join his master class. Rinke had abandoned painting in 1966 in favor of radical body-based performances, which profoundly shaped Müller's early studies. "He was tough," Müller recalls. "I wouldn't even say he was a teacher. The idea was to bring young artists into the academy and expose them, not to a strict curriculum, but to work with experienced creative professionals. The program at the academy in Düsseldorf was very loose and unstructured." Only a few months into the program, Müller was given the opportunity to stage his first public performance (figs. 1–2).

> I had done some performance works, which were basically a series of sequential photographs called *Selbstschutz-Strategien* (Self-defense strategies), where I poured ice water on naked bodies or popped a balloon in your face without any warning. . . . For my performance at the academy, I brought in a dog that had been trained to attack people. We had maybe two, three hundred people sitting around the classroom. And the handler would yell again and again: "Bleiben Sie stehen oder ich schick' den Hund!" (Freeze or I'll send the dog!). And the dog was barking, of course, and going crazy. Then he'd release the dog. I was young and could easily wrestle with a dog. Then I'd ask him to call off the dog and repeat this, five or six times, for increased dramatic effect. I was falling all over the audience. It was very dangerous.

Heavily influenced by Rinke and the performances of Marina Abramović and Bruce Nauman that he had seen locally, Müller, a newcomer eager to make a splash, pulled out all the stops. His relationship with Rinke, tenuous from the start, did not survive the emulative gesture, however. Stumped by his student's sudden prominence and outspoken membership in the leftist Spartacus Student League, Rinke dismissed Müller from his class within a month in a serious blow to the young artist's ego. Still basking in the success of his first performance, Müller suddenly found himself back in basic training, needing to attract another mentor for his senior studies. Eventually, the sculptor Erwin Heerich (1922–2004) took him on as a student and assistant, and the two embarked on a fruitful, near-seven-year partnership that had a lasting effect on Müller's work and career. In the 1950s, Heerich had also studied at the Kunstakademie Düsseldorf, where he and his friend Beuys attended the master class of Ewald Mataré

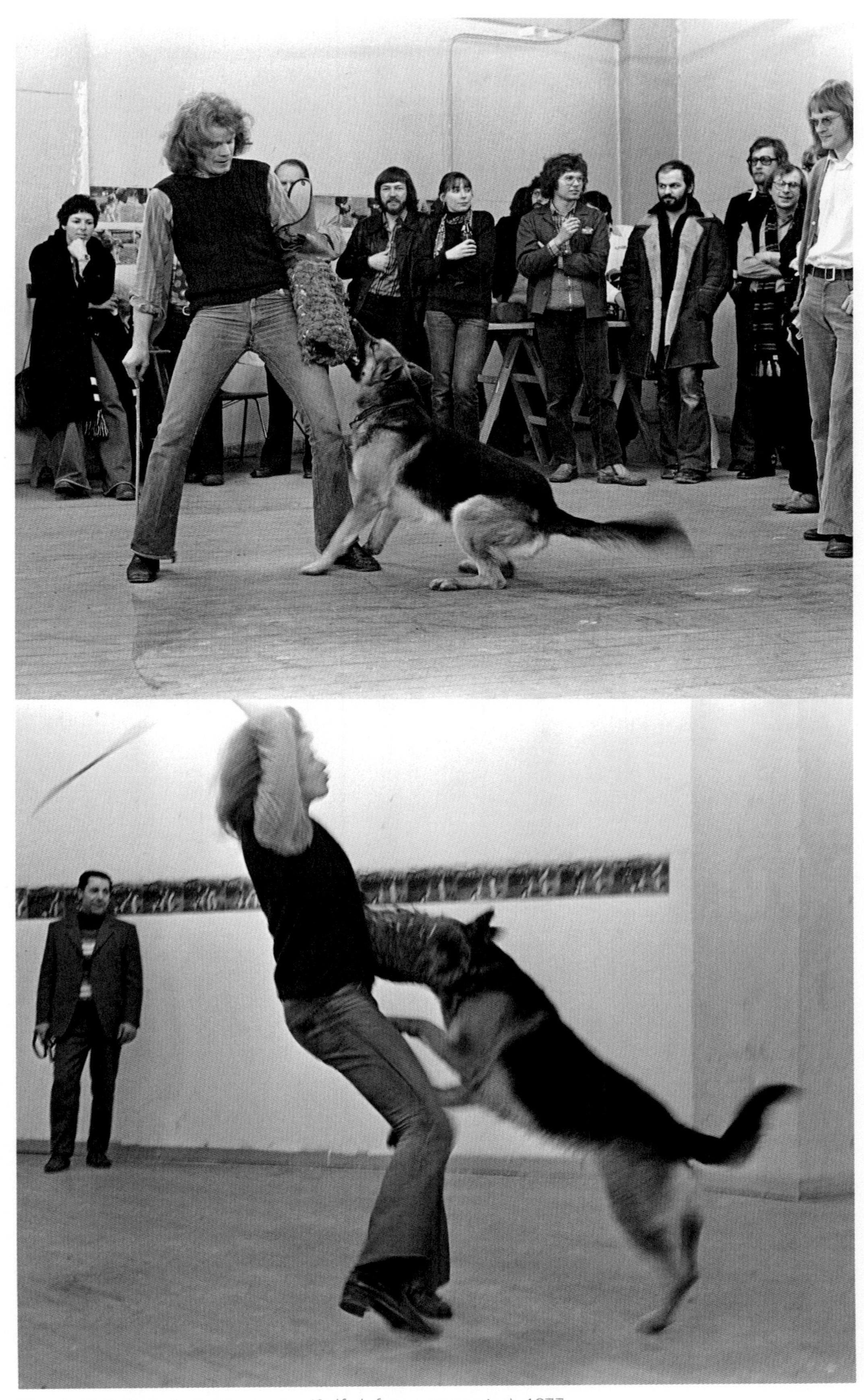

Figs. 1, 2. *Selbstschutz-Strategien* (Self-defense strategies), 1977

(1887–1965), an acclaimed German painter and sculptor denounced by the Nazis as "degenerate." After the war, Mataré was appointed the director of the school, a position he quickly resigned when he realized that many of his fellow professors had pursued successful careers under the Nazi regime. He remained at the academy as a teacher, however, and Heerich and Beuys soon emerged as two of his most prominent students. More than twenty years later, Müller drew deep inspiration from both of them, creating an art that to this day is delicately poised between Heerich's elegant architectural minimalism and Beuys's layered, metaphorical spirituality.

Heerich's abstract sculptures, as Müller came to know them, reflect an abiding concern with simple geometric form. Preferring to work with plain, everyday materials, Heerich noted that for him, "cardboard, like [the plastic] polystyrene, had no specifically aesthetic or historical connotations. The materials are value-neutral to the largest possible extent."[2] An artist with a conceptual outlook on his work, Heerich was not concerned with creating traditional art objects but "with making an idea material in terms of a specific problem: how space can be presented and formed."[3] A two-time documenta participant, Heerich imparted to Müller not only the gift of a supportive partnership but also an enduring appreciation for architecture, simple materials, unadorned compositions, and exacting craftsmanship, which successfully engaged Müller's earlier training as a technical draftsman. "Whatever I showed him," Müller notes, "Heerich was always positive and constructive. He . . . was the greatest motivator and reinforcer." Initially, Heerich's formidable influence resulted in work that closely resembled the teacher's own, like Müller's *Studio Objekte* (Studio objects) from 1981 and 1982. But eventually, Müller conceived of complex geometric wall, floor, and table sculptures using recycled materials, such as *Architektonische Skulptur Studien* (Architectural sculpture studies) of 1984 (figs. 3–4), which took his mentor's legacy in new, interactive directions. Like Gordon Matta-Clark, whose work Müller had seen for the first time at an exhibition in Cologne in 1978, Müller created pieces that actively engaged their architectural settings—punching holes in floors, busting through walls, or jutting out of doors and windows—in an effort to expand the sculptures' physical realm.[4] This approach later led Müller to create elaborate sculptural installations that hovered indeterminately between ready-made assemblage, quiet reflection, and theatrical performance, revealing the significant influence of Müller's other great inspiration, Beuys.

From Beuys, Müller derived a penchant for philosophical inquiry, narration, ritual, and, eventually, a self-reflexive approach that harnessed personal

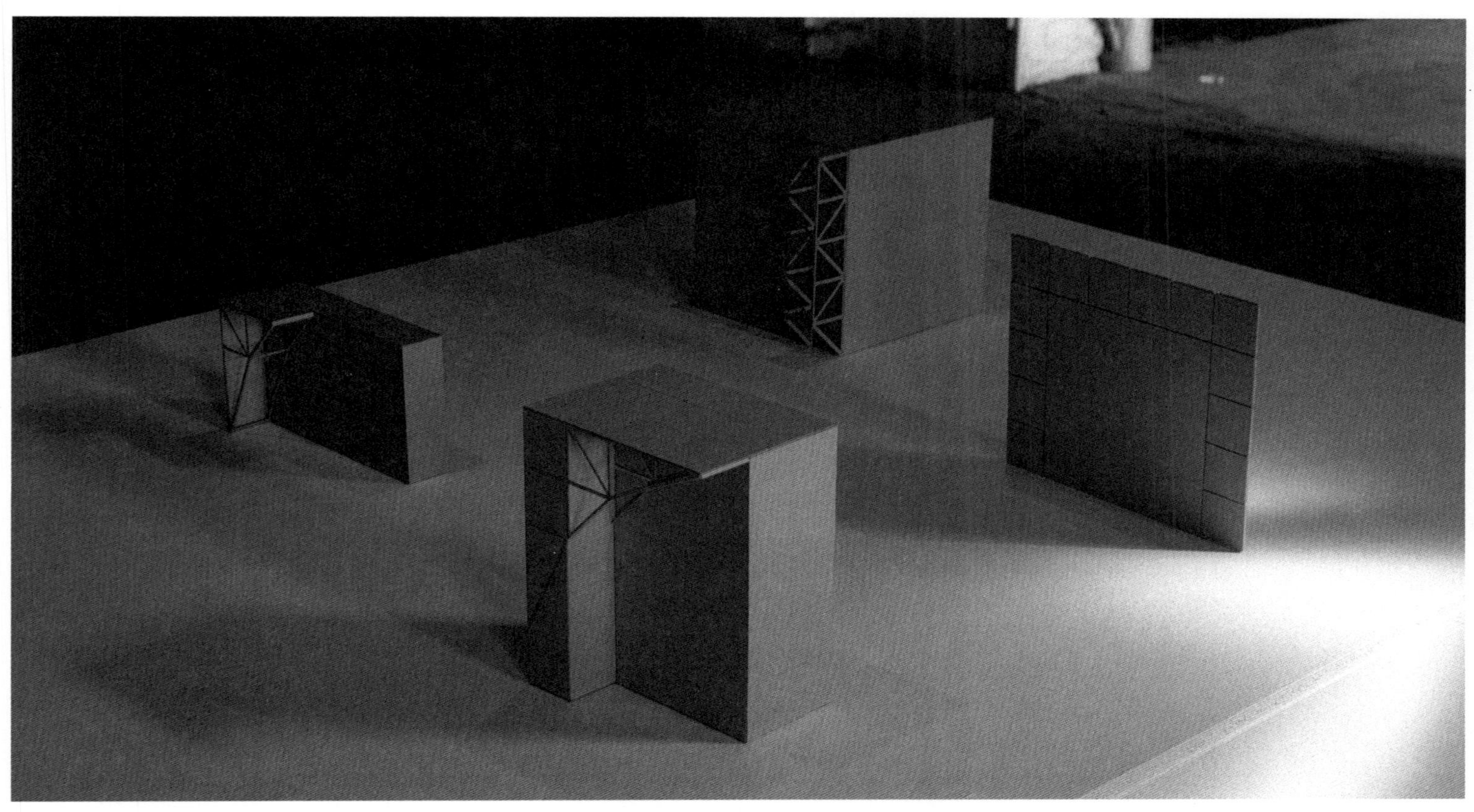

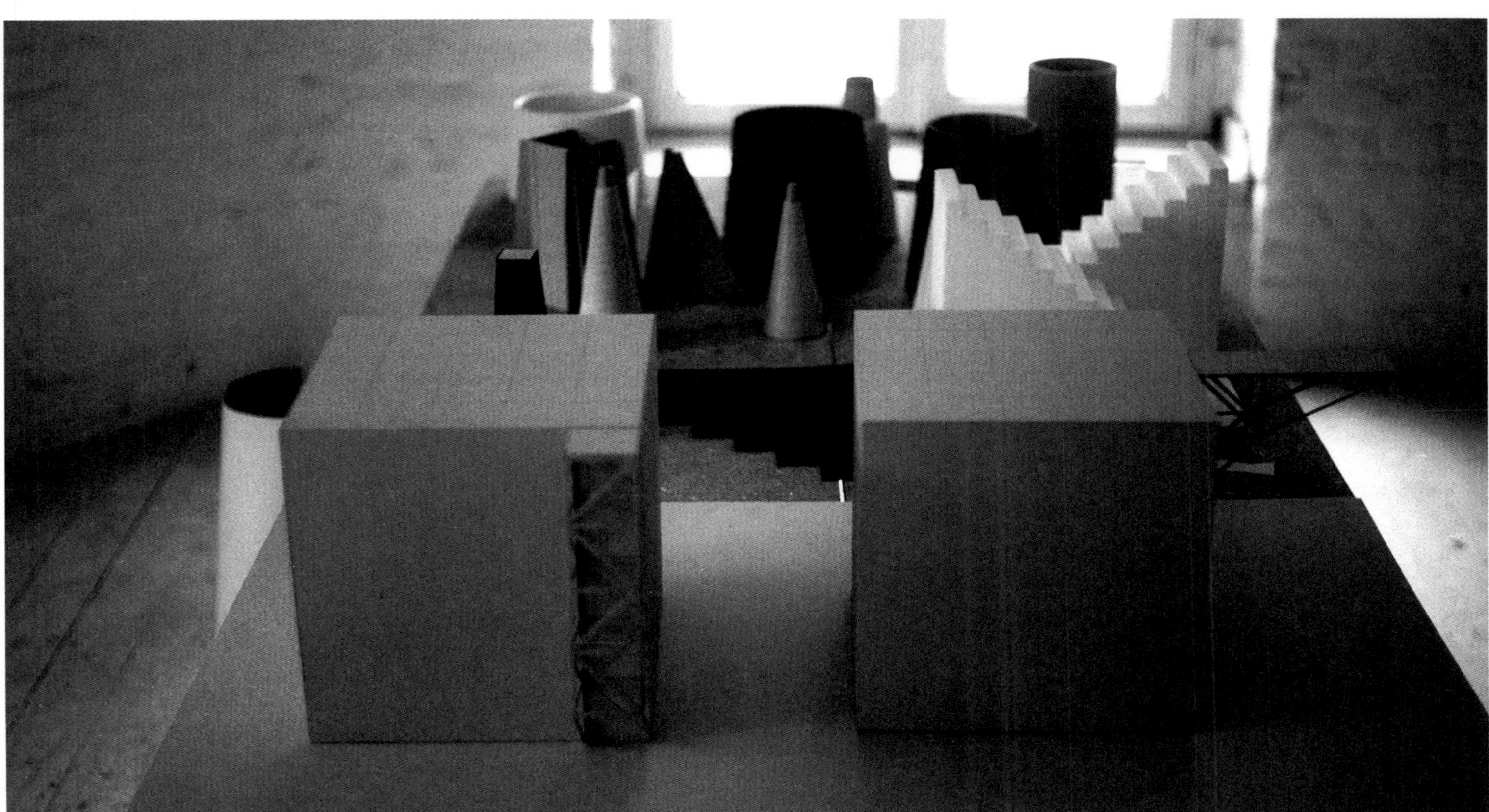

Figs. 3, 4. *Architektonische Skulptur Studien* (Architectural sculpture studies), 1984

trauma in the pursuit of artistic expression. "Joseph Beuys definitely influenced that metaphorical part of my work," Müller says. "You could not live in this area, in Düsseldorf, at this time and not be influenced by Joseph Beuys. . . . There is a deep psychology that is brought out by seeing his work." Engaged in impassioned and often acrimonious debate with his public, Beuys had already been fired from his position at the academy when Müller and other students assisted him during the installation of the exhibition *Prospekt/Retrospekt* (Prospect/retrospect) at the Kunsthalle Düsseldorf in 1976. Mesmerized by the older artist's brilliance and charisma, Müller closely observed how "he twisted things and loaded them with artistic energy . . . how effortless it was for him to bring things together that you would have never thought about before. That made me a Joseph Beuys fan for a time, but [ultimately] that was not the way I wanted to go. You have this iconic work in front of you, and you have no way to do that." Nevertheless, Beuys's sprawling installation *Honigpumpe am Arbeitsplatz* (Honey pump in the workplace) at documenta 6 in 1977 inspired Müller, who embarked on projects like *Schubkarre* (Wheelbarrow, 1981; fig. 5), *Pflüger auf Grund* (Plow on ground, 1982; fig. 6), and *Krater* (Crater, 1981; fig. 7), which are all significantly indebted to Beuys's work. *Krater* was an ephemeral installation involving a large circular mound of black sand, a shallow pool of water, and a blowtorch hissing a tiny flame across the water's reflective surface. This provocative work elegantly blended natural and man-made materials in a philosophical musing on the elements—water, earth, and fire—and industrial modes of production native to the Rhine-Ruhr region, an area that Müller knew well.

Having grown up near the Ruhrgebiet, the Rust Belt of Germany, Müller had an innate affinity for the crude allure of industrial settings. "I got really into these metaphors and ideas about soil, coal, steel, and gas," he says. "I find it captivating: the raw materials of industrial production." Another inspiration for his emerging works were the hard-edged photographs of Bernd and Hilla Becher, who documented the area's vernacular architecture—blast furnaces, kilns, smokestacks, silos, and winding towers—in iconic black-and-white images. Müller particularly gravitated to the photographers' interpretation of these ordinary constructions as "anonymous sculptures," which was also the title of their first and hugely influential book of photographs, published in 1969.[5] The Bechers had started teaching at the Kunstakademie Düsseldorf the same year that Müller enrolled there. Some of their students—Andreas Gursky, Axel Hütte, Thomas Ruff, and Jörg Sasse—supplemented their incomes by taking pictures of their fellow students'

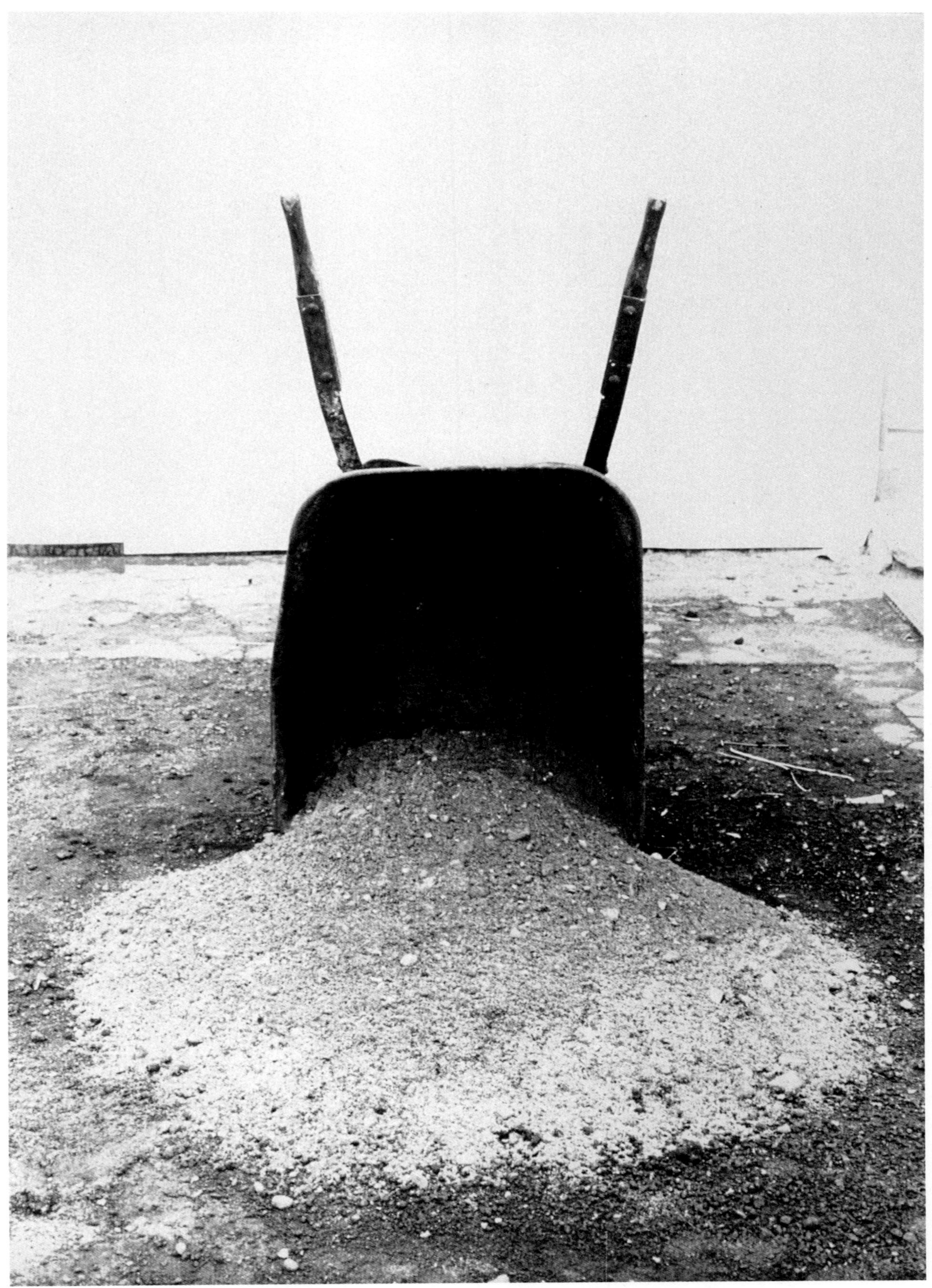
Fig. 5. *Schubkarre* (Wheelbarrow), 1981

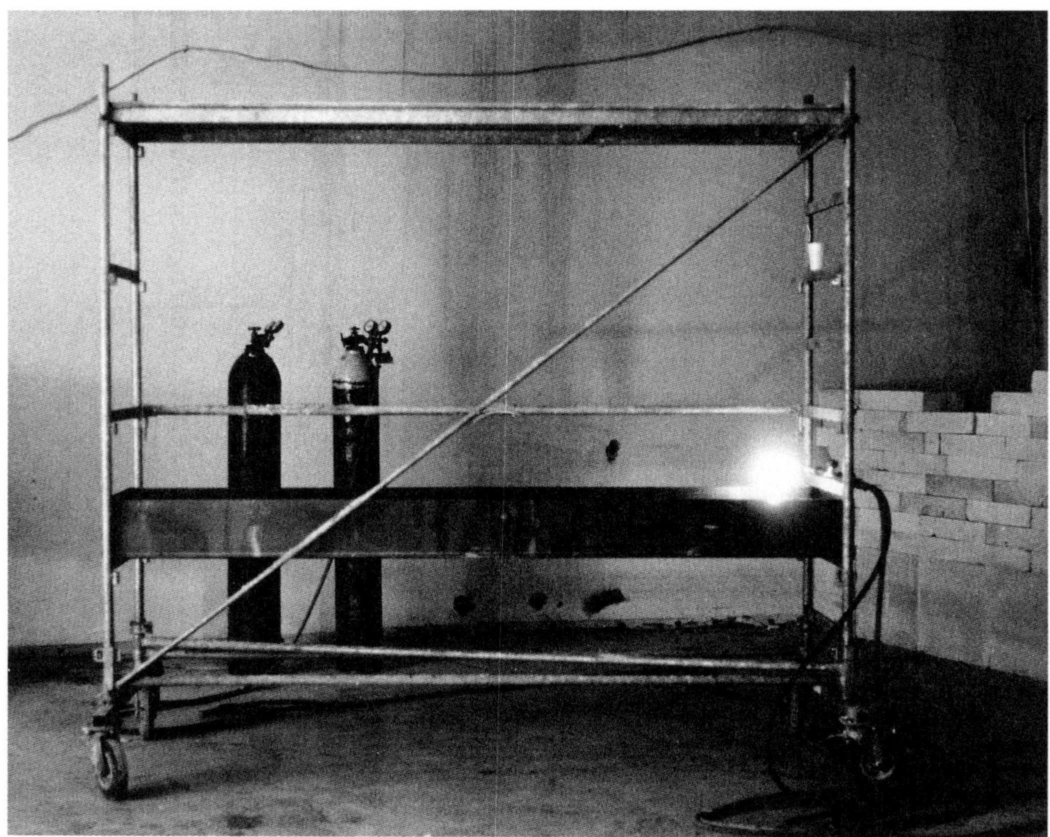

Fig. 6. *Pflüger auf Grund* (Plow on ground), 1982

Fig. 7. *Krater* (Crater), 1981

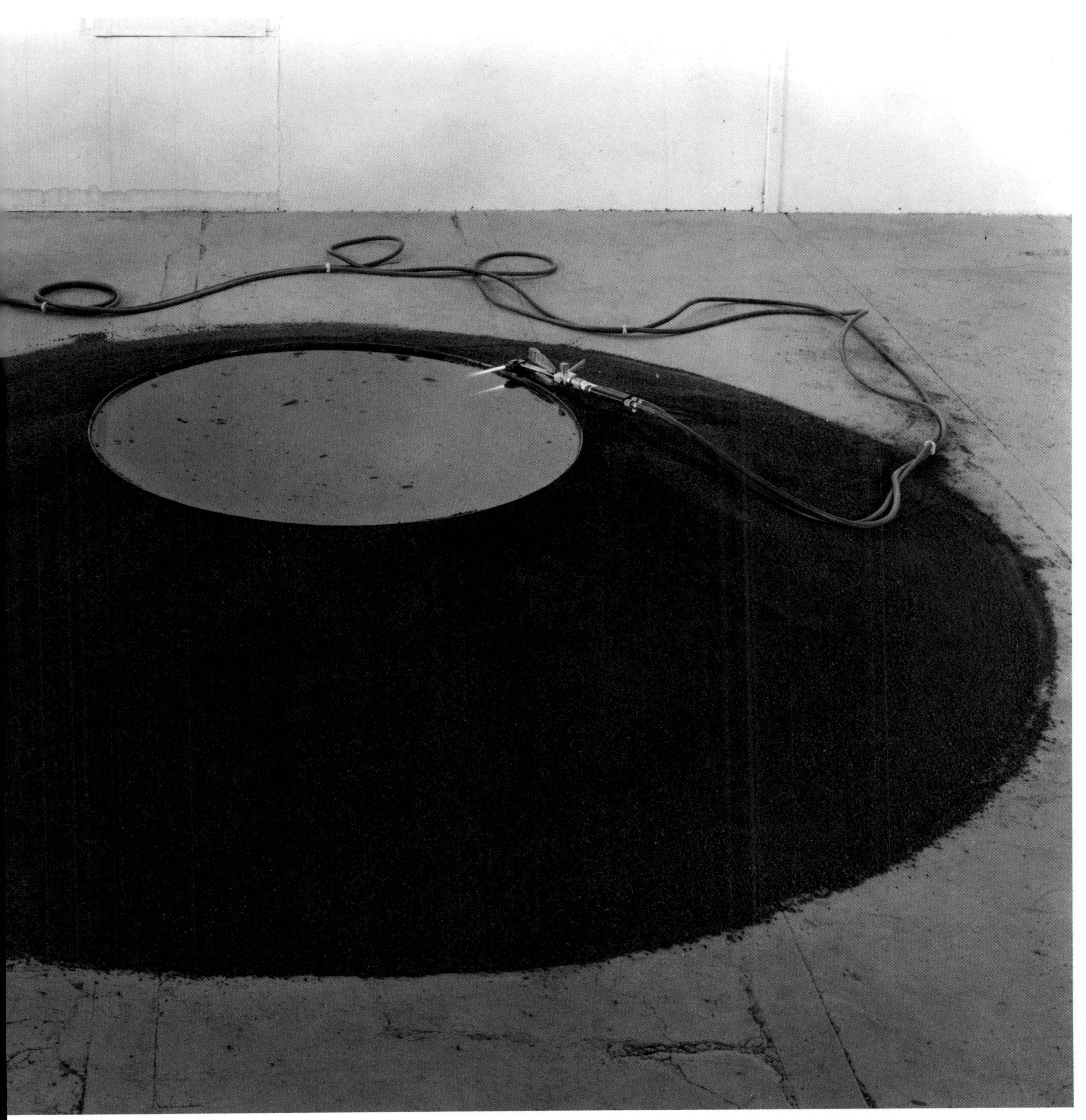

artwork and performances, including Müller's. Conversely, students from other master classes assisted the Bechers in their myriad photography campaigns, setting up cameras or preparing settings for a shoot, both in Germany and abroad. On one occasion, Müller accompanied the husband and wife team to northern France, where he was able to observe their exacting, if somewhat unexpected, working methods.

> They had a big van with all the equipment, including chain saws. If there were trees or bushes in the way, they asked the students to clean them up. It took us maybe five or six hours to set up the camera. There was no one to take care of that, so we just did it. Just cleaned it up. It was fantastic to see how they photographed. There were lots of fights about "move that bush" or "no, put it back," but it was interesting. They were very risky.

Müller was particularly taken by the Bechers' complex interactions with a given site and their near-scientific approach to their subjects. Both tendencies resonated deeply with his earlier professional training and foreshadowed his future work with various environments.

> They approached a shot almost from the engineering side. They first take a picture head-on to get the symmetry, and then they take another picture at exactly ninety degrees, and another at ninety degrees, and so on. That, by the way, is how you create technical drawings. And, of course, it makes sense to make these images under neutral light conditions, which also fascinated me, having been a technical draftsman.

From 1980 to 1983, Müller created a series of *Fotoskizzen*, or photo-sketches, in the straightforward Becher style, focusing on simple wooden constructions of carousels and contemporary fairgrounds, called *Wandernde Kulissen* (Wandering backdrops, figs. 8–11). His multiple photographs of industrial barges floating down the Rhine, titled *Stromaufwärts* (Upstream, figs. 12–15), similarly betray the Bechers' typological approach, highlighting both regional commerce and the boats' inherent sculptural qualities. Architectural photographs remain close to Müller's creative pursuits, though he often enhances them now with chemical splashes and other darkroom manipulations to impart a sense of mystery, ritual, and the handmade.

Following his graduation from the Kunstakademie Düsseldorf in 1981, Müller increasingly came into his own. He moved into an industrial studio at the old slaughterhouse at Ratherstrasse 25 in Düsseldorf-Derendorf,

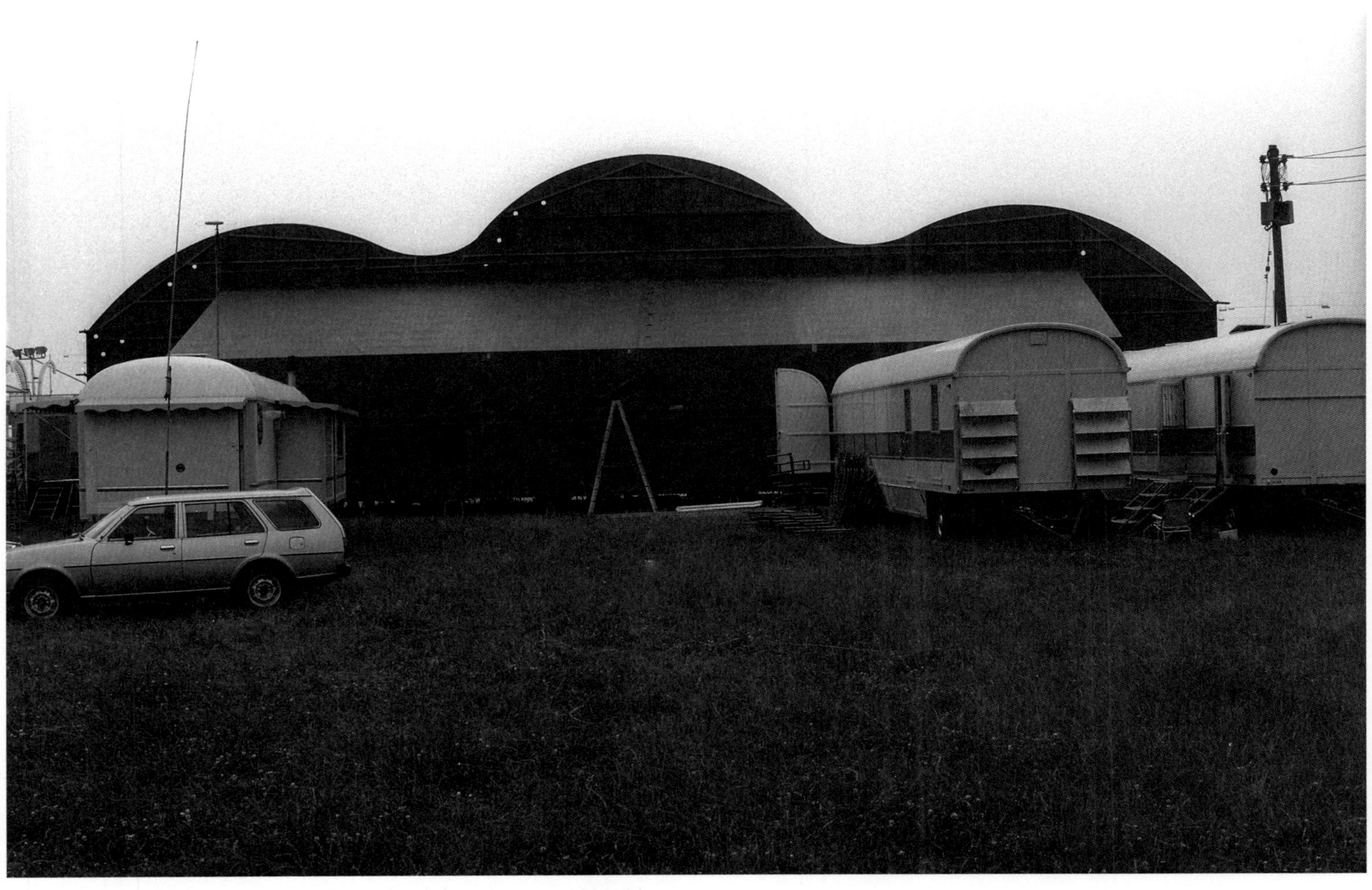

Fig. 8. *Wandernde Kulissen* (Wandering backdrops) series, 1980–83

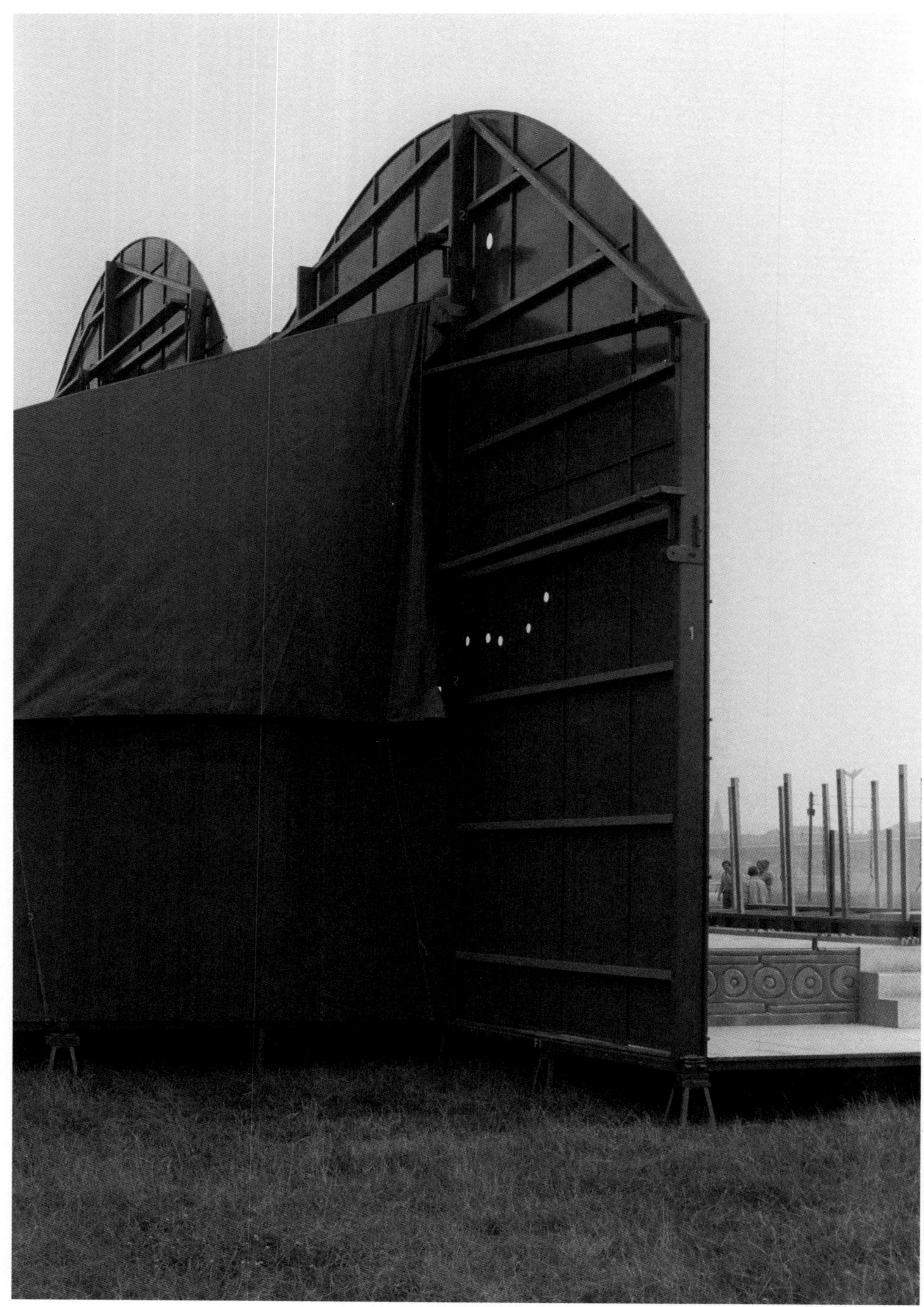

Figs. 9, 10. *Wandernde Kulissen* (Wandering backdrops) series, 1980–83

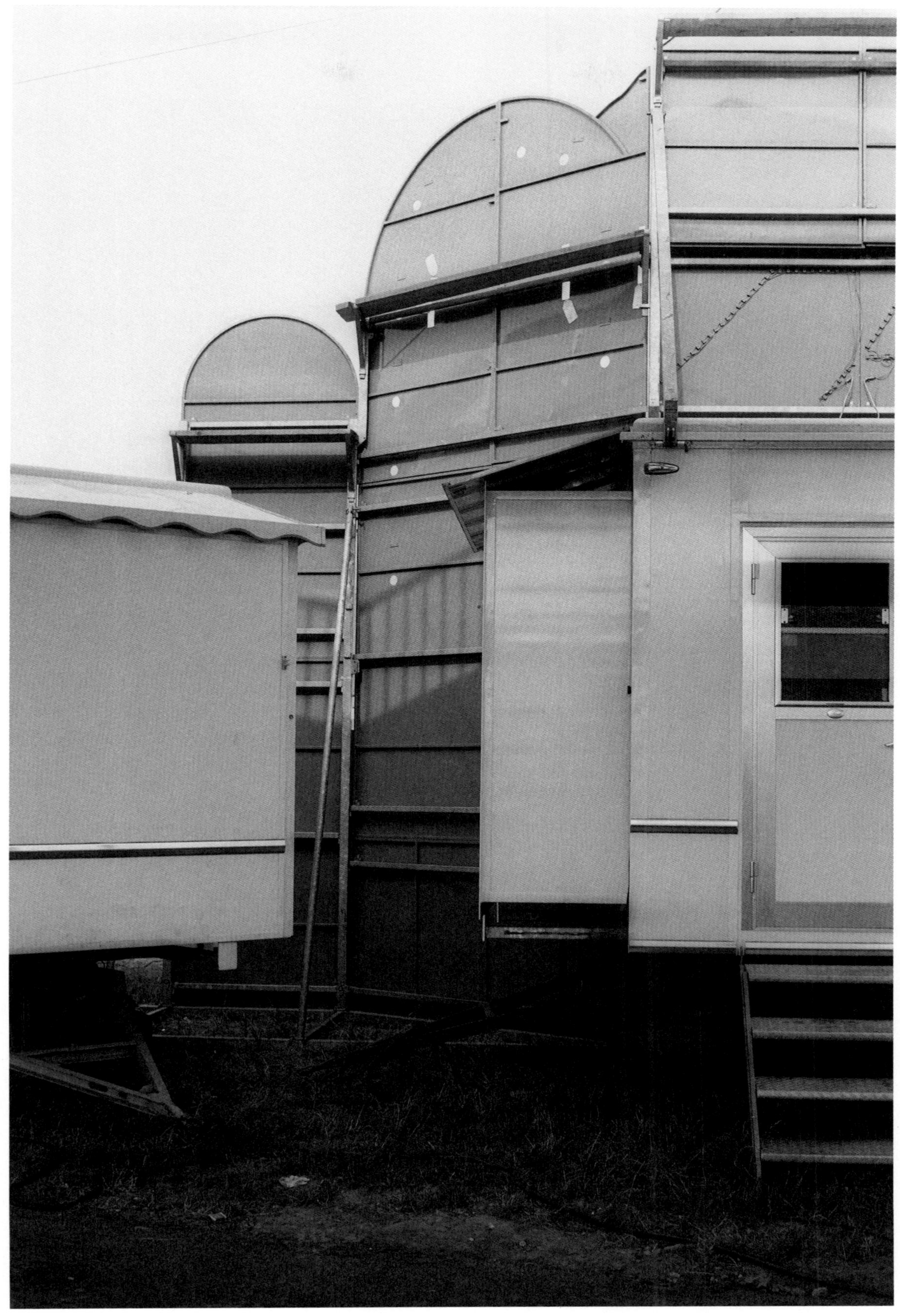

Fig. 11. *Wandernde Kulissen* (Wandering backdrops) fragment, 1983

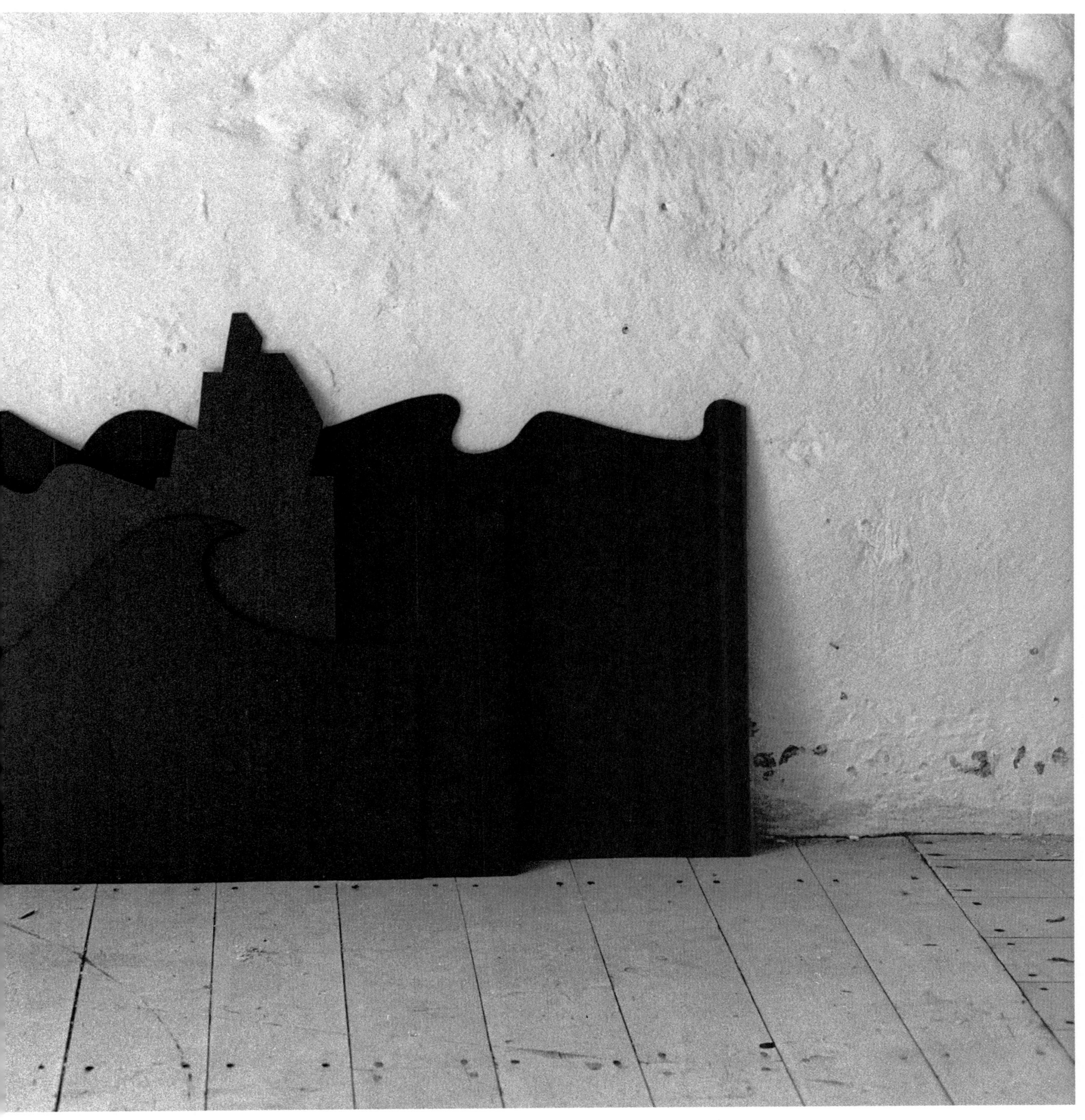

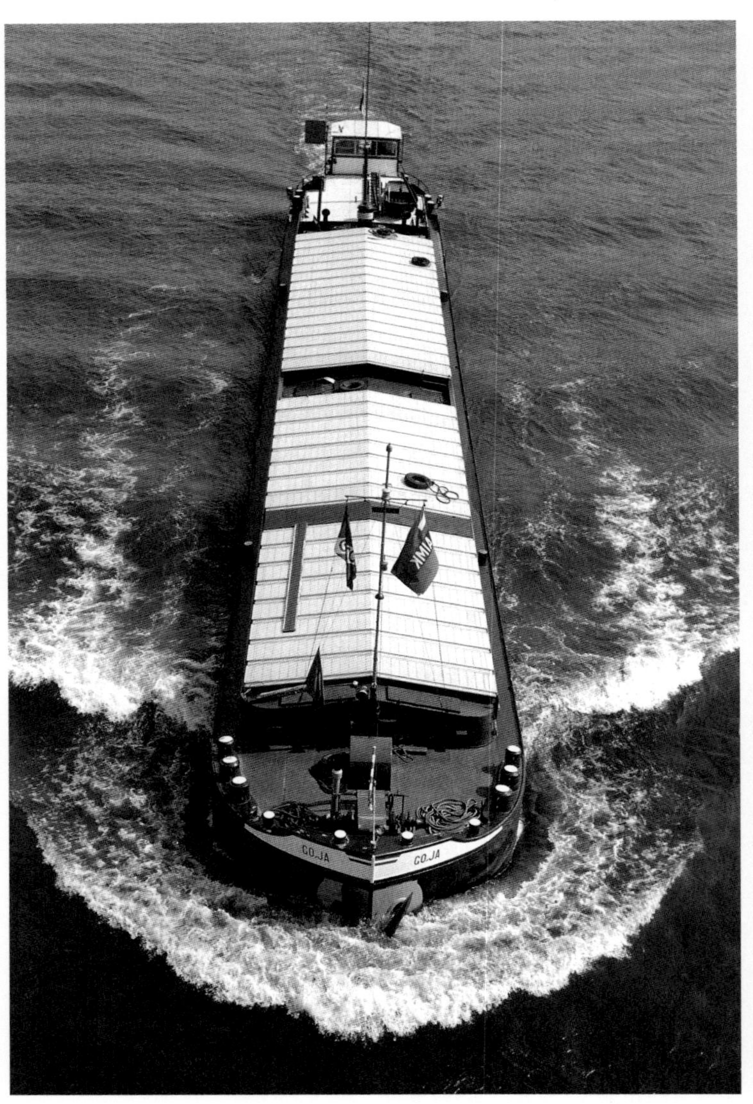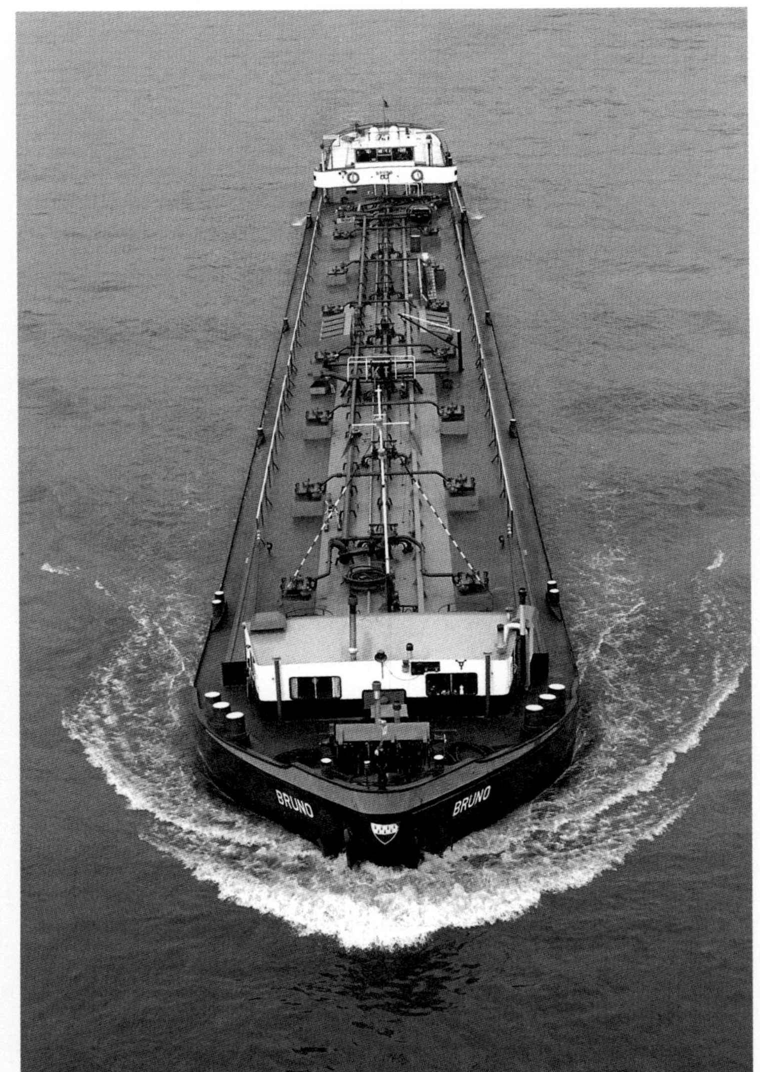

Figs. 12, 13, 14, 15. *Stromaufwärts* (Upstream) series, 1983–86

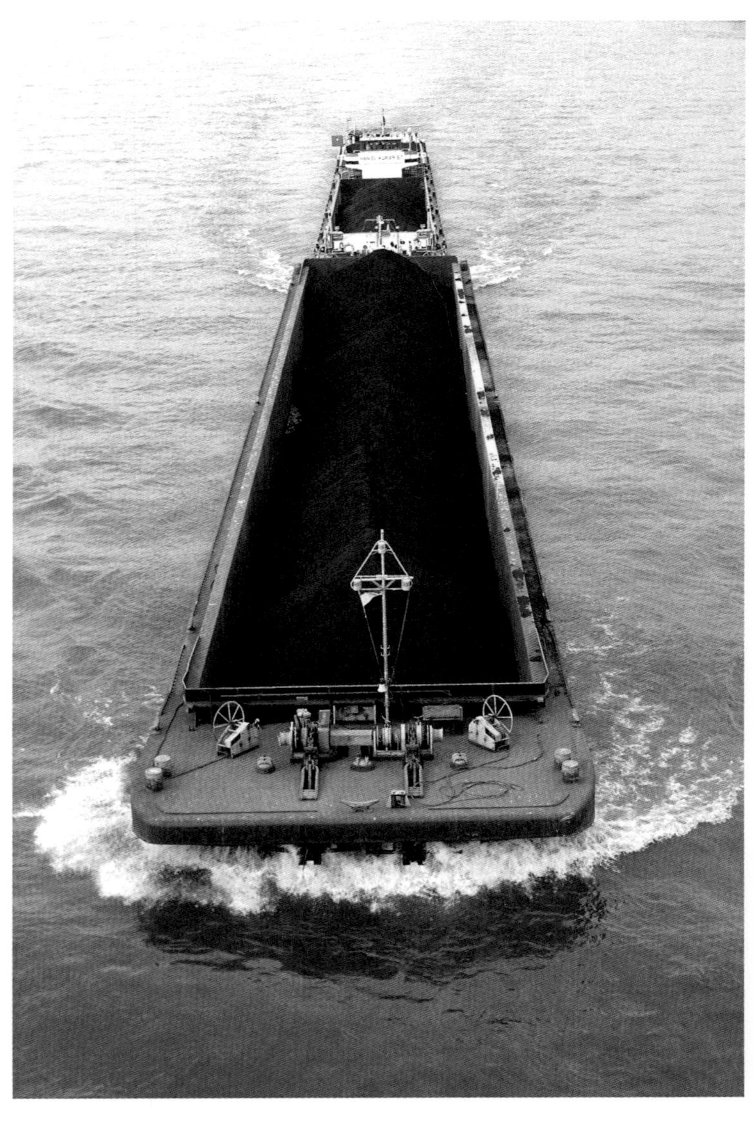

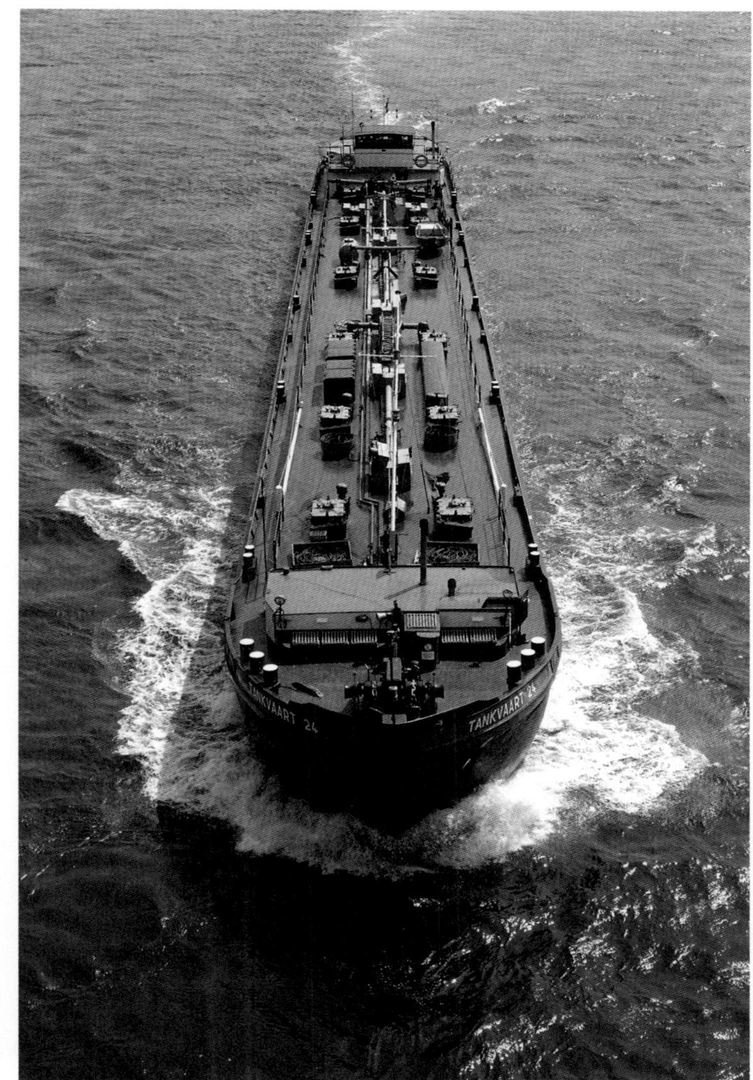

sharing the large space with six like-minded artist-friends: Liz Bachhuber, Ernst Hesse, Annette Leyener, Wasa Marjanov, Christoph Rihs, and Martin Schilken. A six-month residency at the Cité des Arts in Paris had left Müller eager to replicate the collaborative mode of artistic production that he had appreciated there and that hearkened back to his heyday as a union activist. Artist collectives, where emerging artists banded together to pool professional resources, became increasingly popular in the 1970s and 80s, most prominently with the progressive group that surrounded Klaus Jung, Harald Klingelhöller, Wolfgang Luy, and Thomas Schütte in Düsseldorf's Hildebrandtstrasse. A large, self-curated exhibition in 1981, provocatively titled *Reine Weste, tote Hose* (Clean slate, nothing happening), was a first critical success for the young Ratherstrasse group, and they proceeded to work and exhibit together, both in Germany and abroad, for the next several years. Large-scale works, like *Thun Construction* (1983–84, p. 48) and *Black Friday* (1988, p. 77), constructed from industrial scrap materials, operated on the interstices of sculpture and architecture, much like the sprawling installations of the New York artist Alice Aycock. With site-specific works like *Project for a Riverbank* (1981, figs. 16–17), Müller entered the realm of earth, or land, art, commenting on specific natural or man-made sites through sculptural interventions.

> I started to think more in terms of space, of the way art and architecture intersect. . . . This integrating of art, sculpture, and architecture was the foundation for building these early installation pieces—sculptures going through the window, panes of glass, etc. And we made a name with that. That was the time when everything worked.

Lucrative grants, international exhibitions, prizes, and public commissions soon followed, including a small group show, *Paperworks*, in 1987 at T. G. Art Gallery in downtown Los Angeles, which brought Müller to the United States for the first time. He eventually returned to Southern California for an artist residency and another group exhibition, *BoñAngeles*, at the newly founded Santa Monica Museum of Art, creating his work *Wall Street/Boyd Street* (1989, fig. 18) specifically for this show.

> I took a burned piano from a downtown Los Angeles gas station that interested me. The gas station had become a homeless shelter, I found out, and I heard that a neighbor burned it down, because it caused too much trouble. This was on the corner of Wall and Boyd Streets. I took a wheelbarrow and a sort of curtain that spilled onto a table like a waterfall. I had just come back from a show in Germany, where

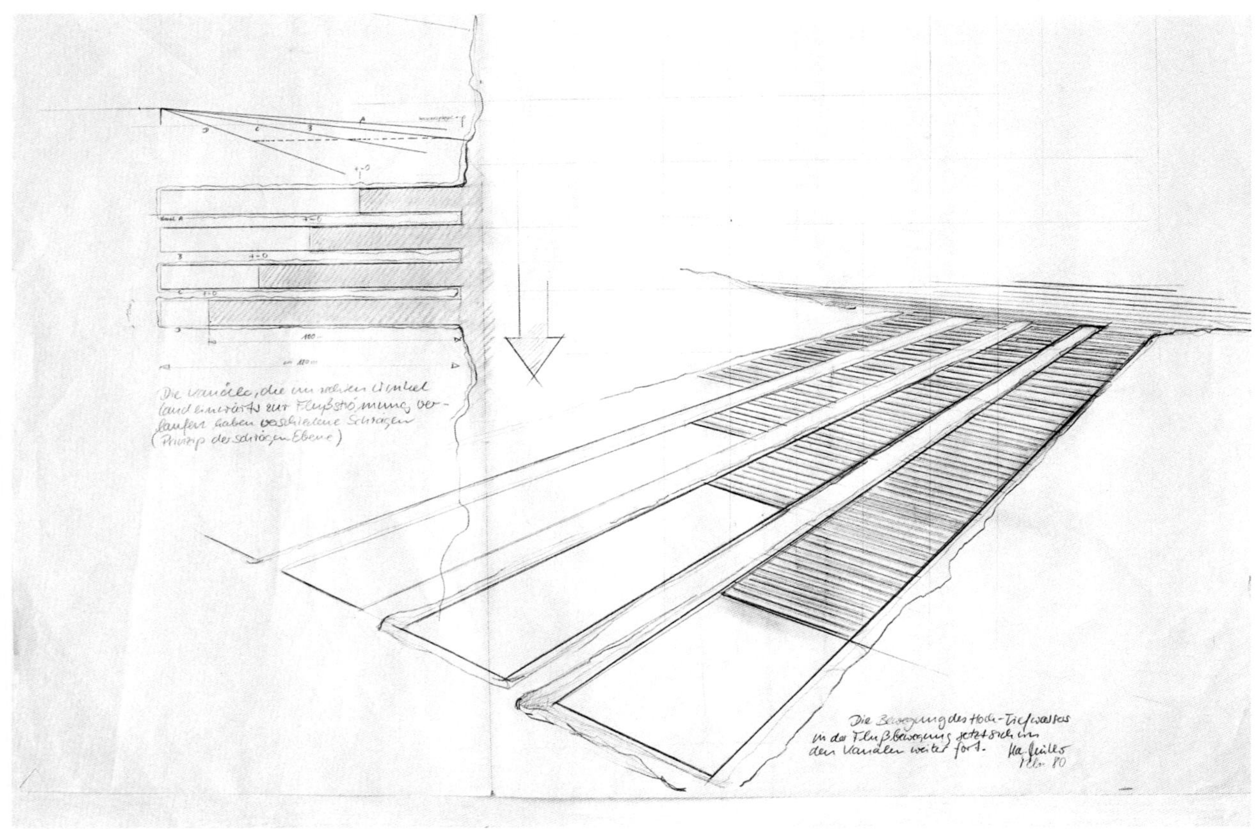

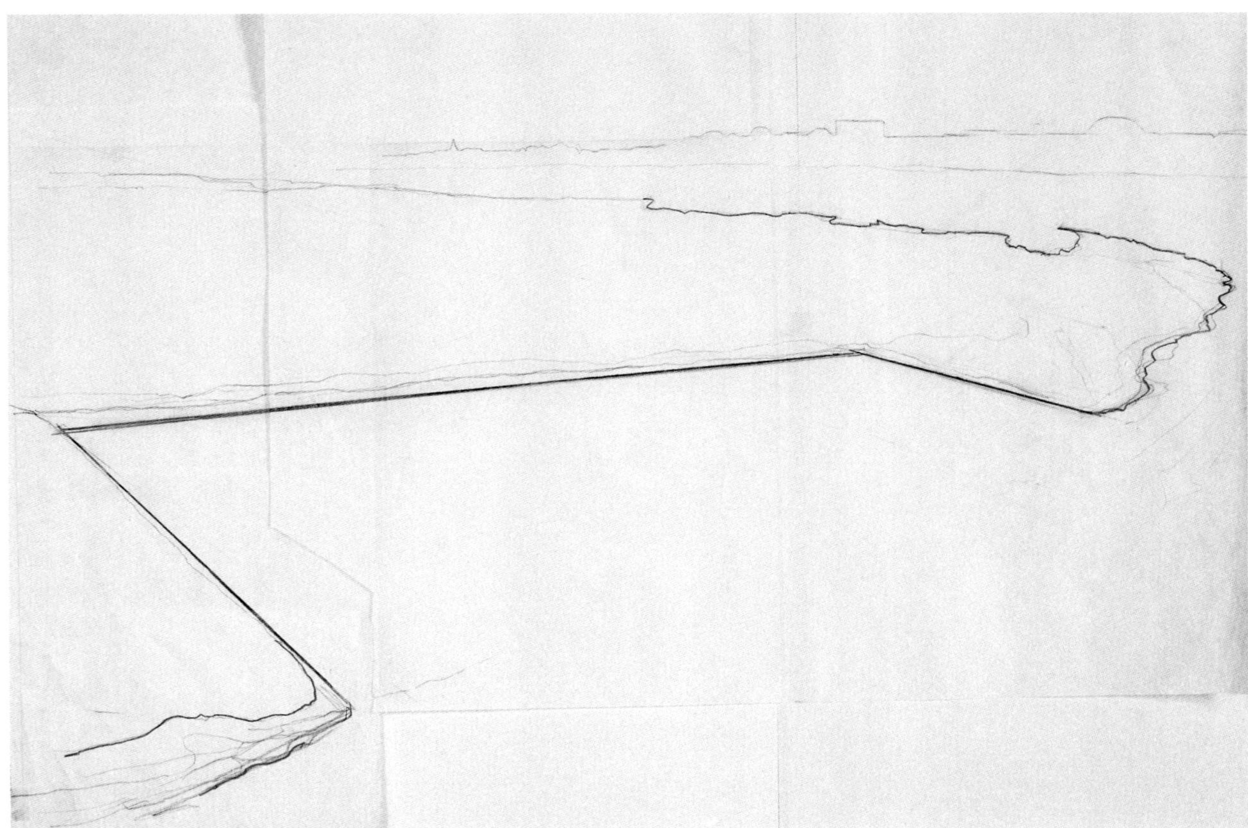

Figs. 16, 17. *Project for a Riverbank*, 1981

In 1989, Müller began to travel back and forth between Europe and Los
Angeles to be with his future wife, the photographer Rose Shoshana,
whom he had met at the opening of the Santa Monica Museum of Art's
inaugural exhibition. Although his move to California brought professional
opportunity, it proved challenging in the long term. "Let's call it opening a
new horizon," he recalls. "This society has different values, different ideas
from where I come from. It was very clear that I had a different historical
background." He rented a large studio at the Santa Monica Airport and
began working on new sculptural works that were fueled by the discovery
of ready-made objects from the area's recently defunct aerospace industry.
Excited by the large-scale assemblages of Los Angeles Surrealist Ed
Kienholz, whom he had assisted as a student during an installation of
his work at the Kunsthalle in Düsseldorf, Müller jerry-rigged American
junkyard materials and Cold War bric-a-brac into multidimensional
sculptural constructions that were at once raw and compelling.

Together with Bay Area artist Christel Dillbohner, Müller organized
an exhibition in 1994 of industrial assemblages, or "combines,"
entitled *Transformer: A Change of Past Perceptions* for the
Contemporary Arts Forum in Santa Barbara, a show that eventually
traveled to Canada. Machinelike and hard-edged, his composite
sculptures possessed an improvisational aesthetic that recalled the
work of the Swiss artist Jean Tinguely. Müller also continued to
work in his Düsseldorf studio, creating large-scale public artworks
like *Ringrotsiebzehngrad* (ringredseventeendegrees, 1997) at the
Universität Münster, a giant steel ring that seems to lean against
the building's wall of windows but doesn't actually touch them.

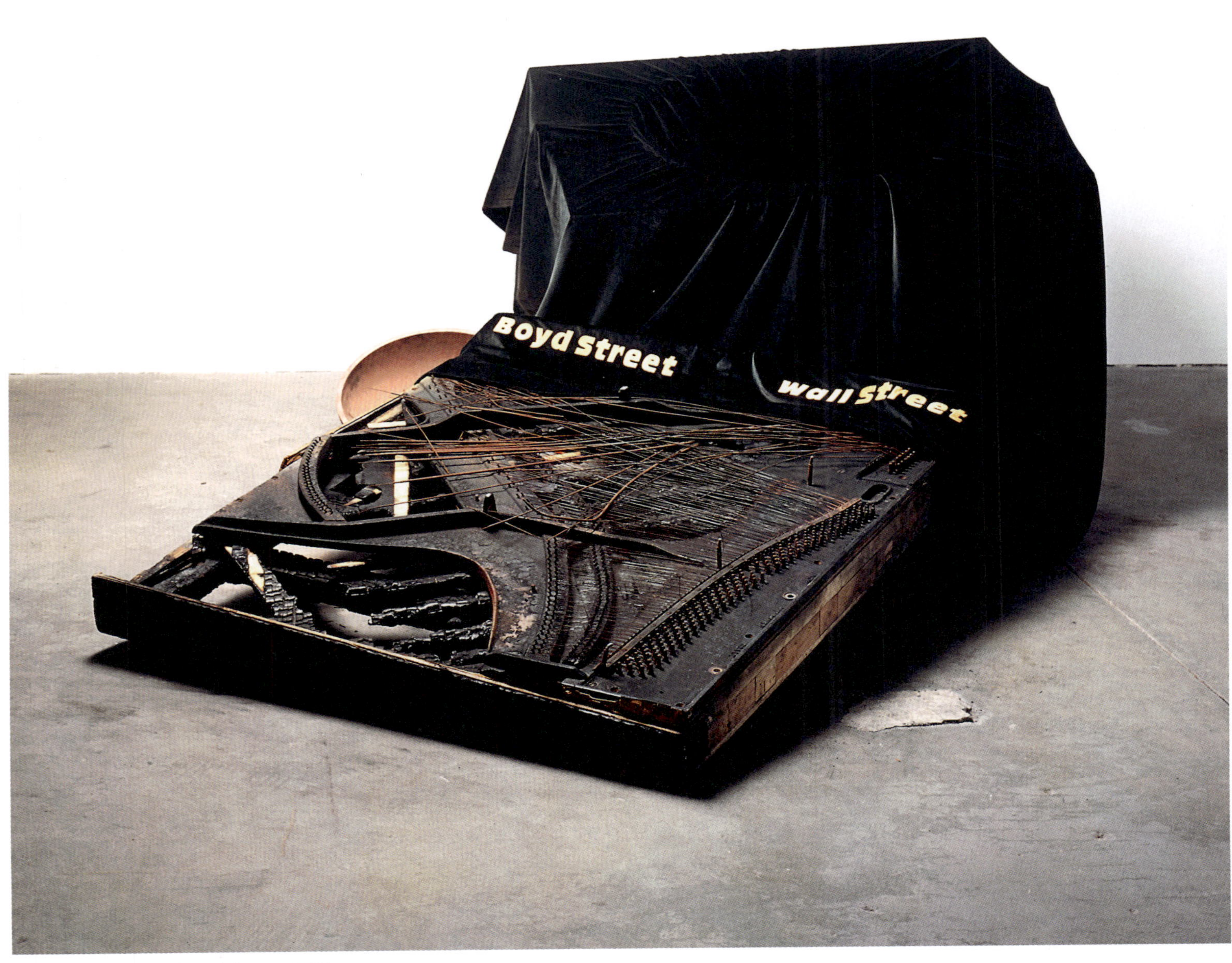

Fig. 18. *Wall Street/Boyd Street*, 1989

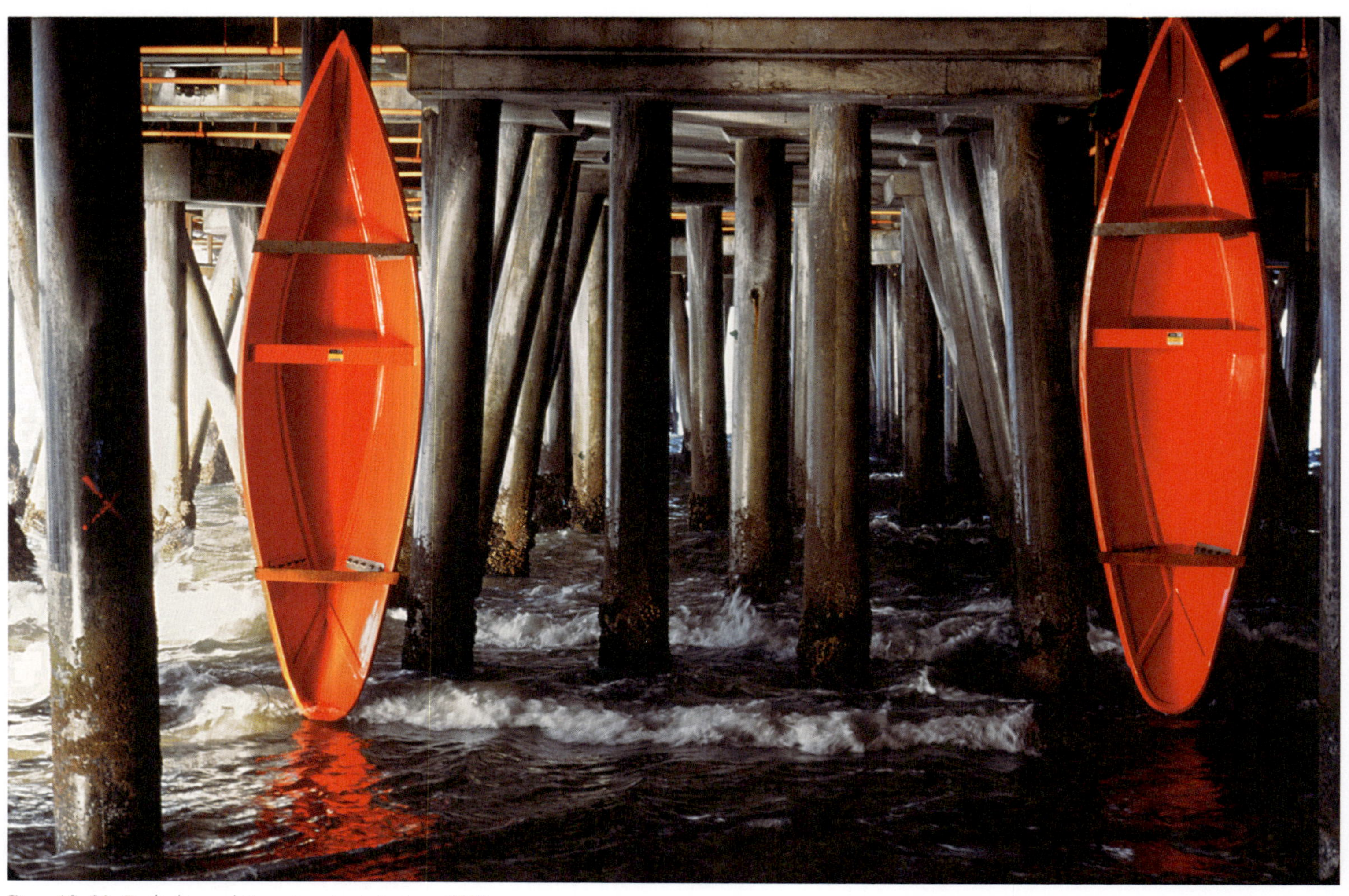

Figs. 19, 20. *Twilight and Yearning*, installation, 1998

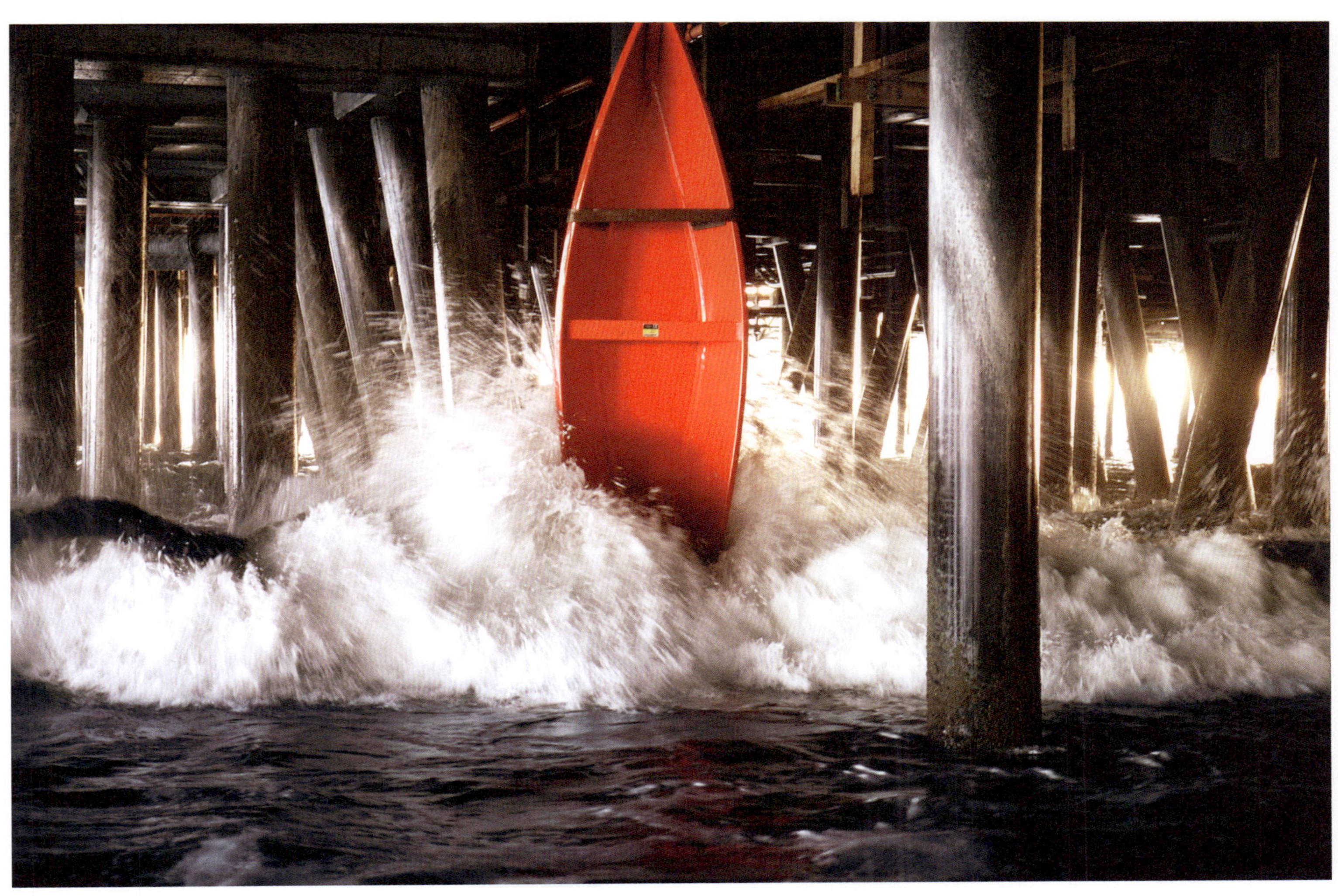

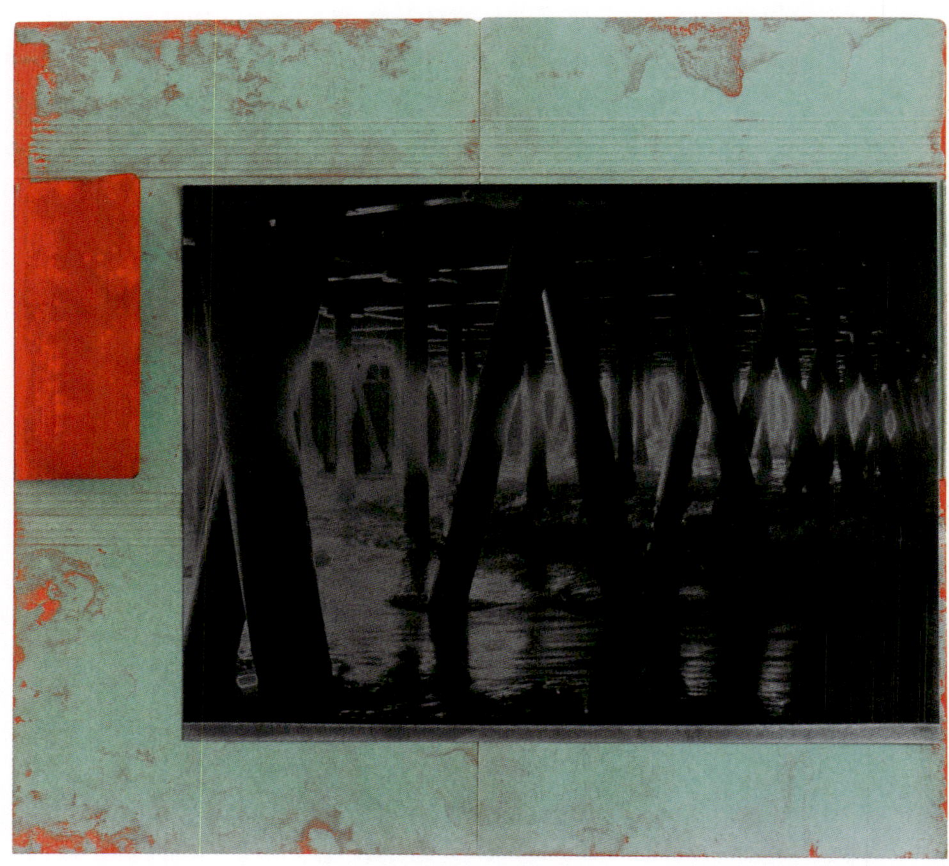

Figs. 21, 22, 23. *Twilight and Yearning*, 1998

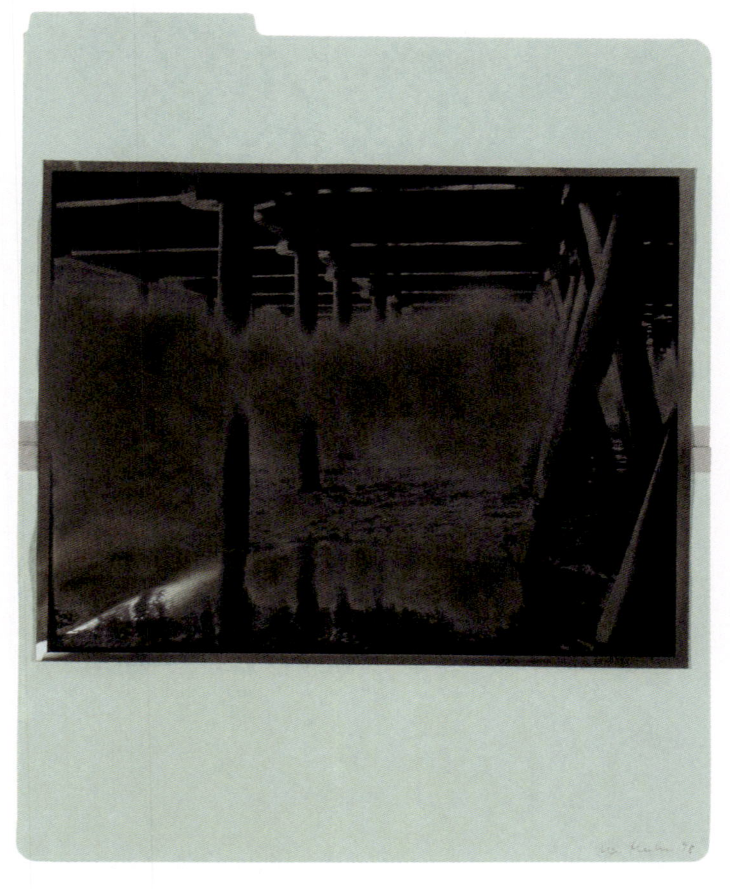 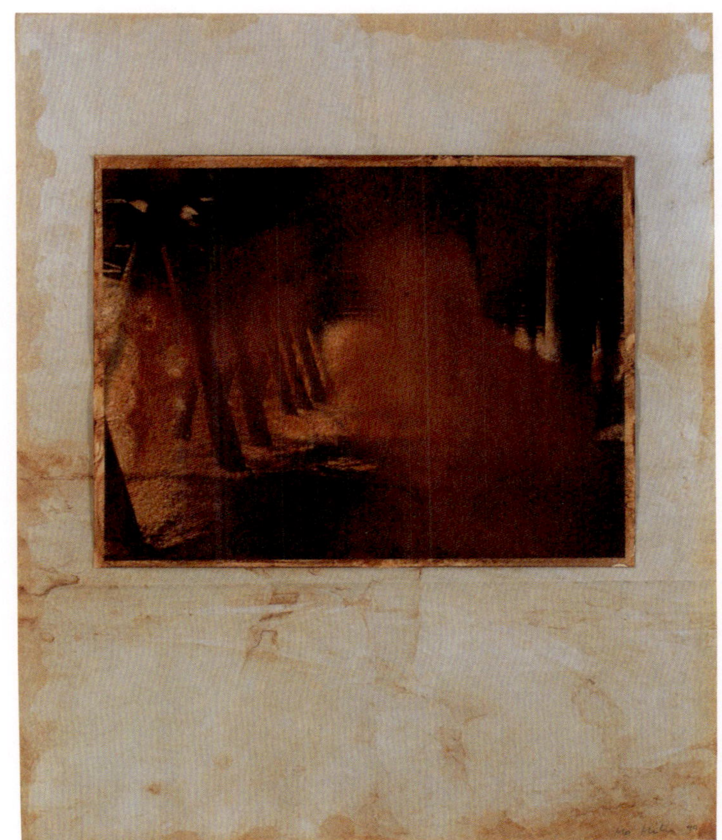

Found objects and environmental interaction remained key to Müller's work. In 1998, after many years of preparation, he unveiled *Twilight and Yearning* (figs. 19–23), a site-specific installation under the Santa Monica Pier, introducing a large American audience to his work. In 1999, just weeks before his accident en route to San Francisco, Müller created a multimedia installation in Mexico City titled *Palacio de Memoria* (Palace of memory, figs. 24–25). Installed at the Museo Universitario del Chopo in an elegant Art Deco pavilion designed by the early twentieth-century German architect Bruno Möhring for an international exposition in Düsseldorf in 1902, the project included an animated jumble of wooden church pews, piled one on top of the other and juxtaposed with a large shelf of handmade ceramic bowls, which poignantly evoked the inevitable social tensions of the early industrial age. Augmented with quotes by the leftist German poet Hans Magnus Enzensberger, *Palacio de Memoria* also reflects the dramatic social upheaval Müller had witnessed for himself in 1992 during the civil unrest after the Rodney King verdicts. "When there were riots in Los Angeles, people didn't go to city hall to rampage," he remembers. "They tore up their own neighborhoods and shot each other. One of the points I hoped to make with *Palacio de Memoria* is that we all live with the potential for aggression close by."[6]

Personal trauma, in the sense of severe shock to both body and mind, hit home when Müller's life was violently disrupted by the car accident in October 1999, at a time when his bi-continental career was reaching a peak. Pried from his overturned vehicle and rushed to the hospital with a fractured hip, rib cage, and shoulder, Müller eventually lost his left forearm to a hospital-acquired infection, which had been discovered and treated too late. It was a devastating blow for an artist, especially one who had prided himself on his physical strength and his very corporeal, muscular art. "It was a big change to go from being this athlete to being handicapped," he recalls. "You have to deal with being handicapped; your capability to produce and to be in this race, to be competitive. . . . It has a psychological effect." It is a lasting testament to Müller's resilience and creative ambition that his art and career barely suffered after the accident. Four years after the game-changing event, he unveiled a large-scale installation at the University of Southern California's Fisher Museum of Art that directly addressed the wounds he sustained on that fateful night in California's Central Valley. *Demo: The Body Shop* involved a one-and-a-half-ton Chevrolet Blazer, tipped on its side and wrapped in one thousand yards of black elastic fabric, reminiscent of industrial-strength packing tape, seat belts, and medical bandages. Silicone casts of his own body

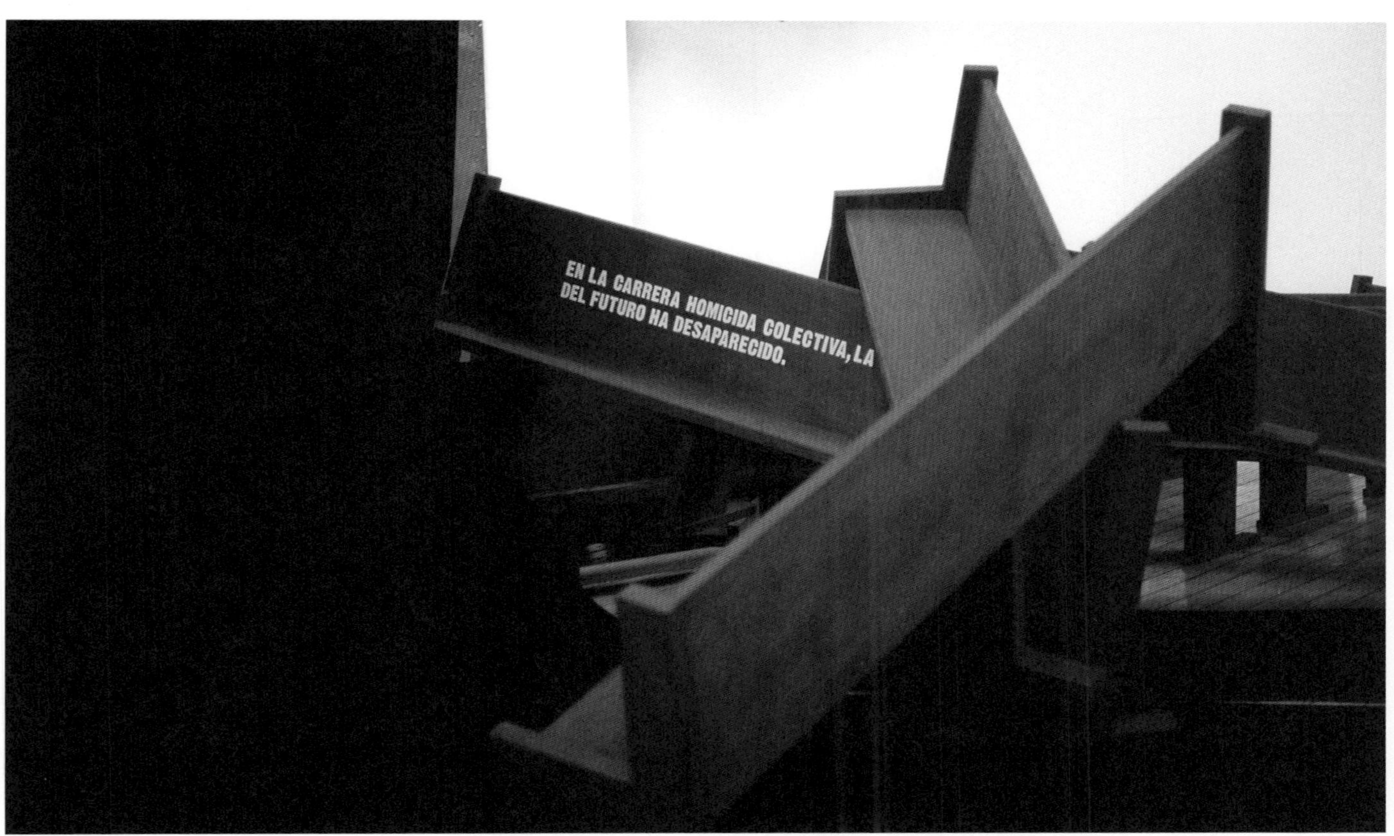

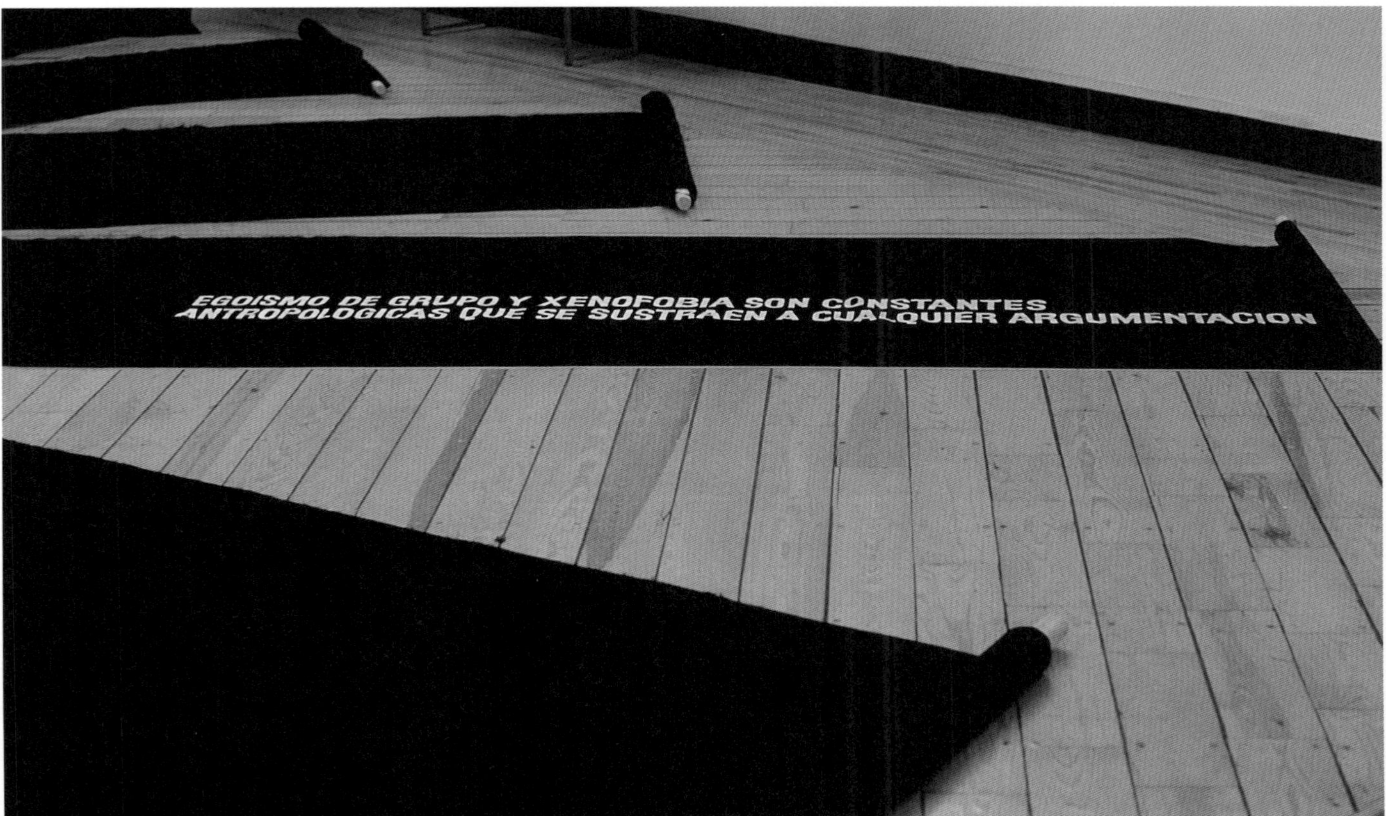

Figs. 24, 25. *Palacio de Memoria* (Palace of memory), 1999

and severed left forearm only enhance a hauntingly personal installation that readily suggests the continued influence of artists like Kienholz and Beuys. Stationed in Russia as an aircraft radio operator during World War II, Beuys had been no stranger to trauma, and he often recounted his own dramatic experience of being shot down near the Crimean front. Although immediately rescued by Luftwaffe search commandos and transported to a German field hospital, he later embellished the story by claiming that roaming Tatar tribesmen had nursed him back to health by wrapping his body in fat and felt, a powerful, if invented, myth of resurrection. Müller's own creative engagement of personal trauma, though therapeutic and hardly surprising, bewildered friends and critics alike. "People were shocked to see how far I went with that, with all the darkness you could imagine. . . . I think there is something under the surface. I was burning to do something like that. . . . It was a reflection of my traumatic accident, but it was also to test how much can I do with one hand."

Working increasingly with the help of assistants, Müller began to rethink his creative approach. He increasingly created drawings and three-dimensional objects made from cardboard or paper, reigniting a passion that reached back to his earliest days as a technical draftsman, illustrator, and graphic designer in Germany. Delicate paper sculptures, like *Coat Survivor* (1999, fig. 26) and his red and white *Preludes* (2010), are subtly scored and richly colored, with surface textures ranging from brushed metal to raw concrete to whitewashed stone. They hover on the wall like forgotten garments, enveloping imaginary bodies that have long since disappeared. Beautiful and monumental, they hug their phantom bodies like sacred shelters, exuding a spiritual power and ritual transcendence that invoke the spirit of Joseph Beuys. The human body, simultaneously strong and vulnerable, had been an element in Müller's work since his earliest performances, but it now returned with a new urgency. Reaching back into his considerable oeuvre, Müller quietly transitioned from large-scale, site-specific installations to lighter, two-dimensional works that intricately engage color, line, and abstraction.

You can't solely survive on installation pieces. It kills you. . . . It becomes uncharming, too rough and harsh. You become like an entrepreneur, too much collaboration. You have to go back in your shell. You have to reflect . . . because it balances you. I often see that in artists who have this talent to make spectacular installations, but who also have the talent of doing these sketches and drawings. You need to exercise your fingers, to refine the technique.

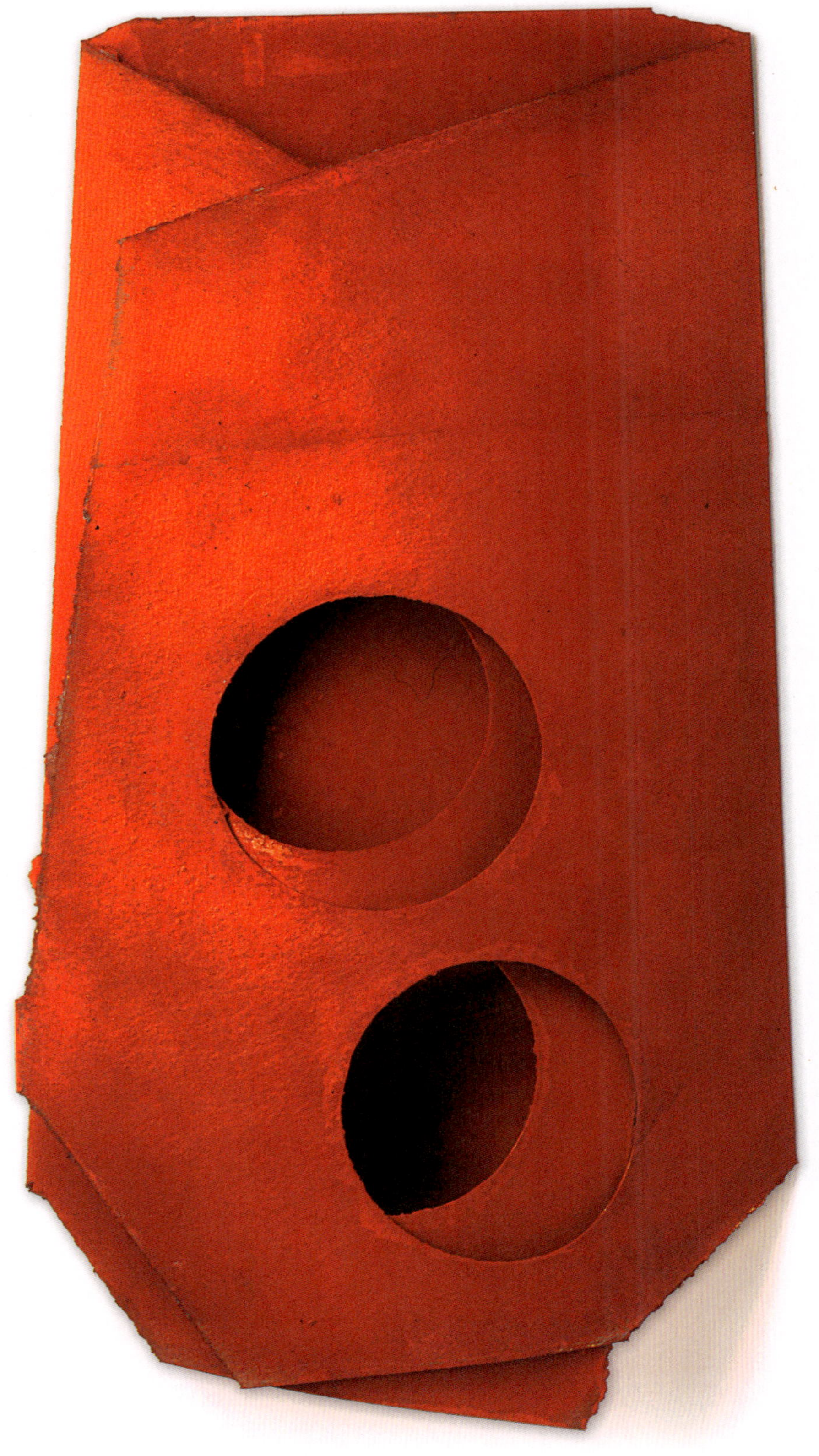

Fig. 26. Coat Survivor, 1999

As a mature artist, Müller continues to avoid unnecessary gestures and empty decorum, striving for the simplest formal expression of an idea. In the summer of 2013, in preparation for his solo exhibition at the Los Angeles Municipal Art Gallery (LAMAG), he created a site-specific environment made solely of light biomorphic paperboard shapes that float on walls and columns (fig. 27). Elegant and still, these ghostly apparitions reach out to the viewer like silent witnesses, attesting to the creative journey of a man who responds to life with great imagination, clarity, and grace.

Notes
[1] All quotes by Manfred Müller are from the author's interview with the artist in Los Angeles between June 19 and July 4, 2013.
[2] Invar Hollaus, "Heerich, Erwin," in *Allgemeines Künstler-Lexikon*, vol. 71 (Munich: Saur, 2011), 44.
[3] Ibid.
[4] Kristine McKenna, interview with the artist, in *Manfred Müller: Any Given Shape* (Los Angeles: [n.p.], 2001).
[5] Bernd and Hilla Becher, *Anonyme Skulpturen* (Düsseldorf: Verlag Michelpresse, 1969).
[6] Ibid., 14.

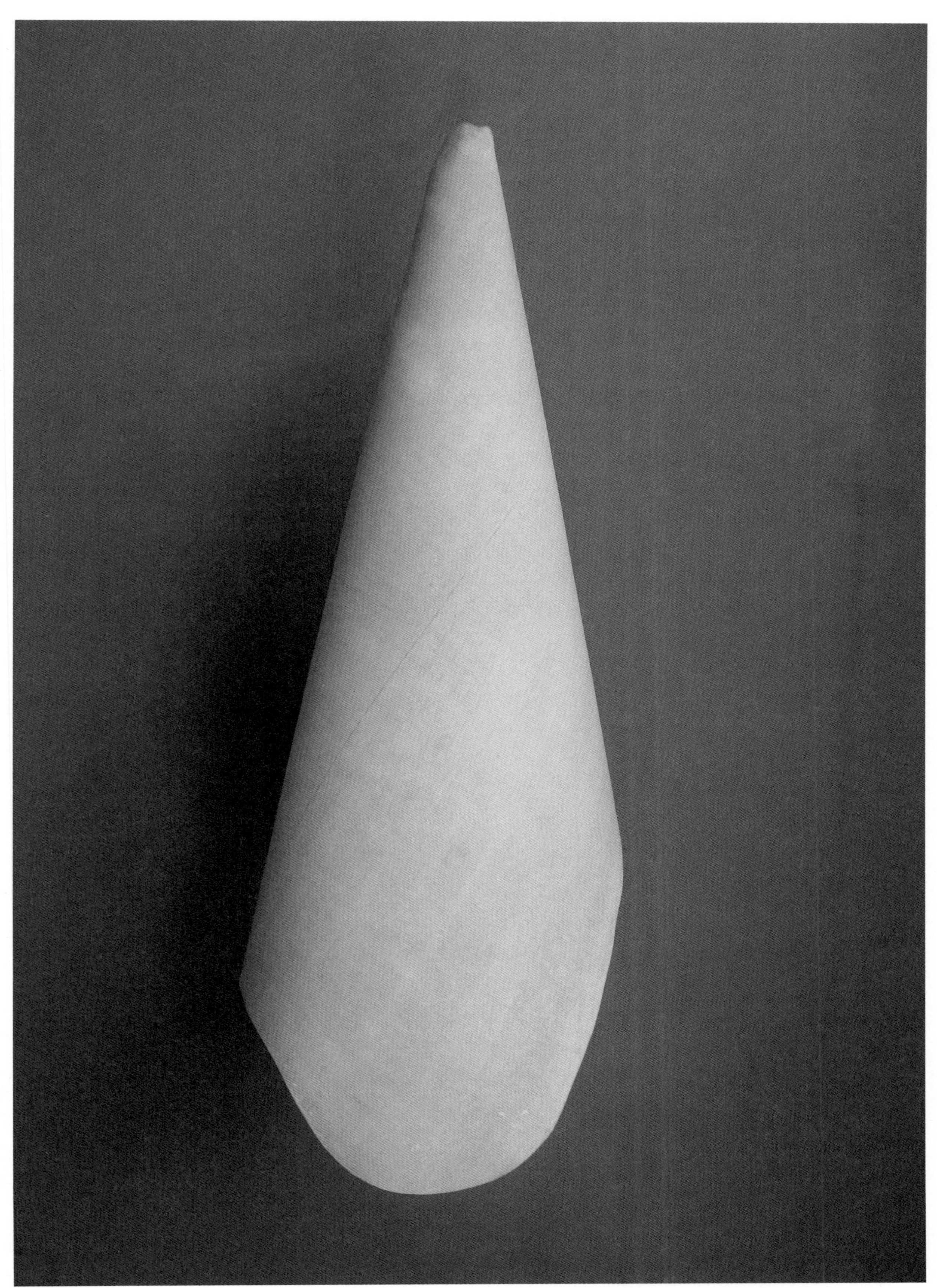
Fig. 27. *White Overture XL 1*, 2013

PLATES
EUROPE

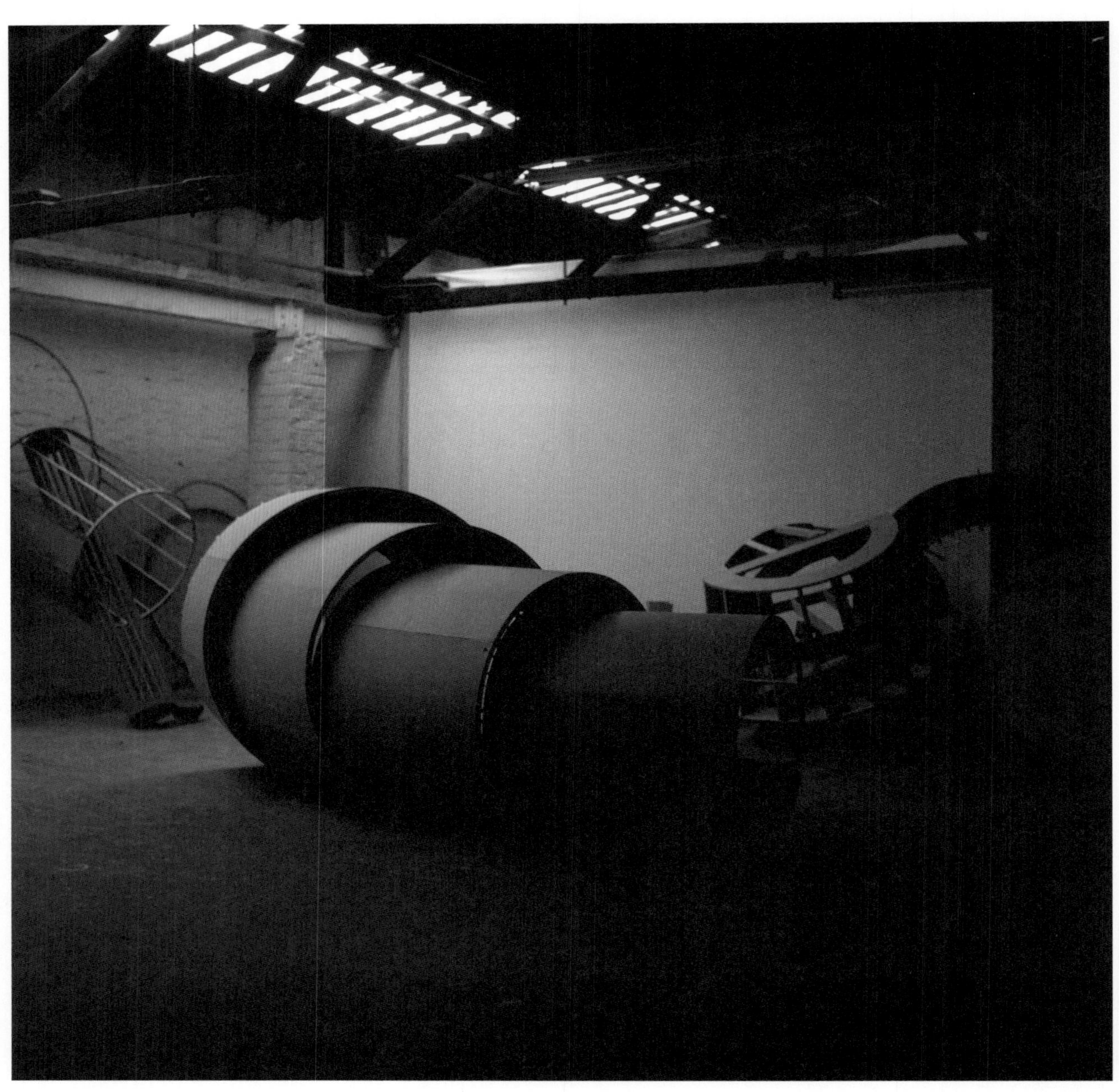

Thun Construction, 1983–84

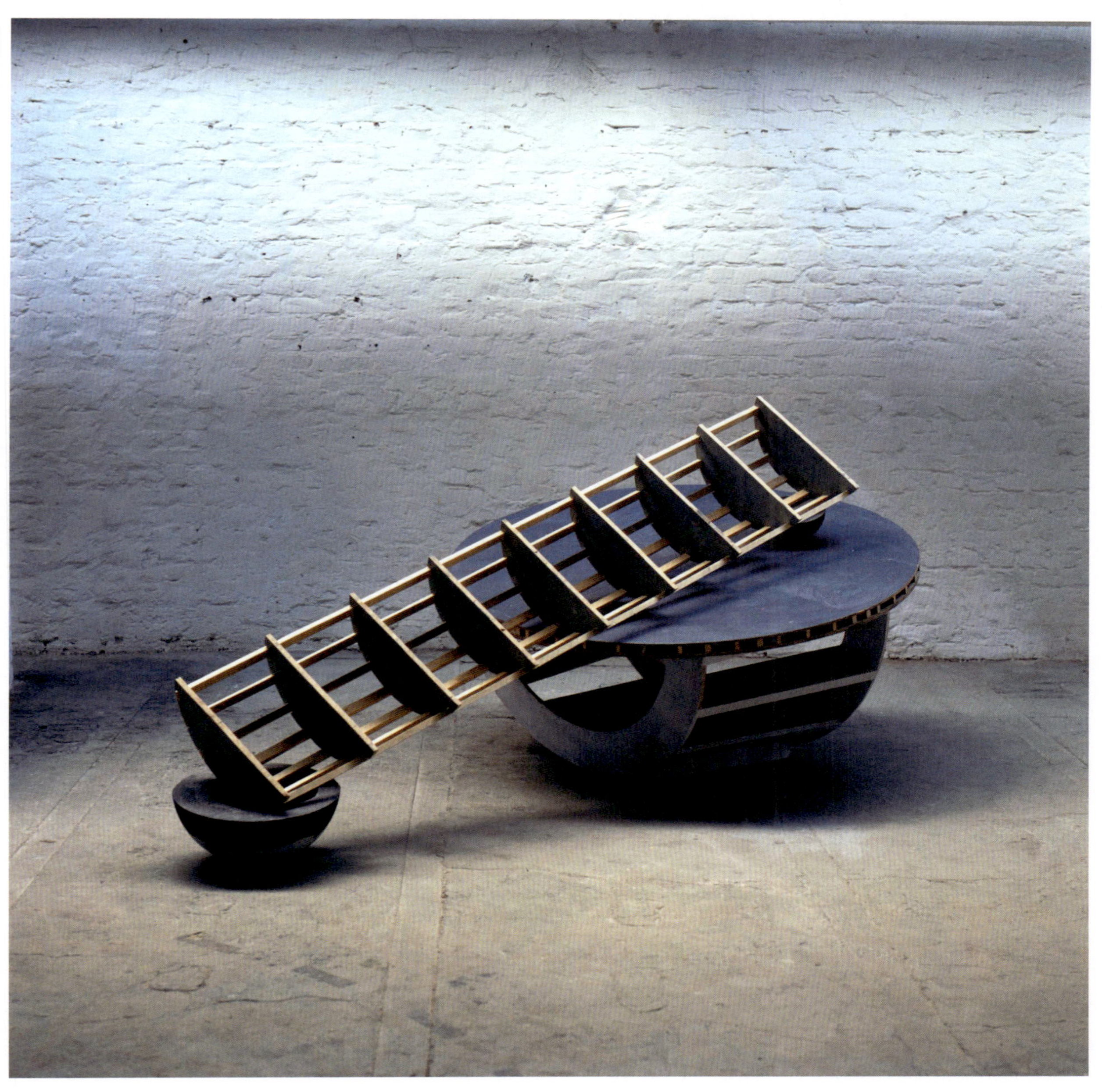

Jöllenbeck Construction, 1985

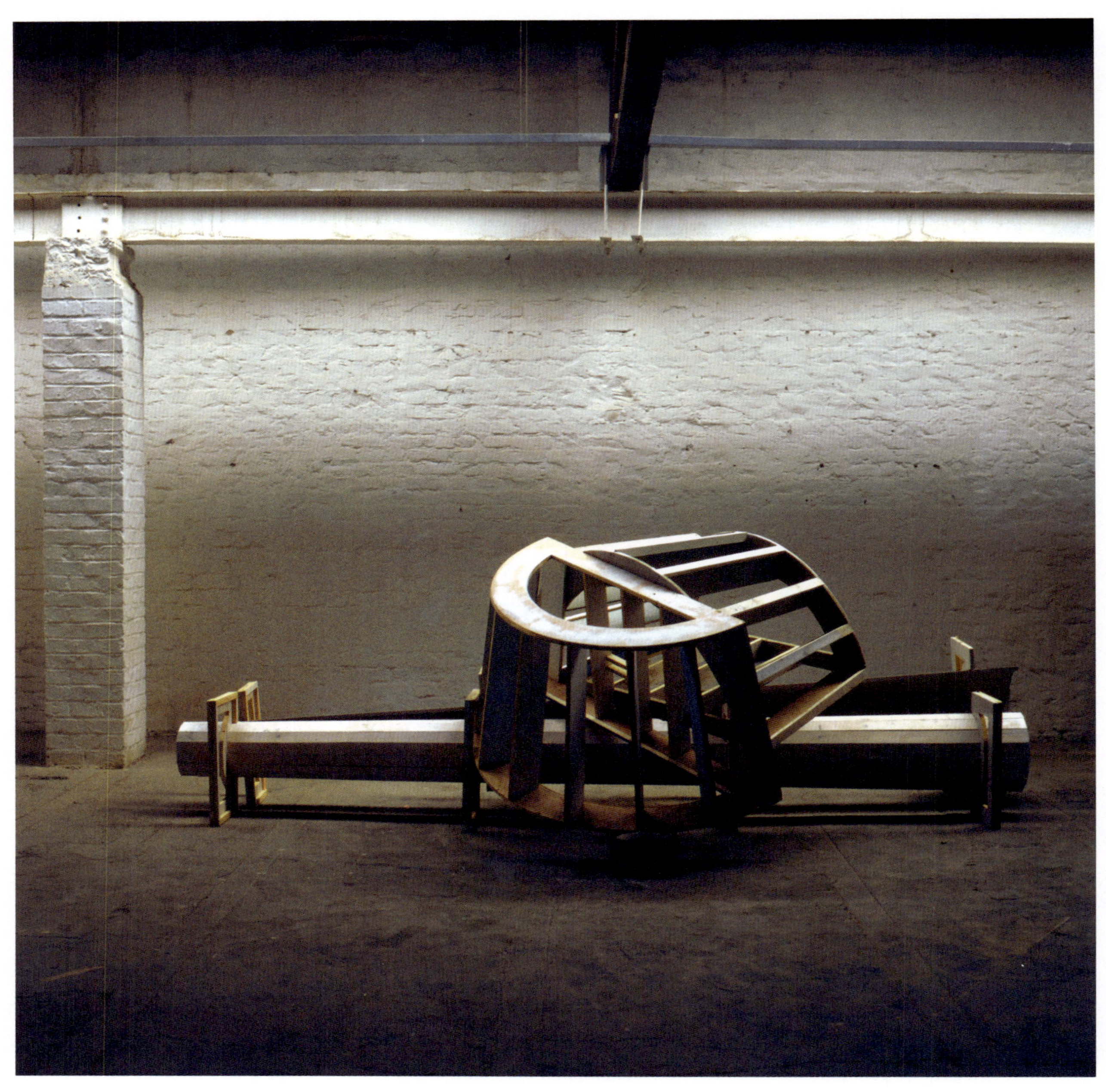

Primavera, 1983–84

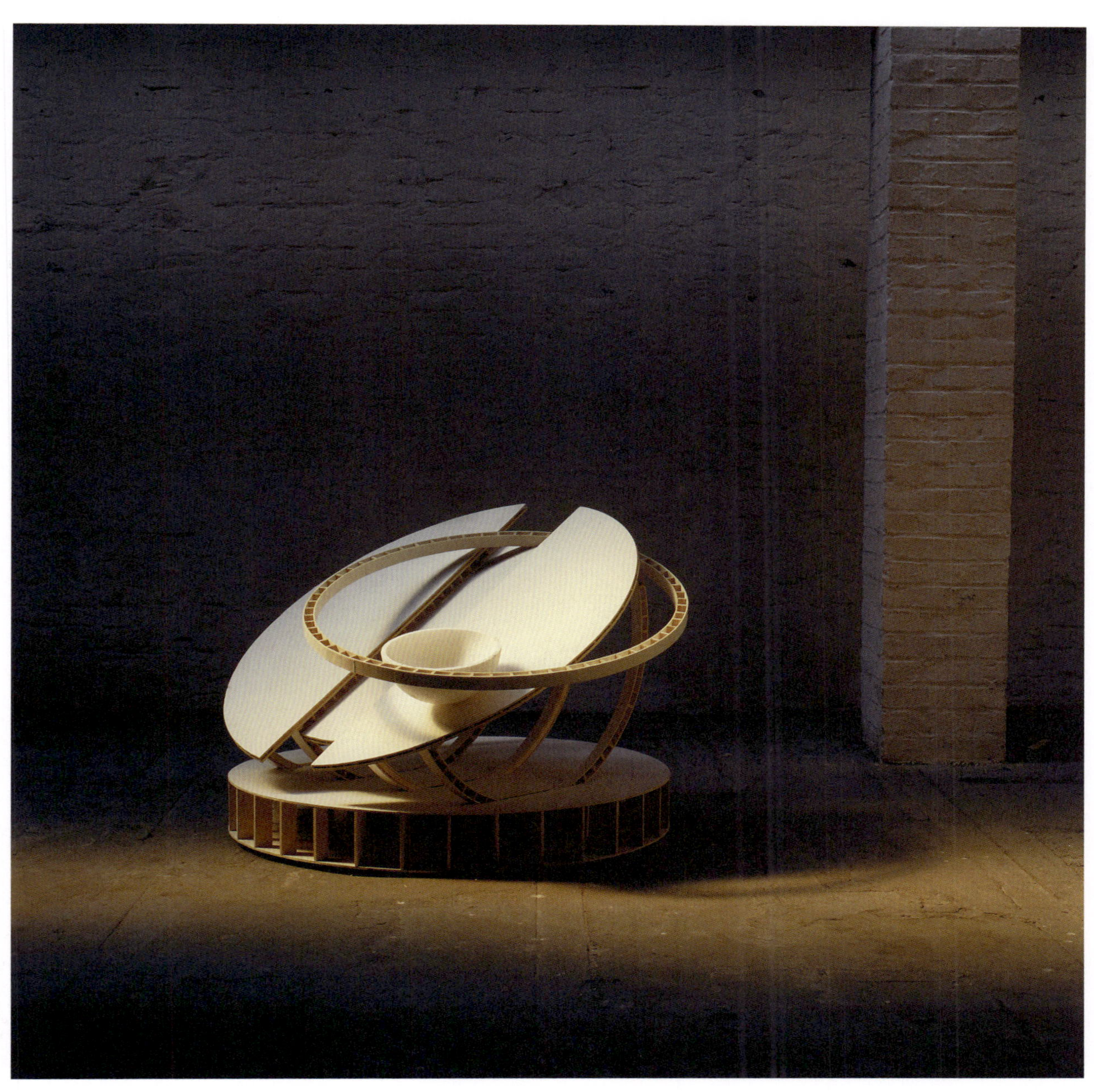

Architektonische Skulptur Studie (Architectural sculpture study), 1984

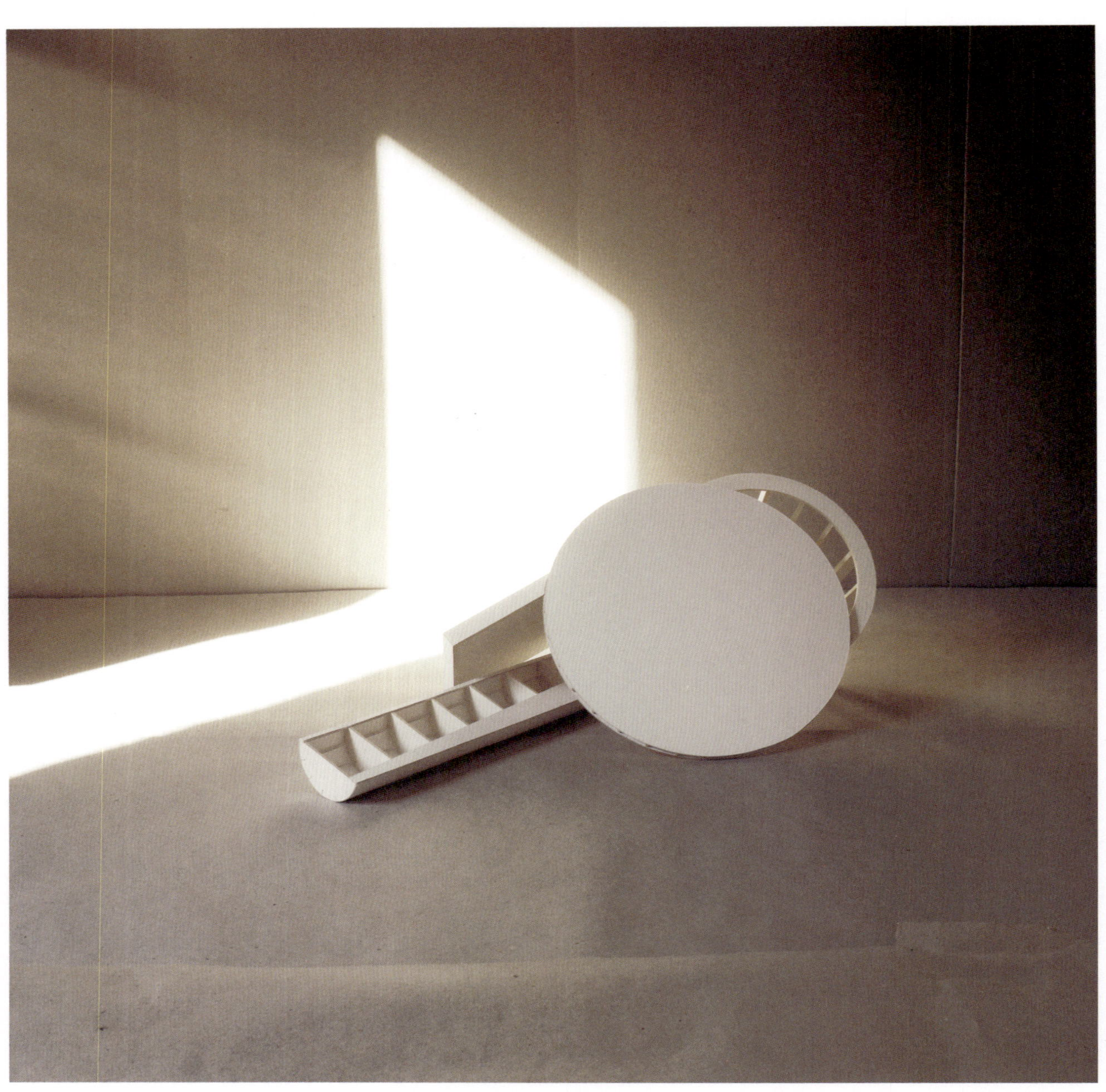

Architektonische Skulptur Studie (Architectural sculpture study), 1982

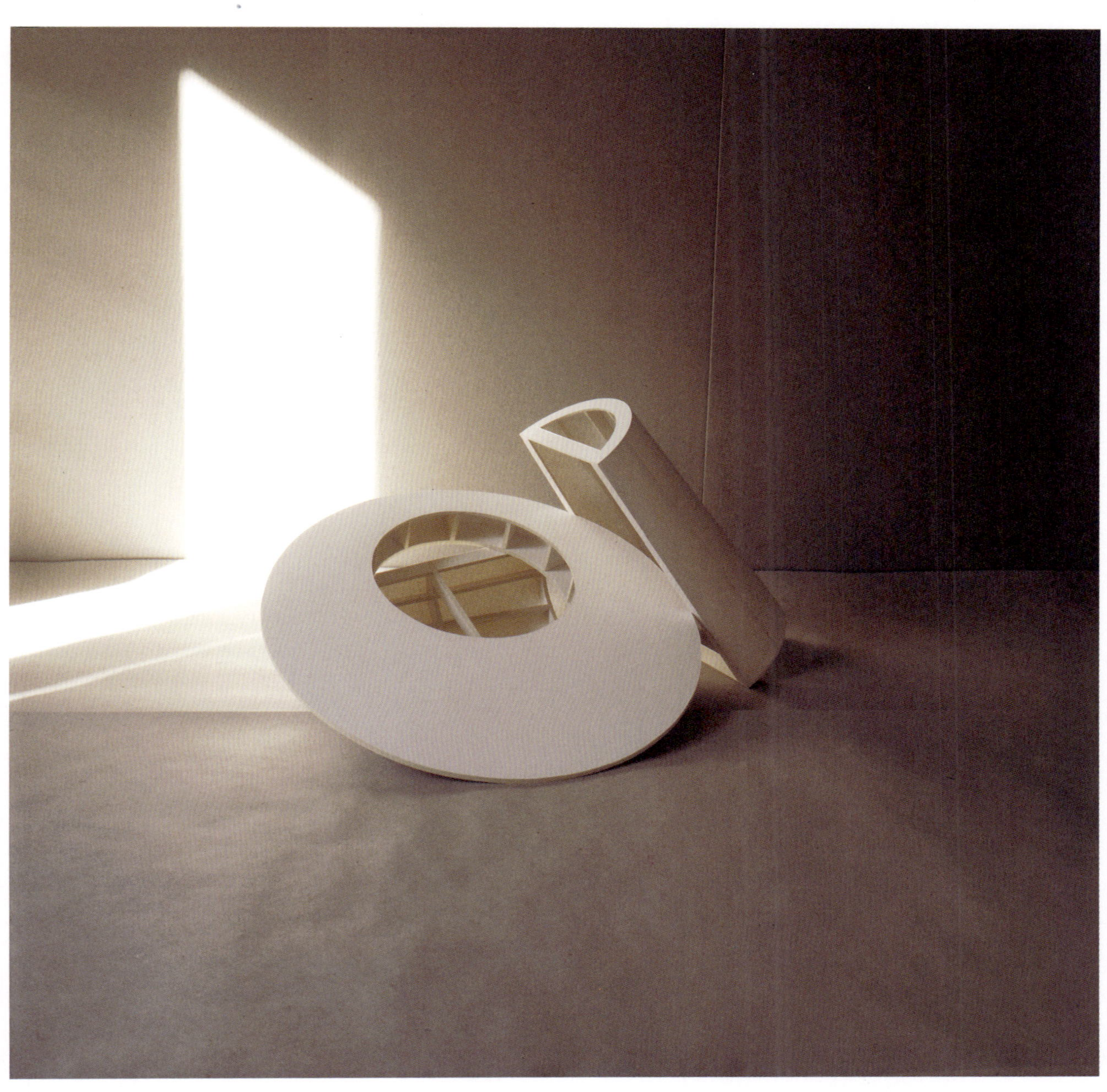

Architektonische Skulptur Studie (Architectural sculpture study), 1982

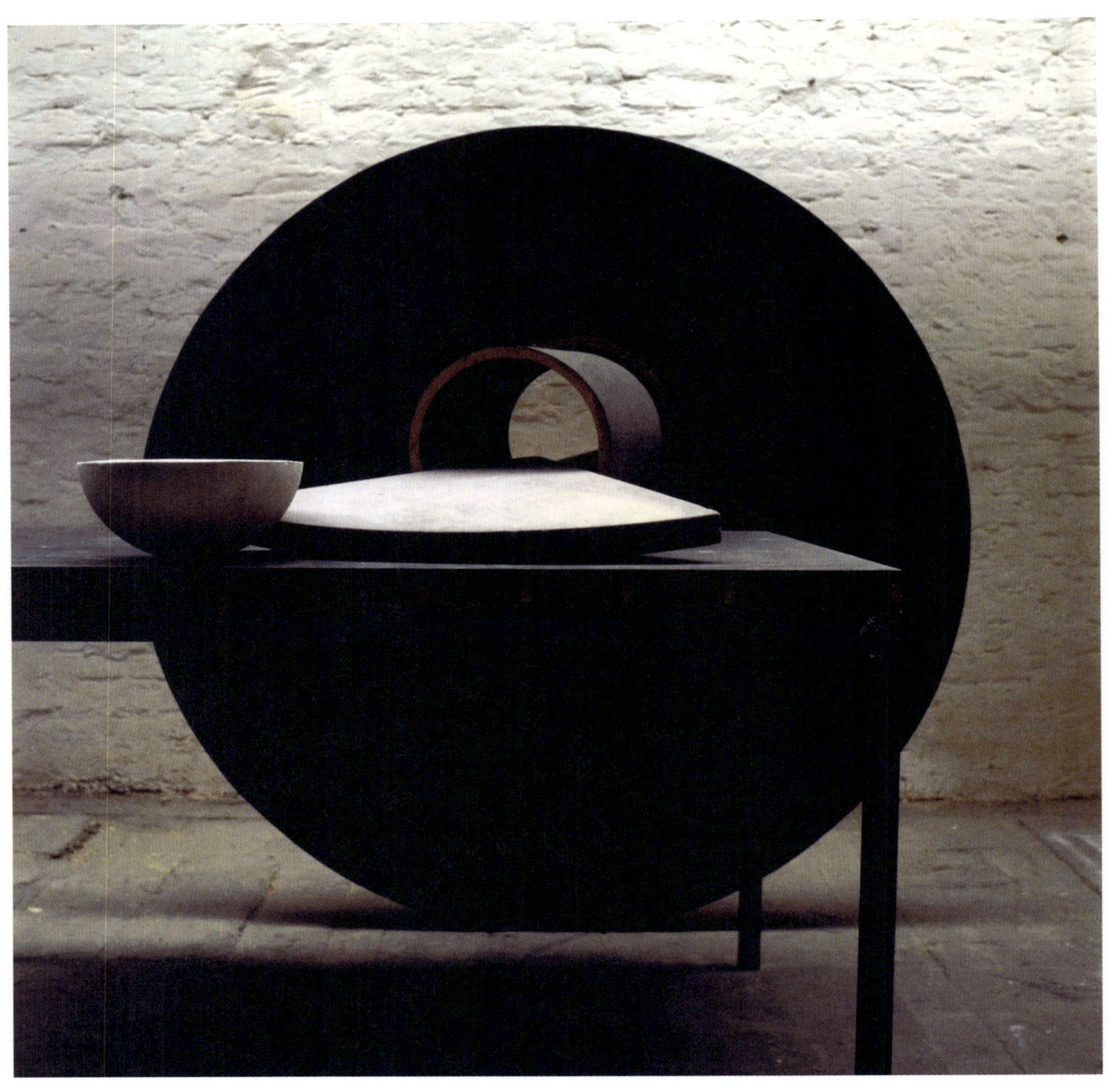

Tunnel Vision, 1983

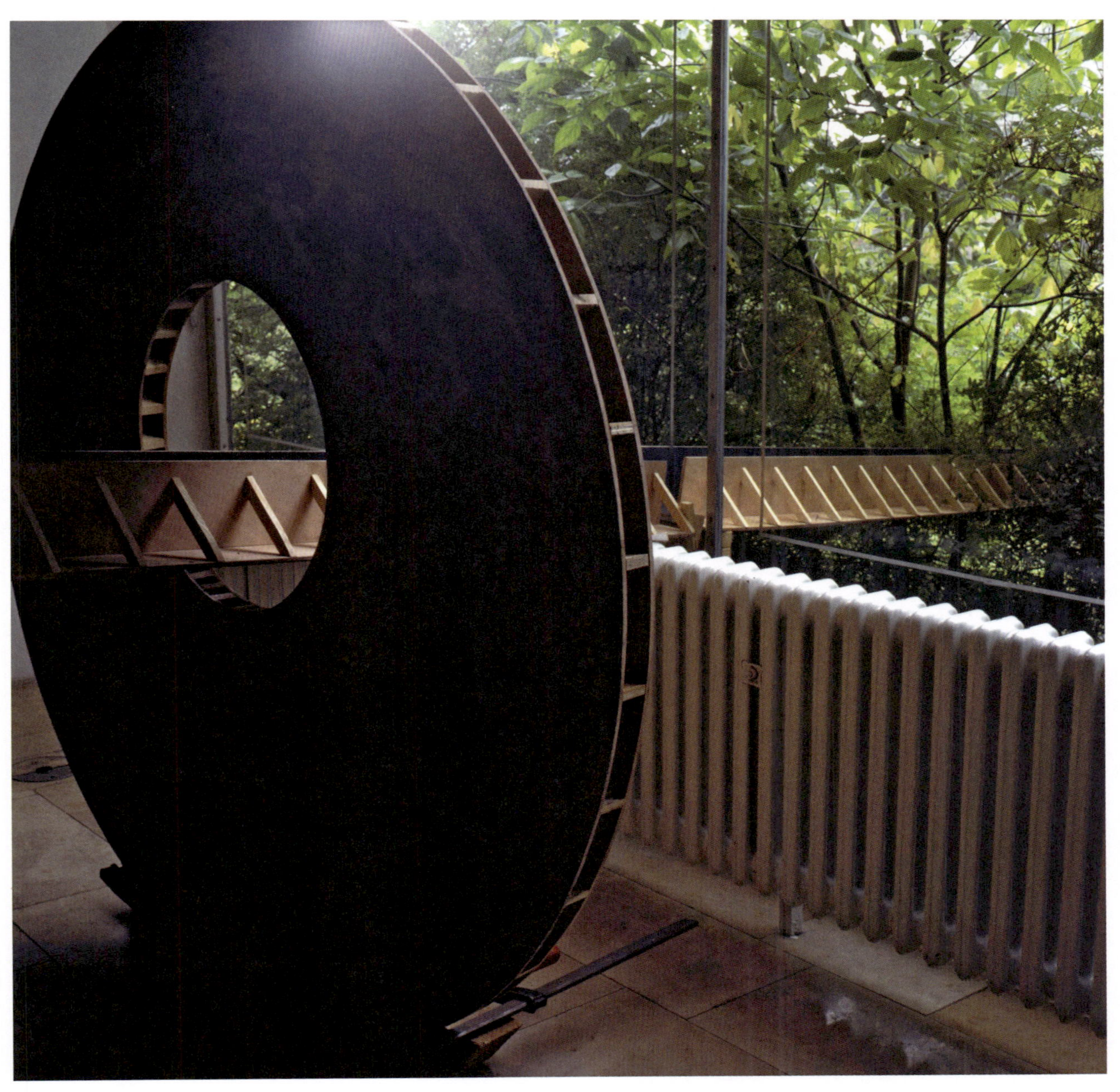

Tunnel Vision: Sculpture Invasion, 1983

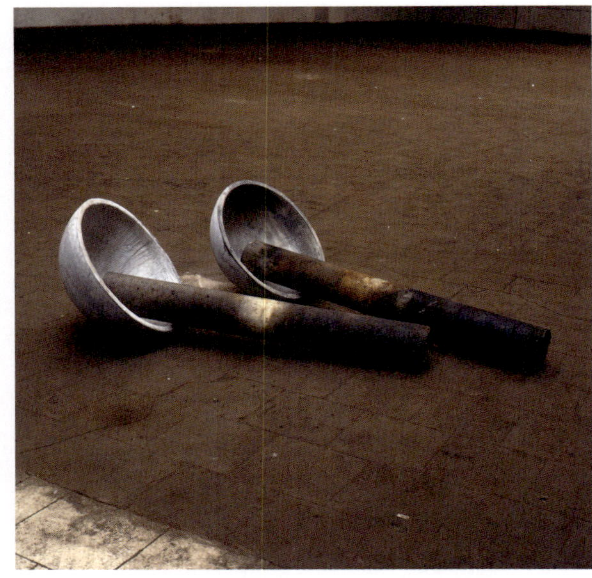

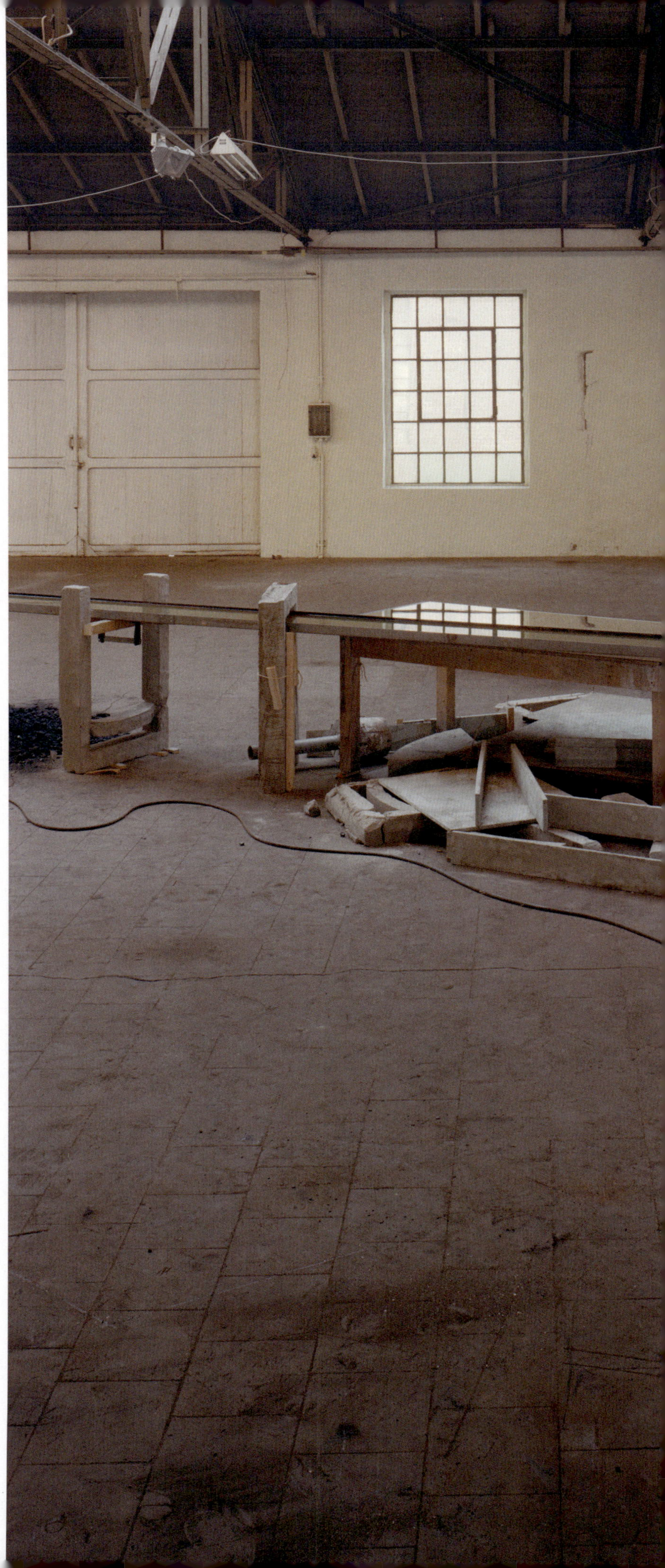

Die ewigen Werte von Gestern (The eternal value from yesterday), 1984–85

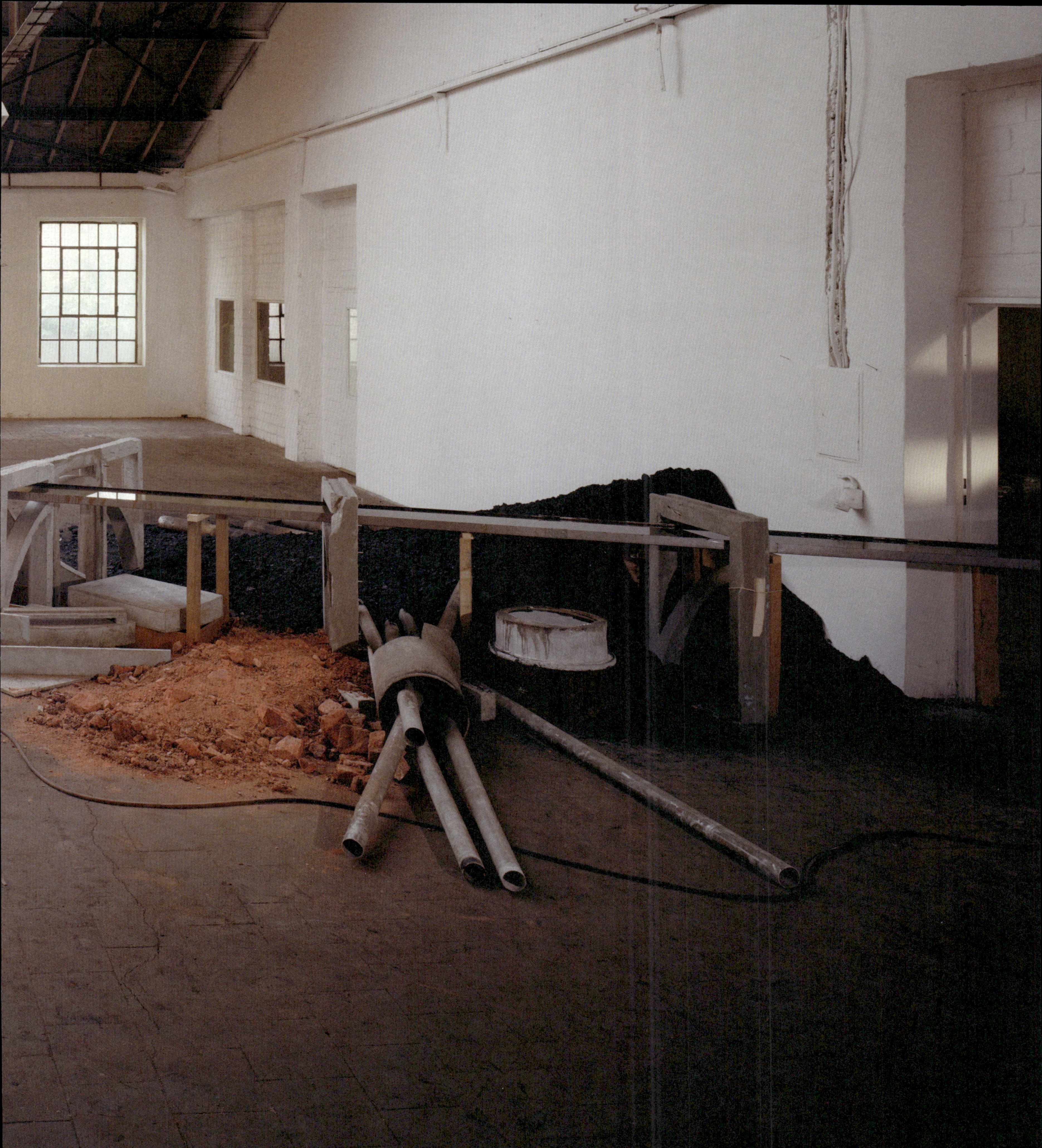

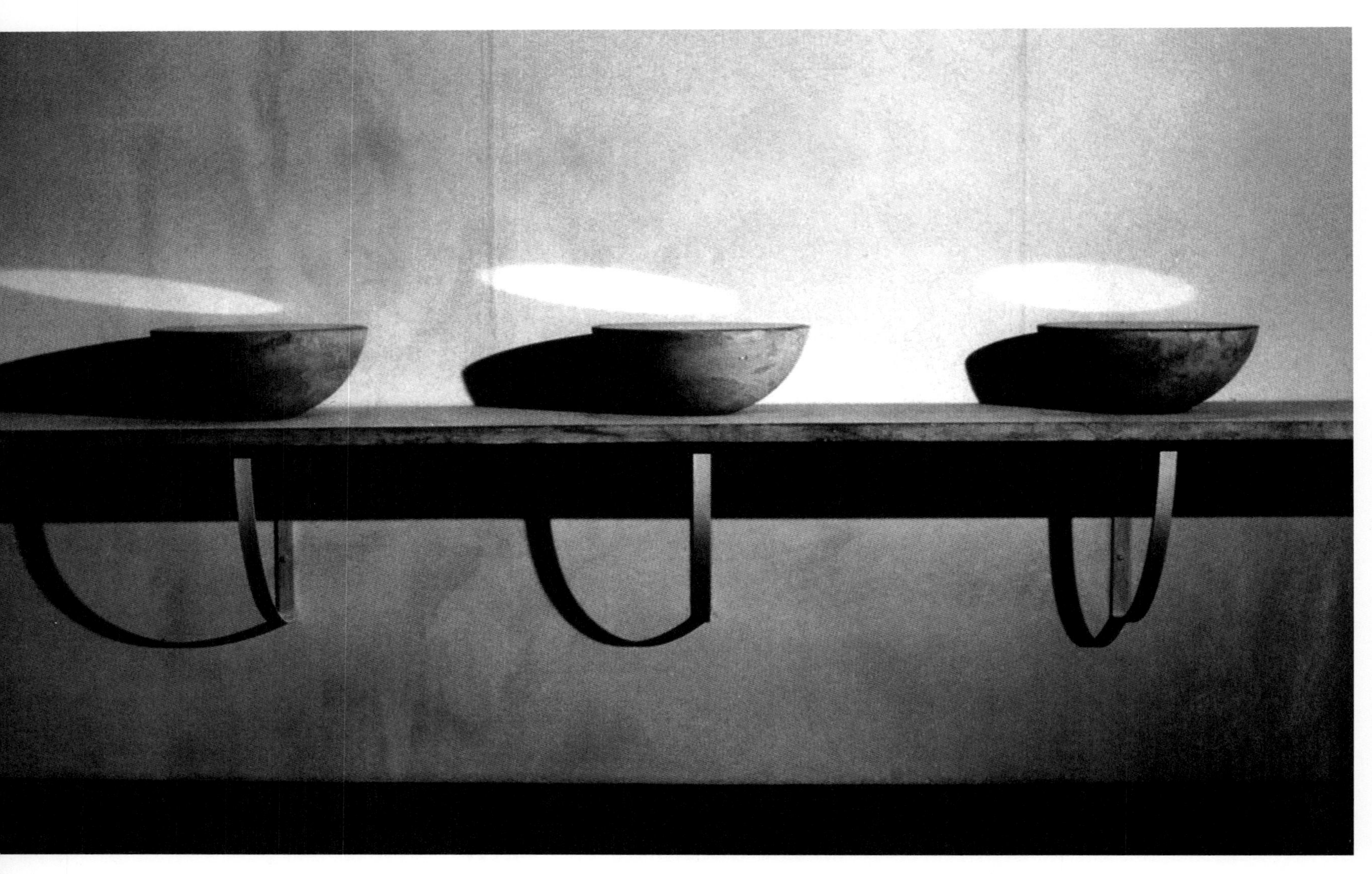

Seven Bowls (detail), 1984

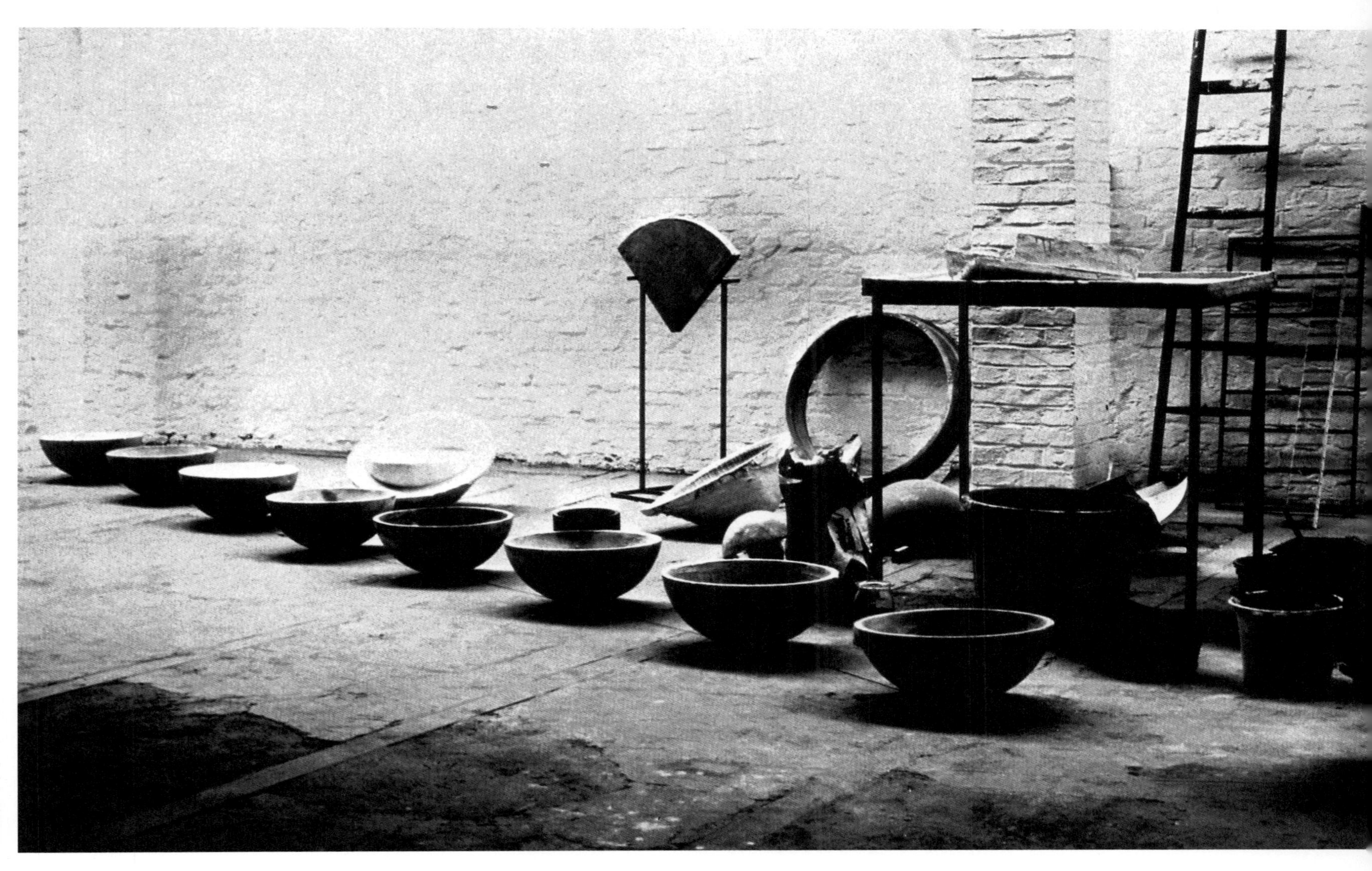

Studio Ratherstrasse, Düsseldorf, Germany

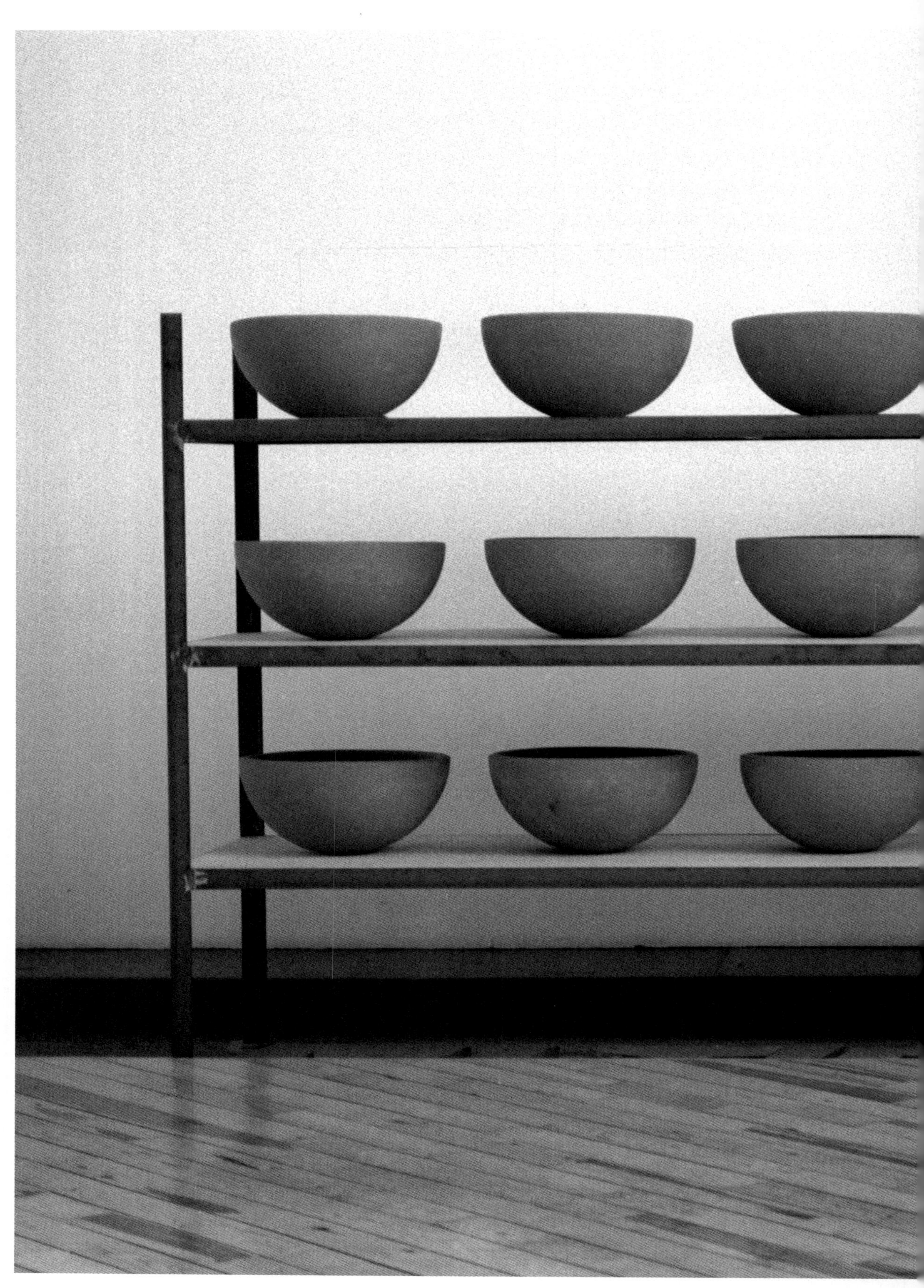

Palacio de Memoria: Mi Tierra
(Palace of memory: my earth), 1999

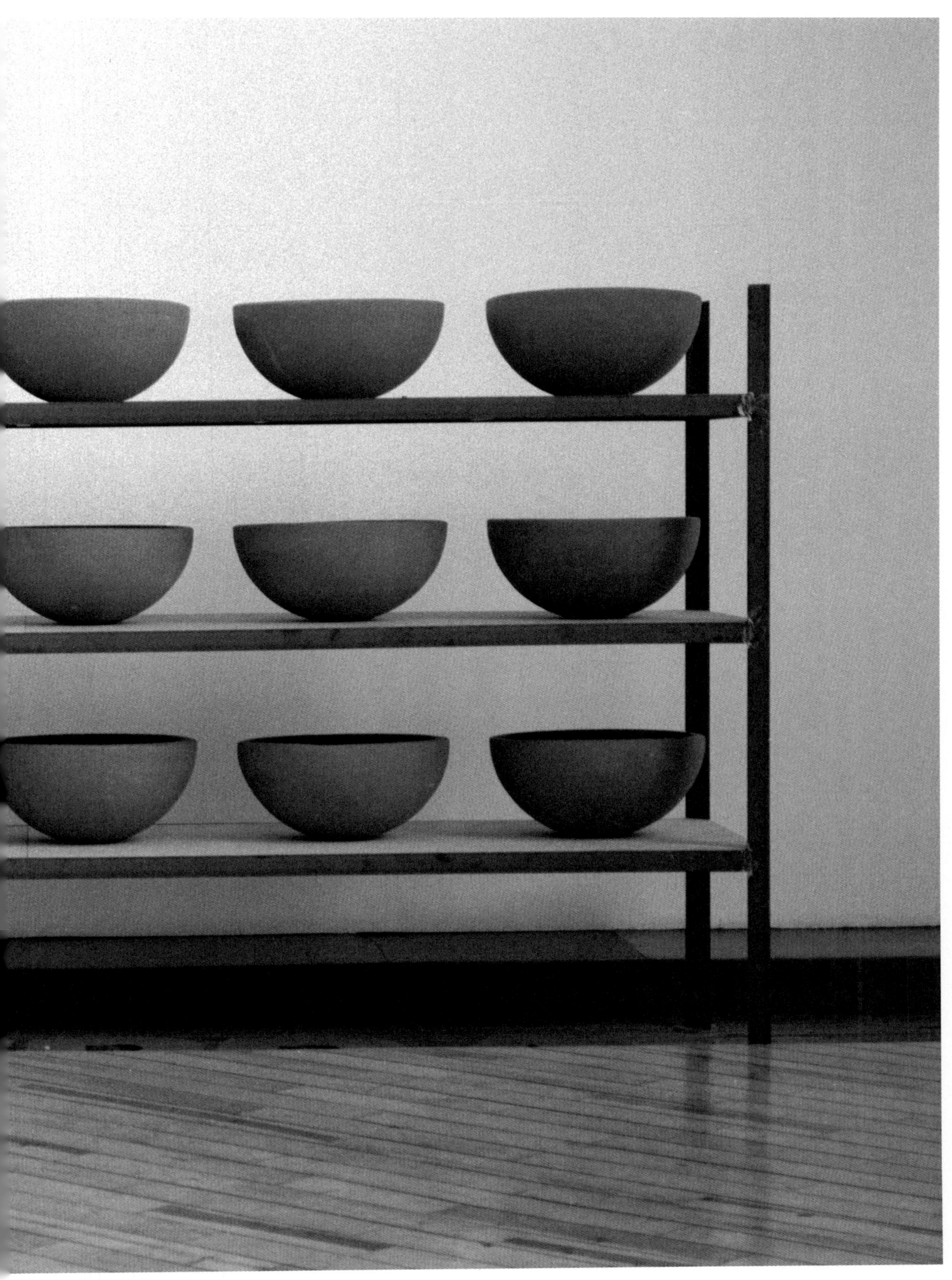

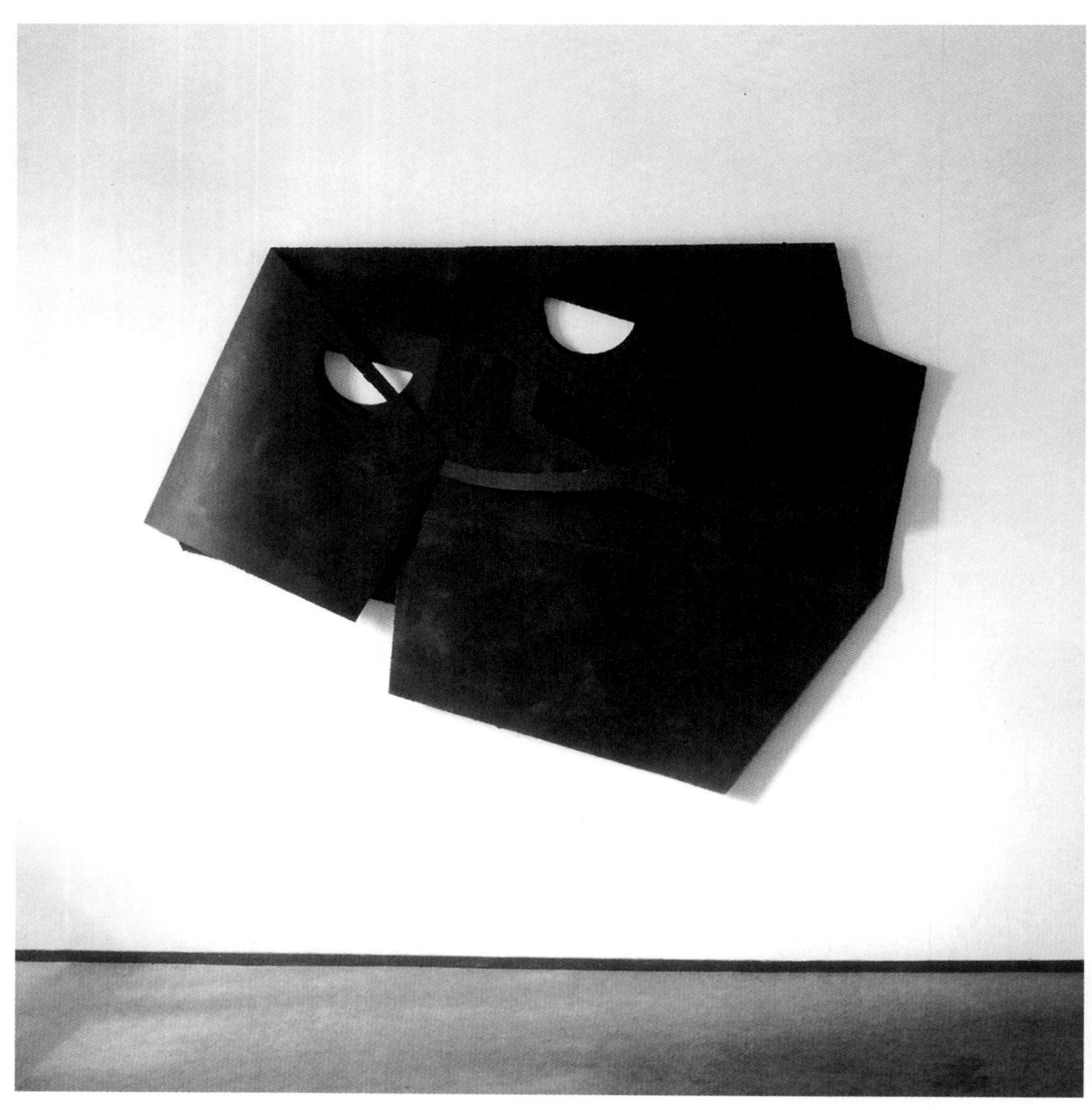

The Exchange "Two Bowls," 1988

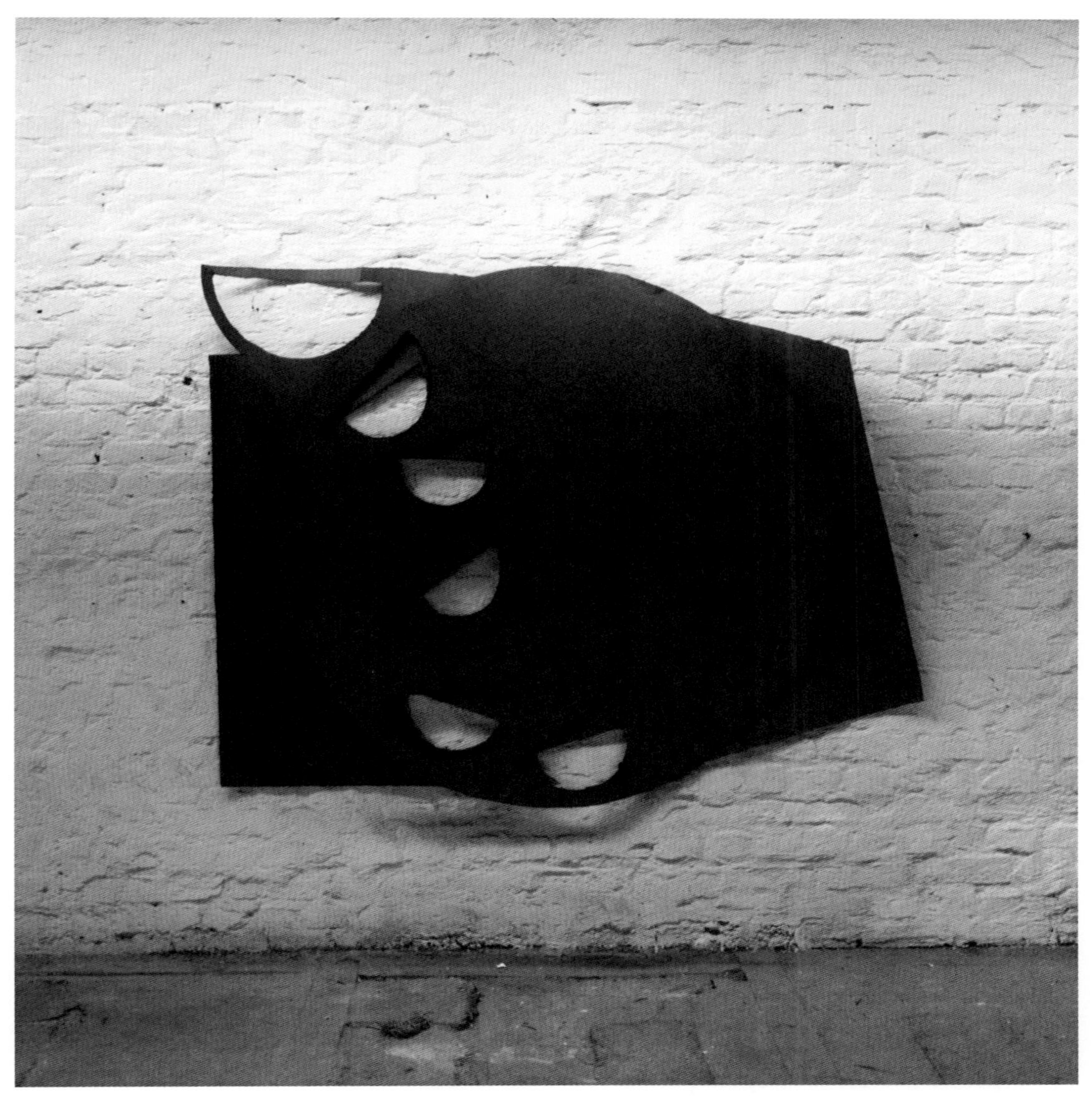

Wall Object, 1984

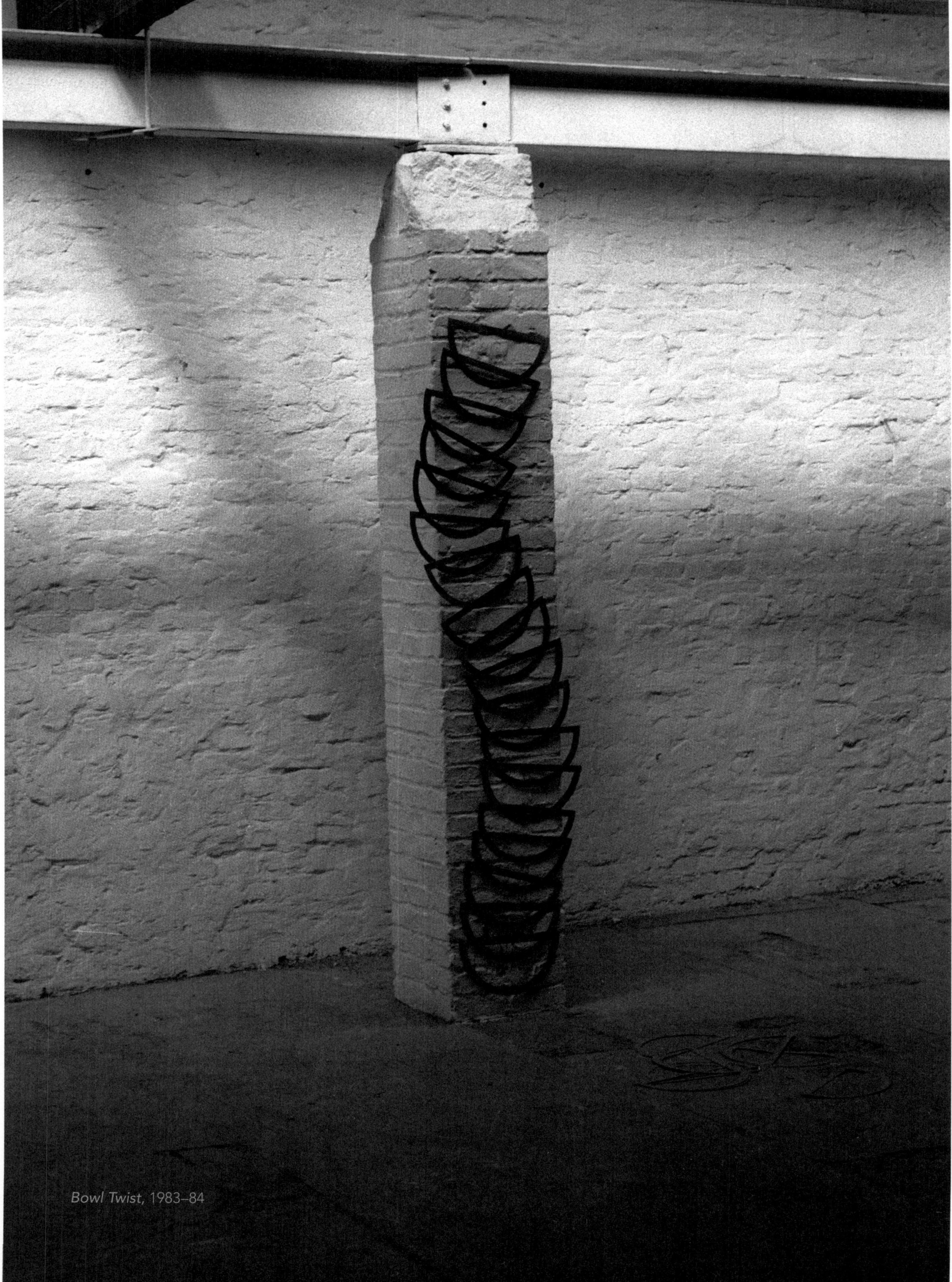

Bowl Twist, 1983–84

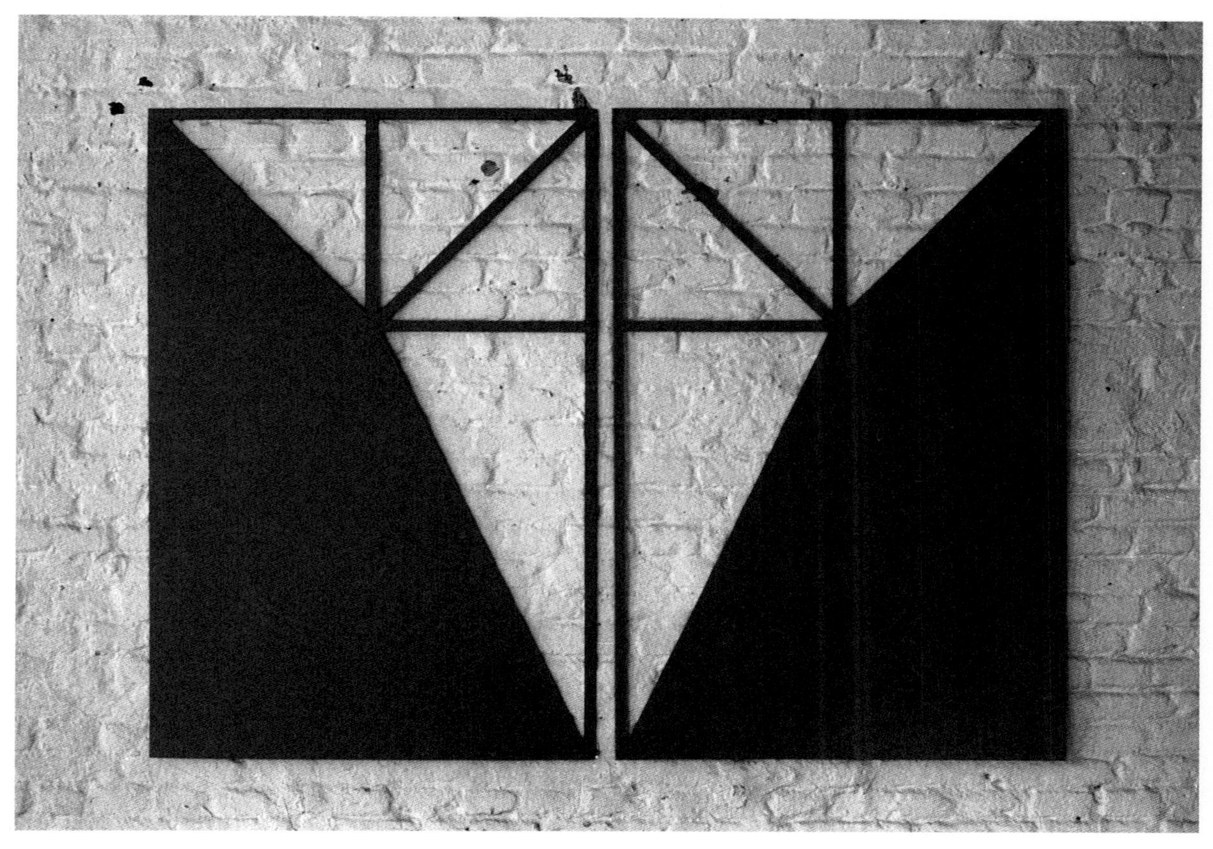

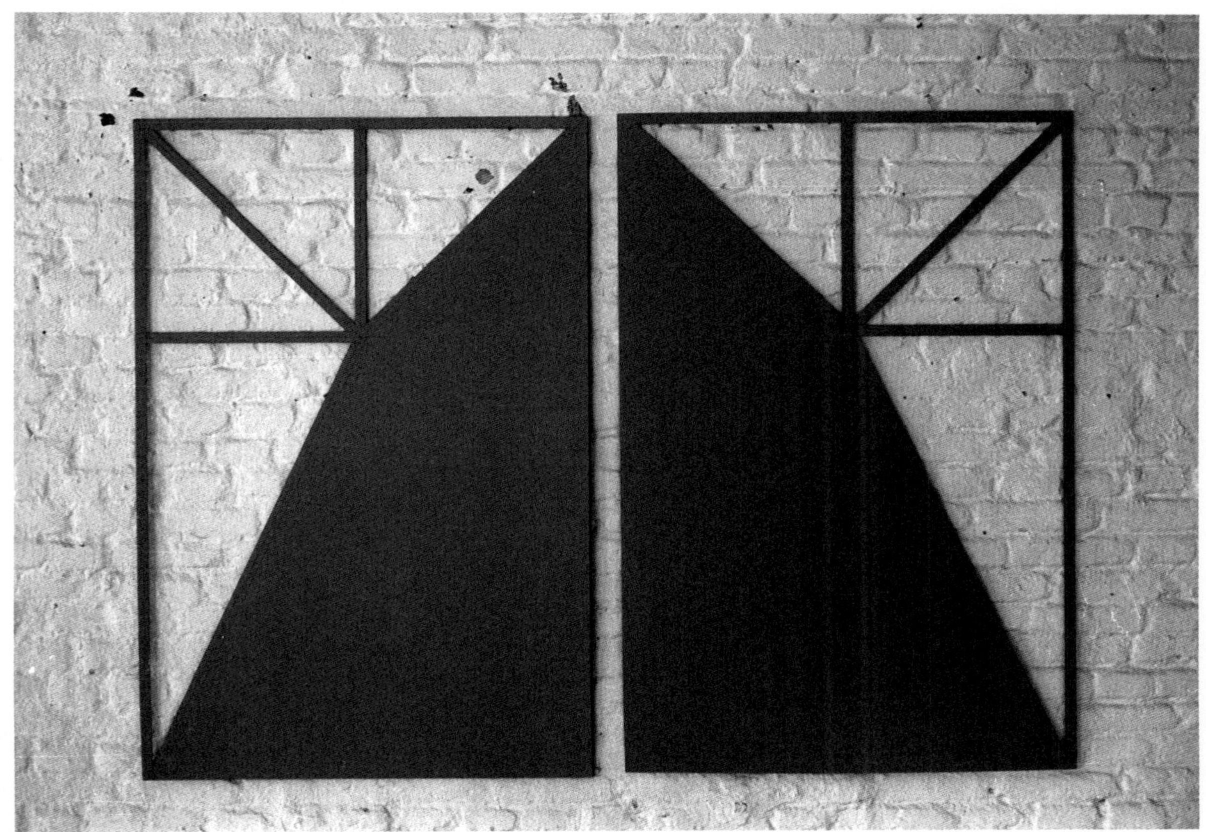

Wall Object, 1983

Wall Object Reversal, 1983

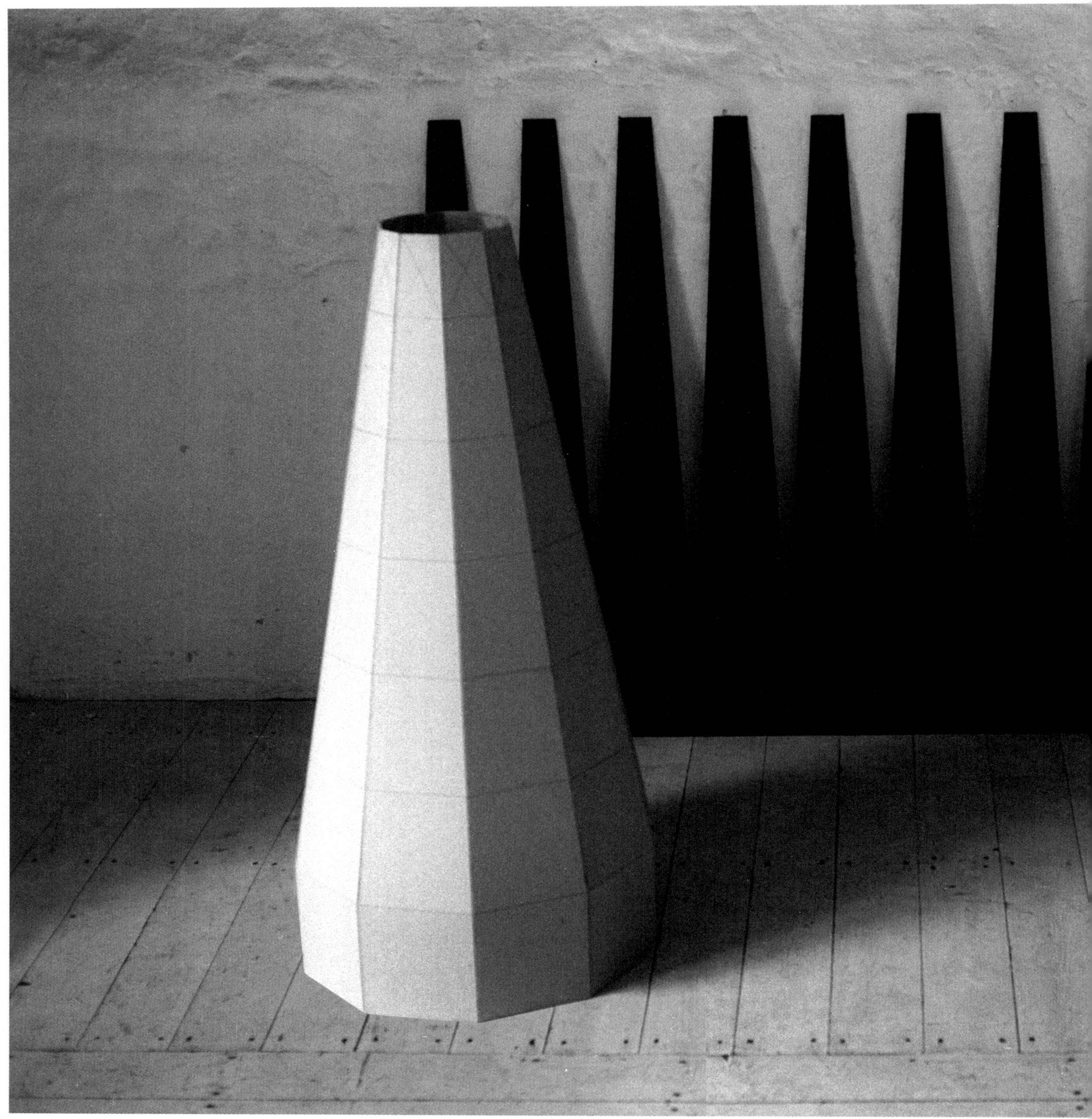

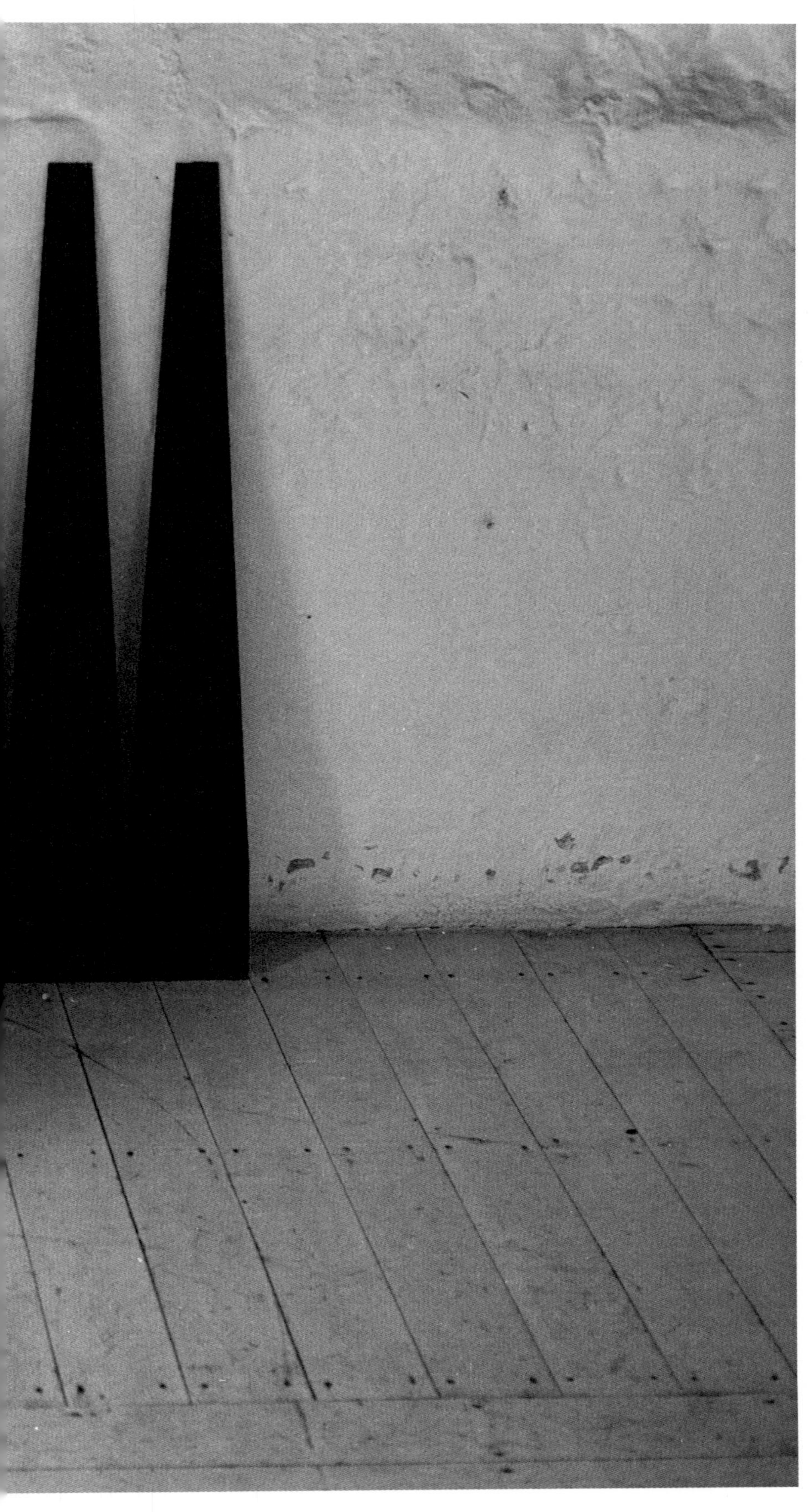

Studio Objekte (Studio objects), 1981–84

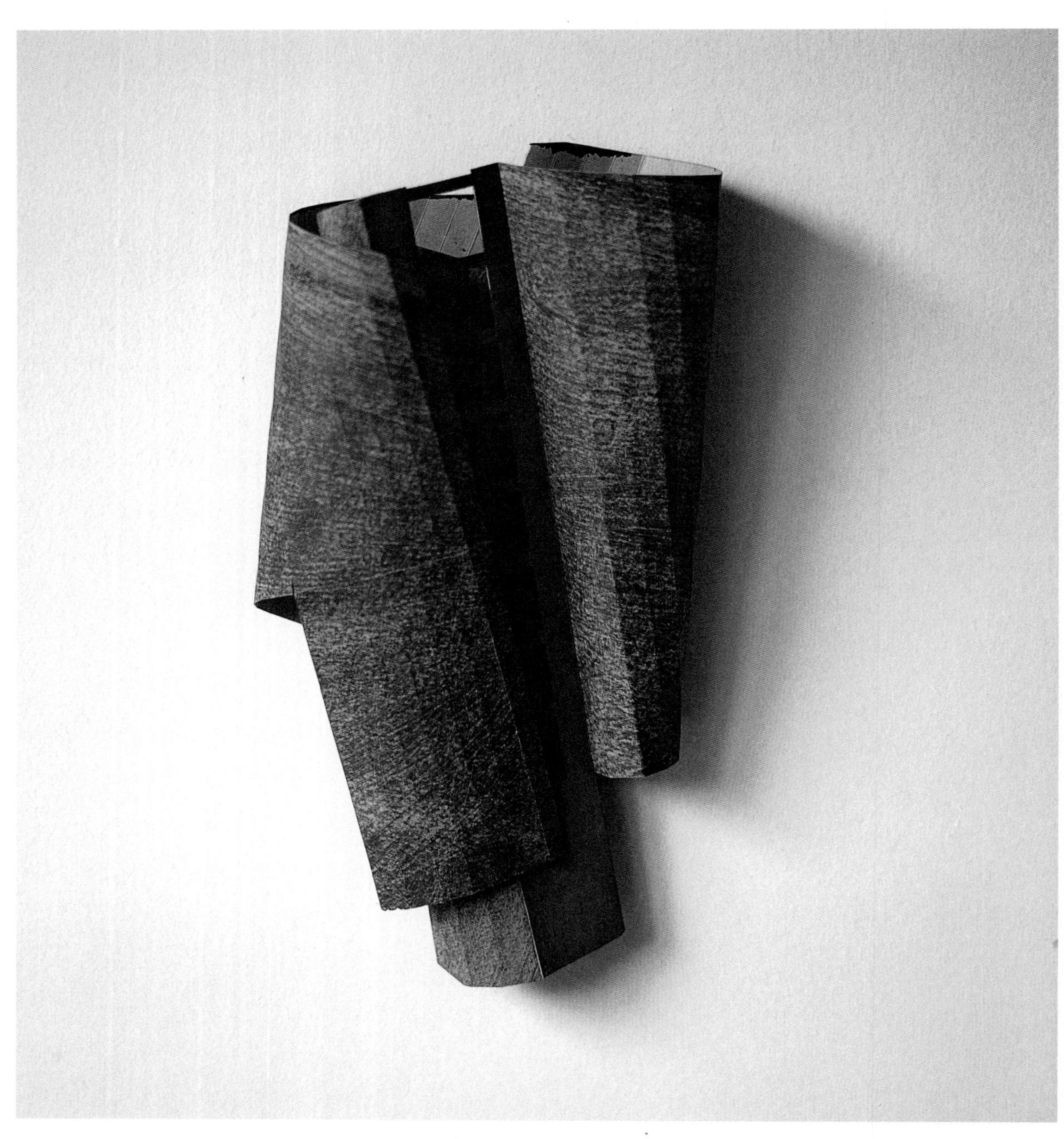

Vintage Prelude Object, 1991–92

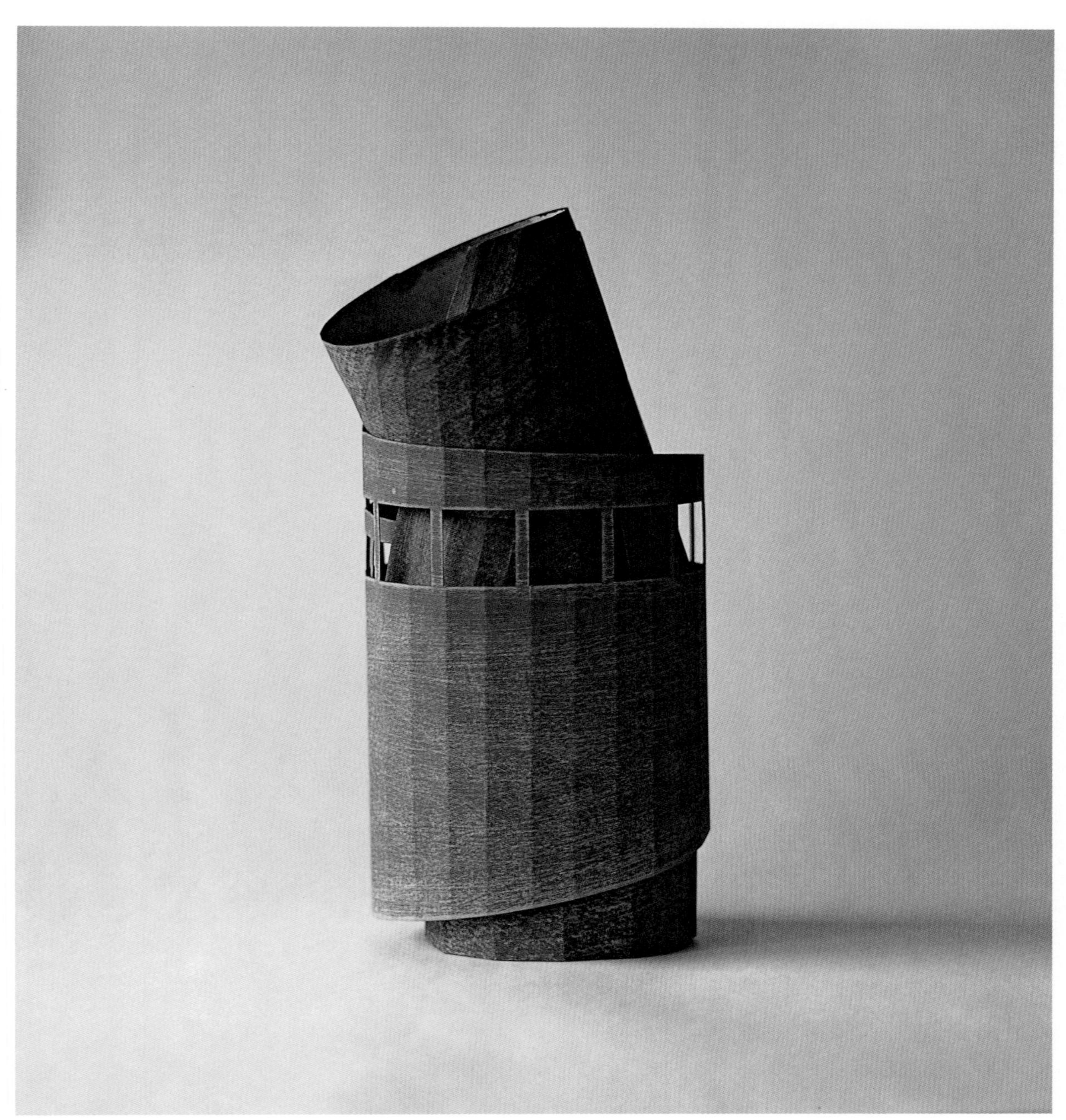

Vintage Prelude Object, 1991–92

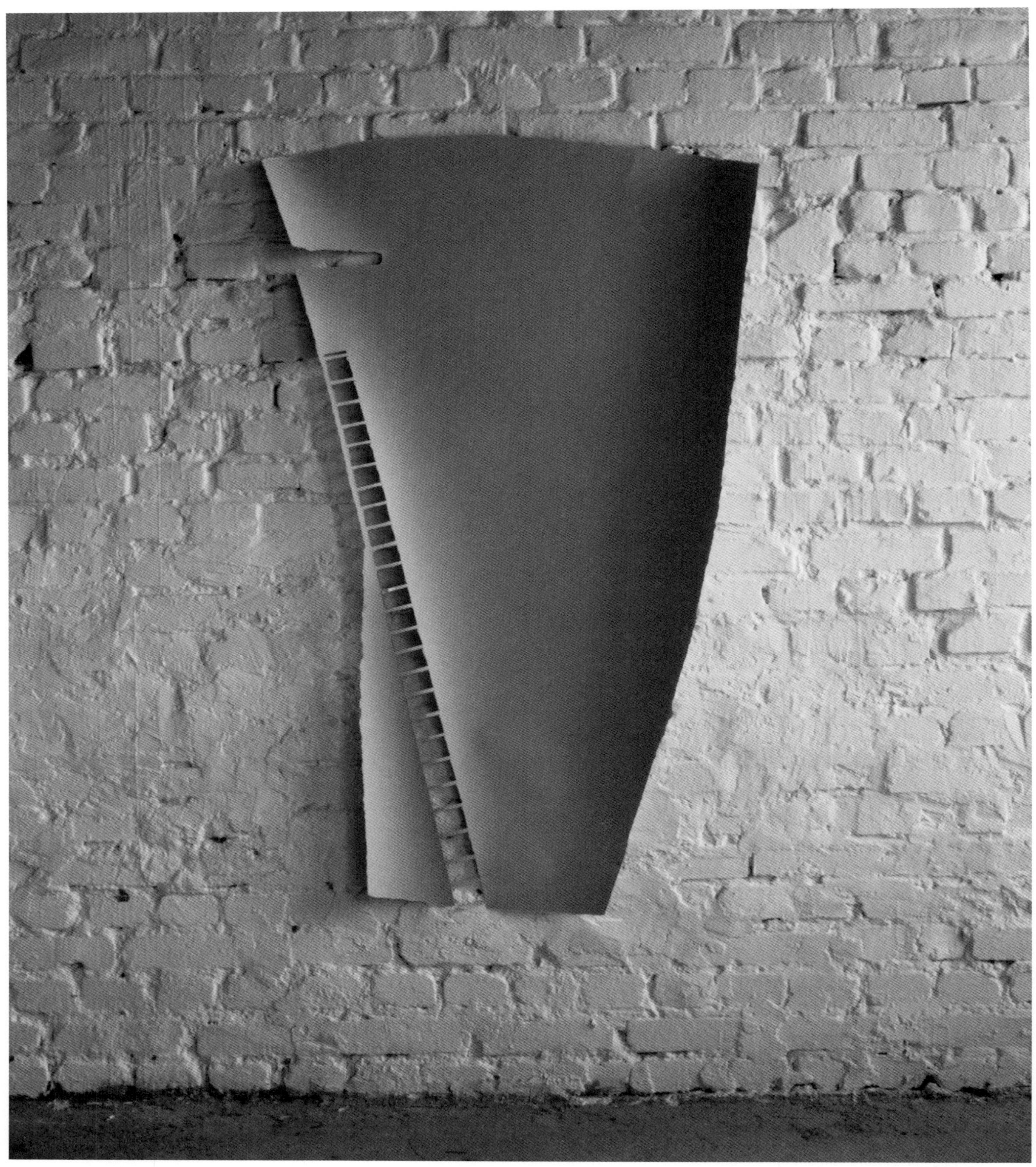

Wall Object, 1982

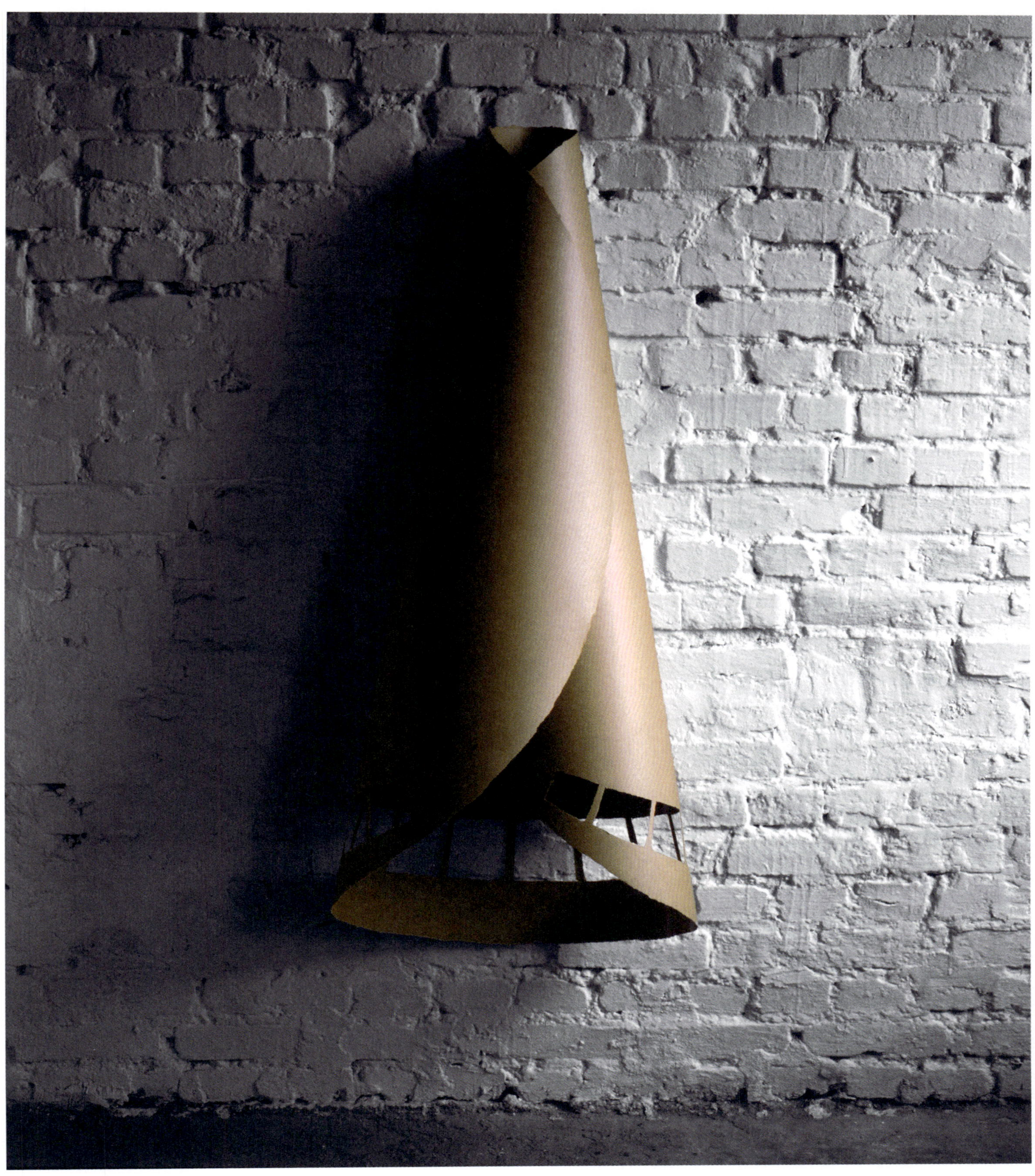

Wall Object, 1982

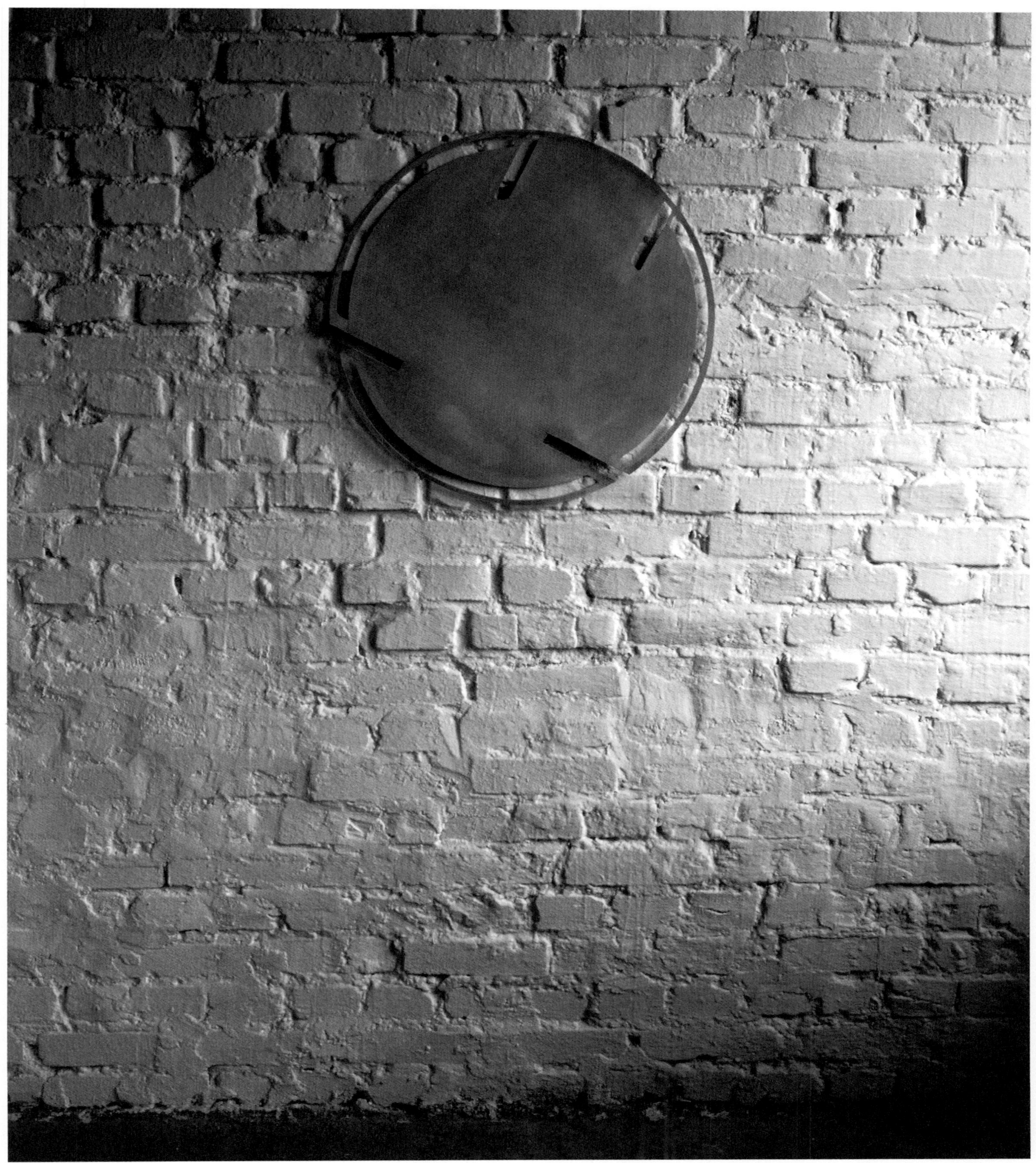

Shield, 1982

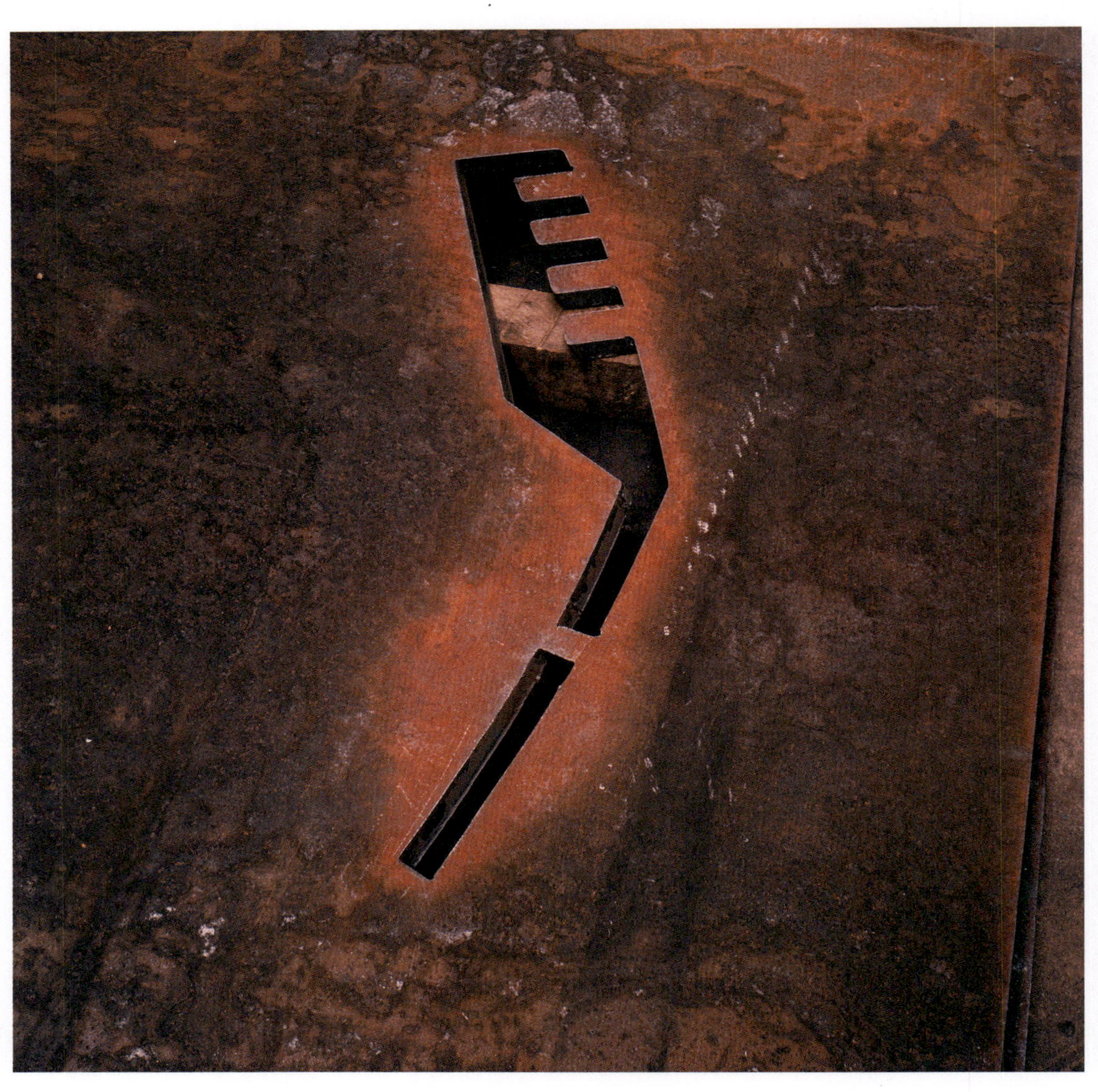

Erdzeichen 1 (Earth signs 1) (detail), 1985

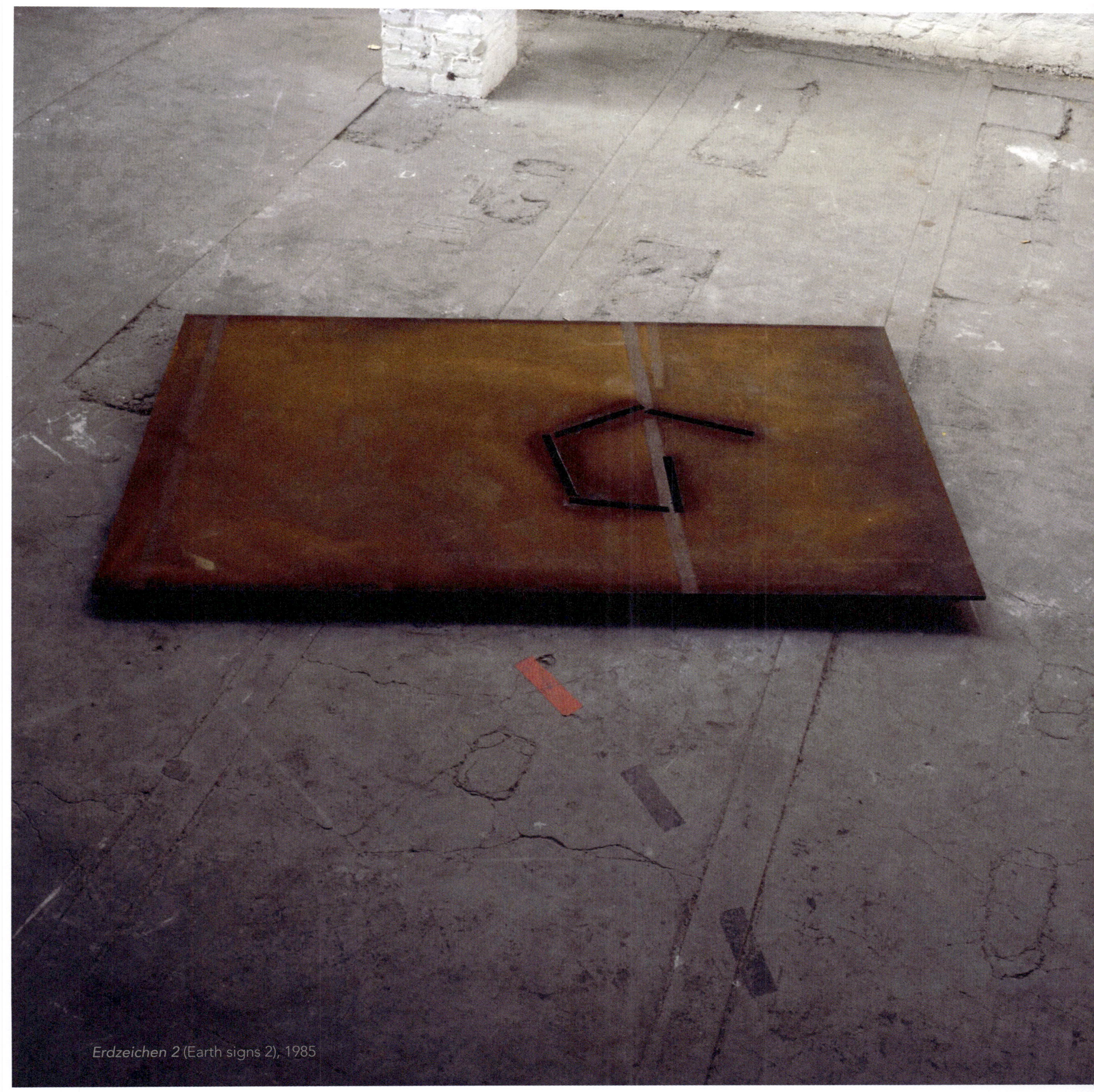

Erdzeichen 2 (Earth signs 2), 1985

A MULTITUDE OF ECHOES: THE ART OF MANFRED MÜLLER

HOWARD N. FOX

The trajectory of Manfred Müller's artistic development has been rich in experimentation and aesthetic discovery, culminating in engrossing results. His oeuvre comprises large-scale, heavy-duty sculptures, assemblages, installations, photographs, paintings, drawings, collages, and molded paperboard constructions. But this diverse body of work in divergent mediums is unified by consistent intelligence and formal curiosity that endlessly engage the physical transformation that the artist perceives to be inherent in his chosen materials.

In the mid-1990s, Müller's early constructions and "combines" (if we may borrow a descriptor more usually associated with Robert Rauschenberg) were fabricated largely from machine parts and industrial "leftovers"—components of automobiles and aircraft, ventilation ducts, electric or gasoline-powered motors, and similar junk goods. Reminiscent of Francis Picabia's early twentieth-century antic collages, which seemed both paeans to and a wry mischief making of machine-age rationality, Müller's constructions defied—subverted, really—the very logic and utility that defines our notion of "machine." These complicated, visually acrobatic sculptures plainly cannibalize extant machinery, repurposing their parts into purposeless presences that assert themselves with flamboyant theatricality. In this period of early artistic maturity, Müller may be regarded as an articulate proponent of large-scale improvisational construction making in the company of historic forerunners, ranging from proto-Dadaist Marcel Duchamp to Constructivists Antoine Pevsner, László Moholy-Nagy, and César Domela to mid-century modernists like David Smith, Alexander Calder, and Jean Tinguely to contemporary colleagues, such as Mark di Suvero, Alice Aycock, Dennis Oppenheim, and Müller's own mentor, Erwin Heerich.

Working in Düsseldorf, Germany, in the early 1980s, Müller had jerry-built many similar improvised sculptures from industrial discards. When he moved to Los Angeles in 1989, the post–Cold War aerospace industry was beginning to downsize from its heyday as a major economic engine in Southern California, and giant corporations like McDonnell Douglas and Lockheed were disposing of heavy-duty aviation and rocketry innards in salvage yards; some of those components ultimately migrated into Müller's improbable constructions. *Black Friday*, a work from 1988 (partially refabricated in 2013 for the present exhibition, which is otherwise composed mainly of work originating from the mid-2000s to the present), is constructed from a cylindrical steel section, about the diameter of a large water main, juxtaposed with a vast industrial

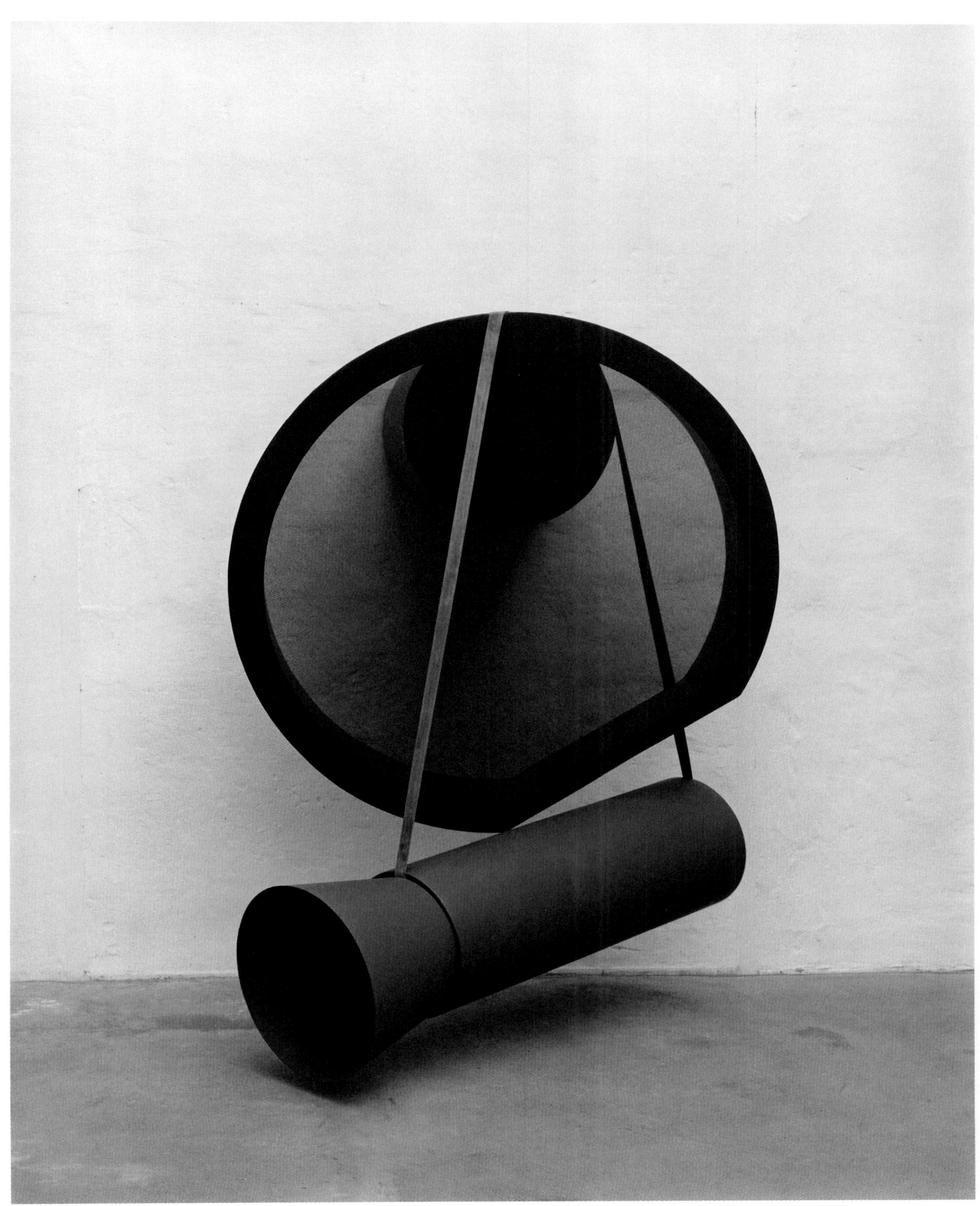
Black Friday, 1988

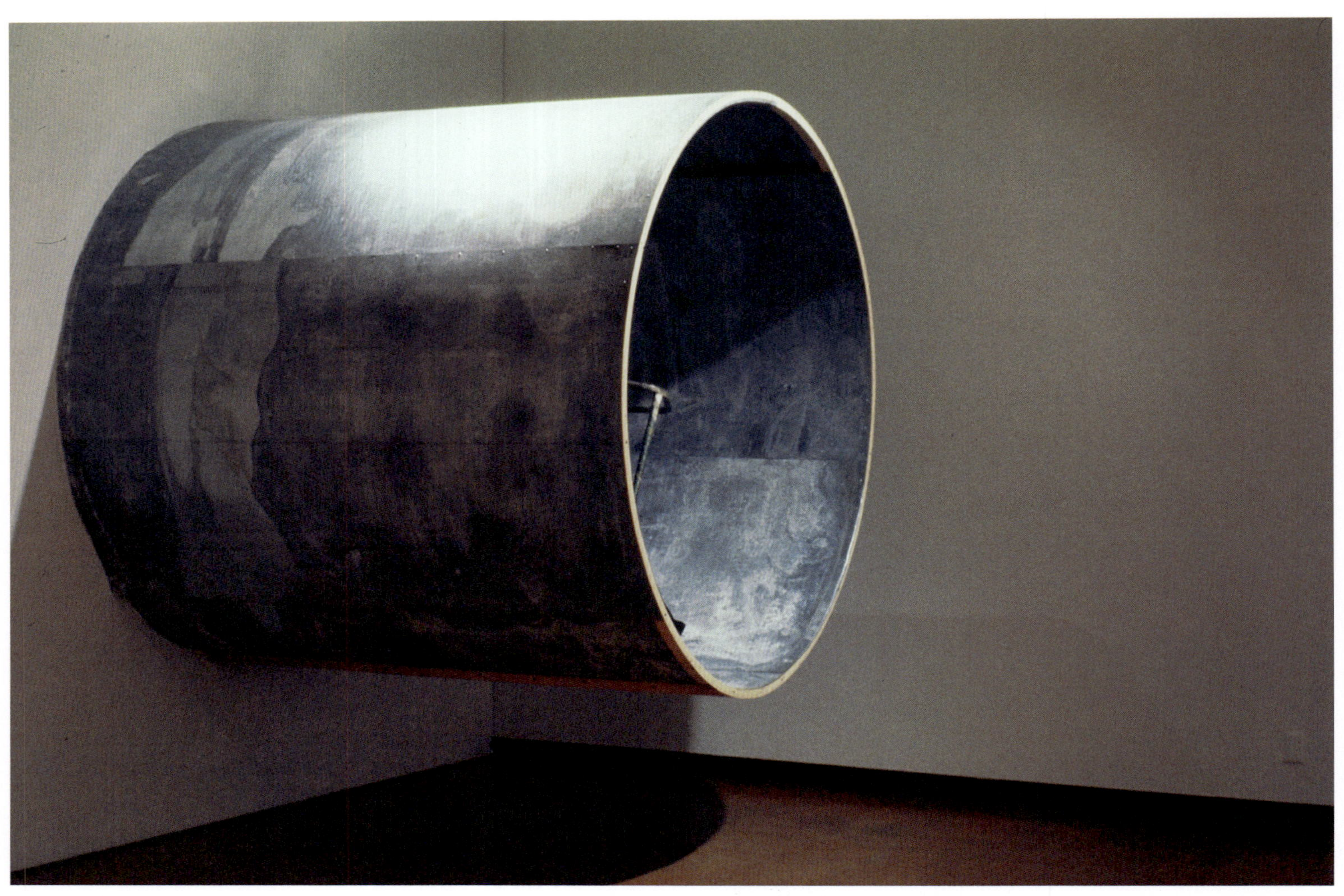

Concept for a Border Town, 1992

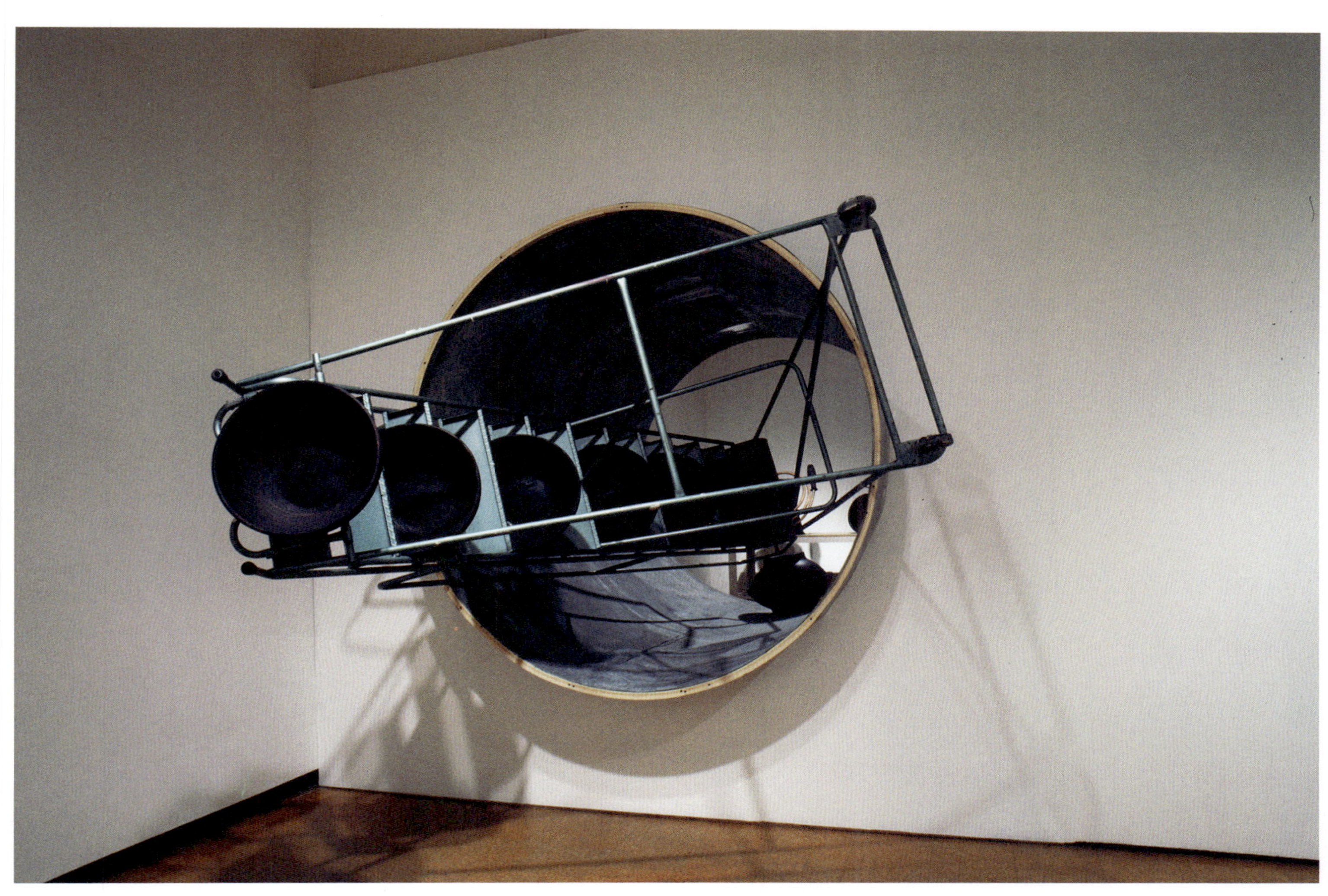

fan attached to the wall. The fan looms pendulously, encroaching on the viewer's space like the Incredible Hulk. It's a daunting elephant in the room. It is characteristic of Müller in his large-scale combines to willingly—perhaps willfully—challenge the comfort zone of the gallery space and the viewer's place in it. Many of his works from the mid-1980s, whether suspended from the ceiling, attached to support columns, or breaking through a wall and claiming dual spaces as they traverse from one room into the next, engage the surrounding architecture.

Müller's fascination with unseemly juxtapositions and intrusions also surfaces in a body of photographic works beginning in 1998 and continuing sporadically since then. These works often feature what he describes as a Romantic photograph—that is, a visually dramatic one—of a public space, such as an open drawbridge spanning the Chicago River, or a view of that city's skyline, or the shore beneath the Santa Monica Pier amid that structure's supporting timbers and the deep shadows they cast on the sloshing tidal flow. Then he alters the black-and-white image, quite intruding upon its intrinsic visual magnetism, through solarization (an old darkroom technique of briefly exposing the photographic paper to bright light while the image emerges in its chemical baths, causing the final picture to appear more like a photographic negative than a normal print) and/or bright pigment dissolved in medium applied randomly to the surface of the finished photograph. Sometimes Müller subsequently places a pigmented sheet of construction paper—a uniform color field with no imagery—to abut the printed image, to jarring effect. These interventions into conventional photography call into question both the inherent properties of the medium and Müller's artistic appropriation of it into the realm of deliberate alteration and aberration, an intervention not only into the facticity of the particular photographic image but also into the aesthetic project of pictorial photography itself.

Müller's early audacity contrasts with his more recent paper "drawings" and sculptures made of construction paper and paperboard. Intuitively conceived as formalist entities and exquisitely executed with careful precision, they have a spare elegance and a no-nonsense approach to form and materiality. These so-called drawings are actually collages, pieced together from monochrome sheets of paper, which are hand-painted and razor-cut by Müller to incorporate into sophisticated compositions. The anatomy of these compositions is in part determined by their perimeters, their silhouettes; but a more subtle, less visible yet equally real activity transpires in their interior

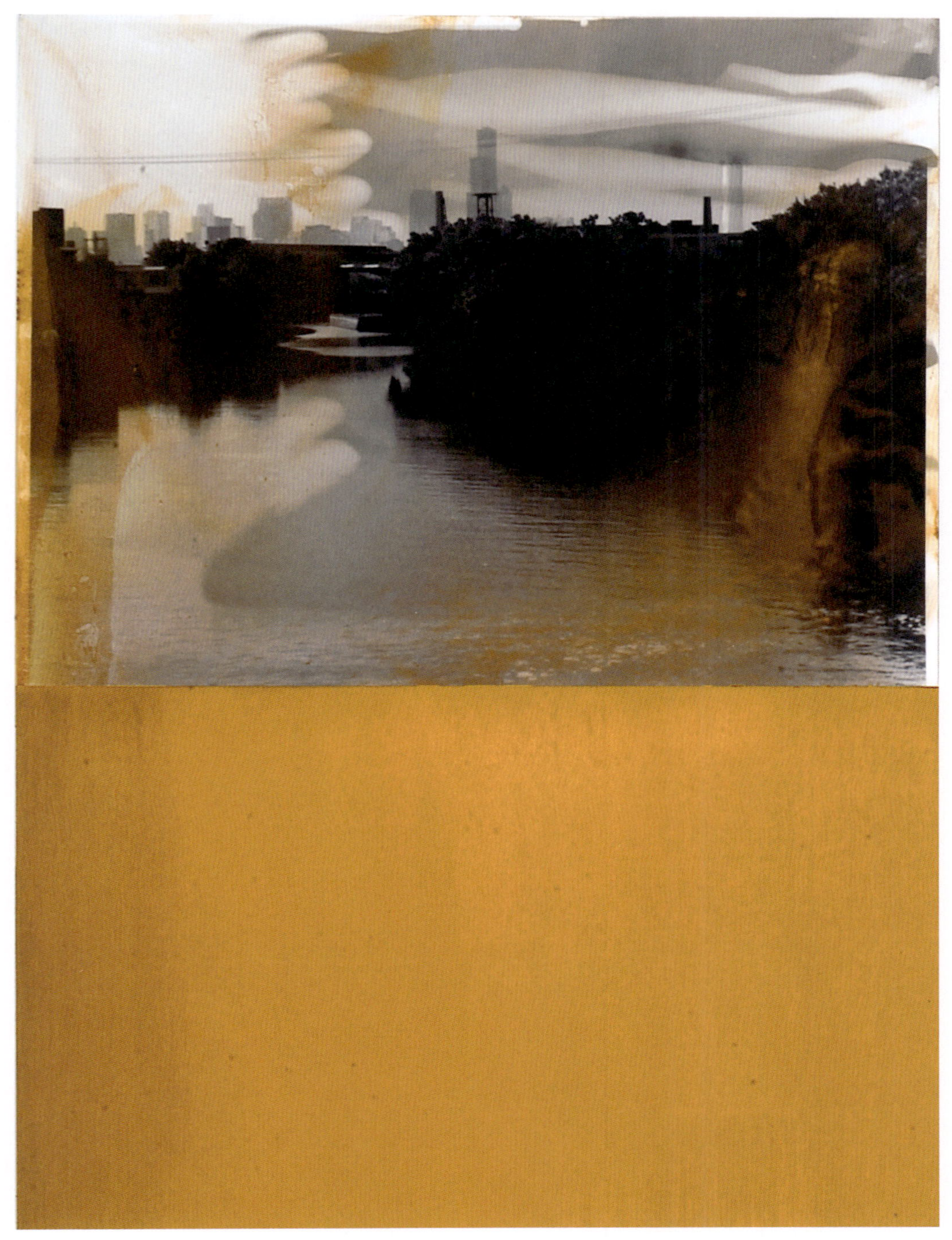

Unique Hidden Cache: River Scene, 2004

space, where paper is laid over paper or sheets are matched edge to
edge atop their paperboard backing. These paper-to-paper "mating"
acts are almost imperceptible at first glance, and the viewer may
have to squint a bit to discern the seams where the papers meet.

Müller's aesthetics of the edge can be tricky. The border of a three-
dimensional expanse expresses its two-dimensional property: the edge
acts, in effect, as a line or a line segment. In Müller's concise, quiet
paper compositions from the 2000s, the edge is where the drama is.
Some of these collaged "sketches," as Müller calls them, use ordinary
store-bought manila folders that he "enamels" with a surface of, for
example, black oil pastel. He then affixes those planes of treated
paper to a ground of white or colored board. Simple enough—indeed,
quite minimal in technique and execution—but the folders' die-cut
rounded corners and the declivity of their tab cuts serve as major
visual drama, analogous to an unanticipated key shift in a Haydn string
quartet or a coloratura trill from a bel canto aria in a Mozart opera.

In other works, Müller may underscore a charcoal-gray plane of paper
with an umber-colored paper substrate that extends perhaps no more
than a sixteenth of an inch beyond the surface paper's edge, evoking
what Müller describes as a "halo effect"—a vibrant nimbus of color that
"levitates" the paper layer atop it and jolts the viewer's mind and eye
with sudden evidence of nearly hidden—and nearly intrusive—vitality.
And that visual interruption is so physically slight that it might not show
up clearly in a printed reproduction of the object, yet it is electrifying to
anyone who sees it up close and personal, perceiving it for the object
that it truly is. Müller subtly but insistently engages and manipulates the
work's materiality. Often the sheets are lightly scored with grooves that he
"draws" into the surface using the side of a screwdriver blade; the effect
is scarcely visible at a quick glance, but it imparts passages of textural
definition that course across certain areas of the picture plane—and not
across other areas. Sometimes you have to look hard to discover these
marks, but they impart a definite drama and eventfulness to the final work.

Despite the centrality of these flat works in Müller's art during the last
eight years or so, he also works three-dimensionally, using expanses of
construction paper that hang loosely off the wall as relief forms and in
an ongoing body of volumetric paperboard constructions. The recent
paperboard constructions, especially, strike the eye as careful, formal
études, or meditations, on composition, materiality, and color—visually

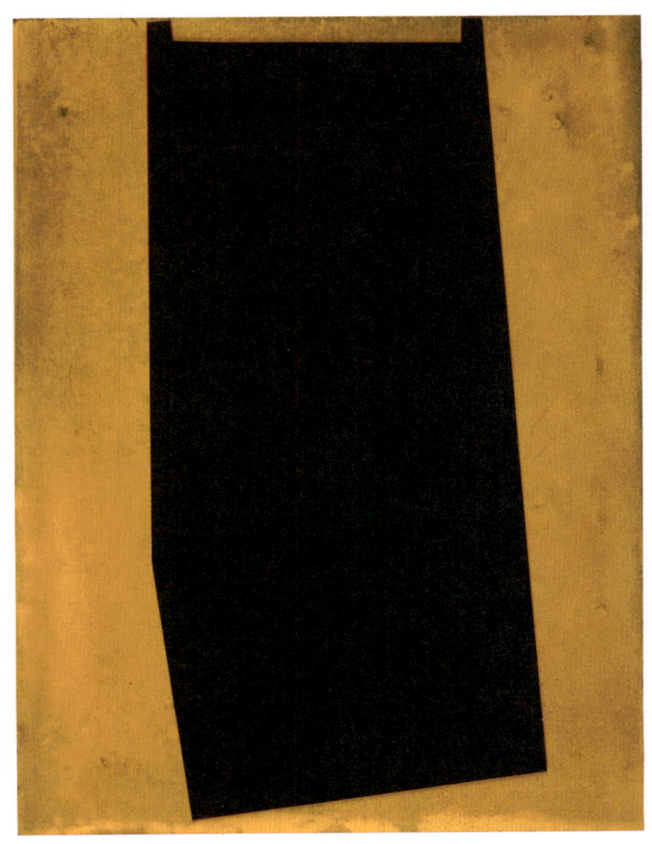

Oxid Yellow, 2007
Oxid Yellow, 2007
Oxid Yellow, 2007

Under My Skin 22/131, 2007

Under My Skin 4, 2007

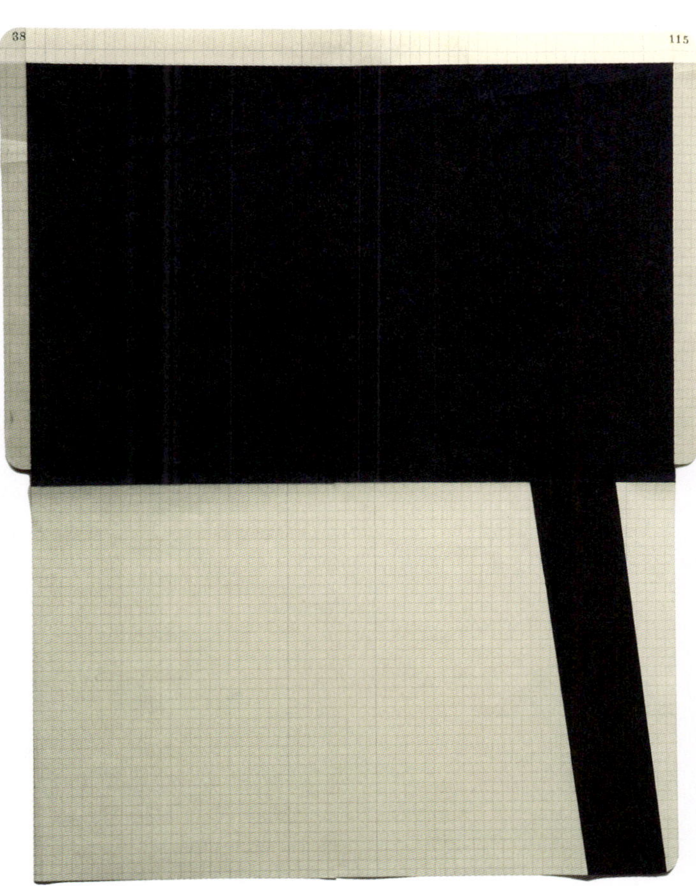

Under My Skin 38/115, 2007

quiet, self-contained, and intimate, maybe even a tad prim. But, in fact, they are imbued with a multitude of echoes of worldly things outside of themselves. For as formalistic as they are, they are also about process and their own facture. They are decisively sculptural, yet they are formed from flat paperboard that Müller molds through moisture into biomorphic, shapely, hollow volumes that may be either freestanding or wall mounted. He occasionally cuts irregular holes into their surfaces, which serve as windows of a sort, allowing glimpses into the forms' interiors. The undulations and dimensional modeling, which engage light and shadow, are wrought entirely from material that was originally flat and brittle—a feat of manipulation and transformation that has little to do with the "inherent" properties of Müller's chosen medium.

Further, they appear monochromatic—usually white or earth-toned— yet they are swarming with vestiges of the transformative application of pigment, either translucent water-based washes or more opaque oil pastel. When seen in concert, they reveal myriad softly colored yet unmistakable and intriguing variations: the range of hues that might be generically called "white" are more accurately described as ivory, sand, buff, alabaster, titanium, oyster, snow, eggshell, and so forth. Their color value may be variously luminous and brilliant, chalky and glaring, or dusky and smoldering. And their application is patently observable as hand-applied—not brushed, not sprayed, not daubed, but rubbed on, by hand. They are white, yes, but they are also so much more.

Like Jean Arp's sculpture, their biomorphic shapes suggest organic, protozoan life forms. But they are not simply *bio*morphic; even at their most abstract, they are more *anthropo*morphic, evoking, specifically, the *human* body. Some works in Müller's studio at the time of this writing (July and August 2013) are wall bound, loosely resembling torsos or the crucified Christ's shoulders and outstretched arms. Absolutely no pictorial image is limned or depicted—all of the objects, whether wall bound or freestanding, are non-objective abstractions—but these works' volumes, shapes, and scale are anthropomorphic and engage viewers and their own bodies one-on-one, cohabiting the beholder's space as if they were stand-ins for human entities. Put simply (perhaps too simply), they are personable presences in the viewer's presence—they are not shaped paperboard "things" to be clinically observed so much as formalistic "phantoms" vaguely referencing the human physique.

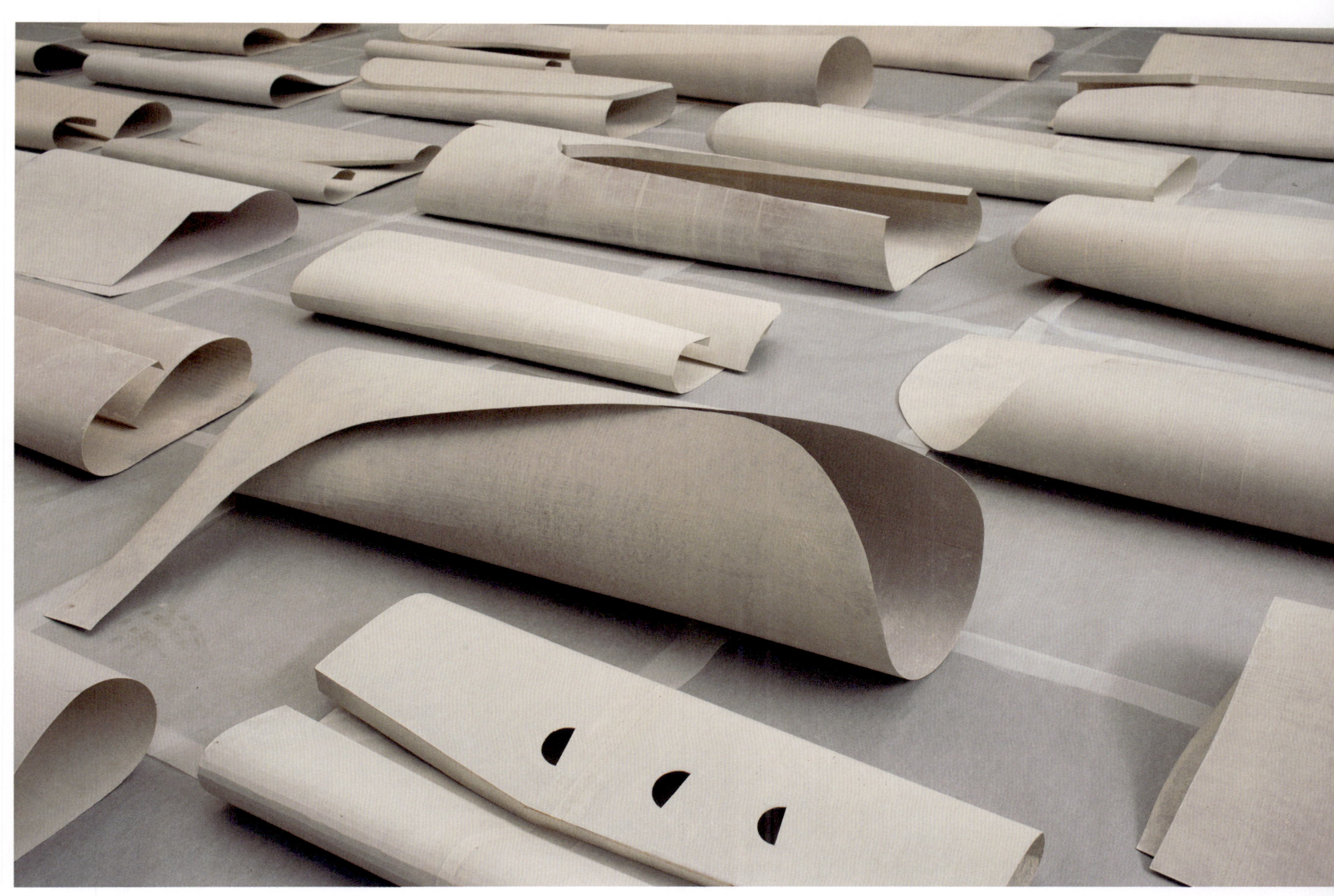

White Preludes at Federal Avenue studio, Los Angeles, CA

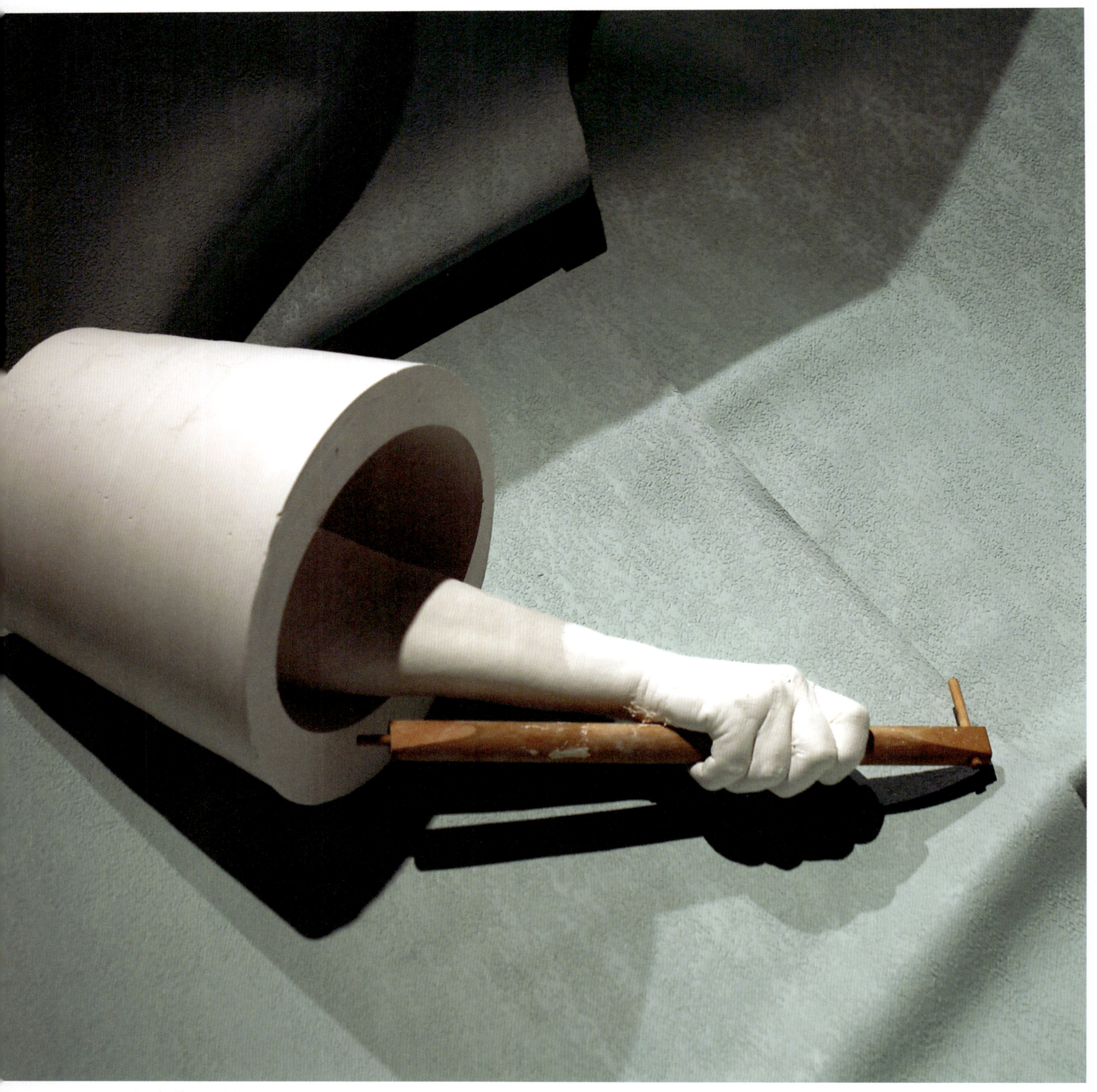

Body Shop, 2003

It would be disingenuous to omit mentioning here that in 1999 Müller lost his left hand and part of his forearm in an automobile accident. While he subsequently undertook a body of work (including a complex installation piece) related to the physical, emotional, and artistic consequences of that trauma, the artist acknowledges that the injury changed his technical working methods in very specific ways and it altered his studio practice—that is, his aesthetic approach—generally. The accident transformed his art's aims, techniques, inquiries, and insights. However, it would be equally disingenuous to read his subsequent evolution as a playing out, or an acting out, or an assertion of his unfortunate accident; rather, it seems that the event catalyzed artistic possibilities and potentials implicit in his work all along. For example, in his earlier recombinant improvisations, there was an implicit, fundamental acceptance of the convertible nature of all things, whether through natural processes (such as rusting, corrosion, or breakage) or through human intervention (such as the "junking" of old equipment, the chancing upon it, and the repurposing of it). At its core, Müller's art has always acknowledged and embraced the properties of transience, mutability, and dynamic process.

With all this talk of two- and three-dimensionality, it seems appropriate to remark that Müller's art, in fact, lives in four dimensions. This is nothing special; everything that has material form exists in three-dimensional space and fourth-dimensional time. But Müller's art has always very much *engaged* time, largely in the visible record of its own manufacture. To some extent, he is a faithful devotee of what in the 1970s used to be loosely described as "process art," and which remains a fundamental working method for many artists today. But Müller was among its early explorers.

Process art, upon its earliest articulation, was an indication, an index, of the artist's engagement with his chosen materials and their nature; the result of that involvement was not presumed to evince the artist's virtuosic mastery and dominance over his materials, like a feudal lord controlling his serfs, but to reveal a kind of complicated dance, or encounter, or wrestling match, or "copulation" of the artist and the material part of the world that attracts his attention and activity. The resulting artwork, whether an object or an installation, is the record of that physical, imaginative, and aesthetic encounter. The philosophy of so-called process art resists the notion of the artisanal "hand" of the artist as a register of individual artistic "genius" and "vision" to produce a "precious object" but instead asserts the primacy of the maker's involvement with his or her materials and technical procedures and the facticity of the resulting work

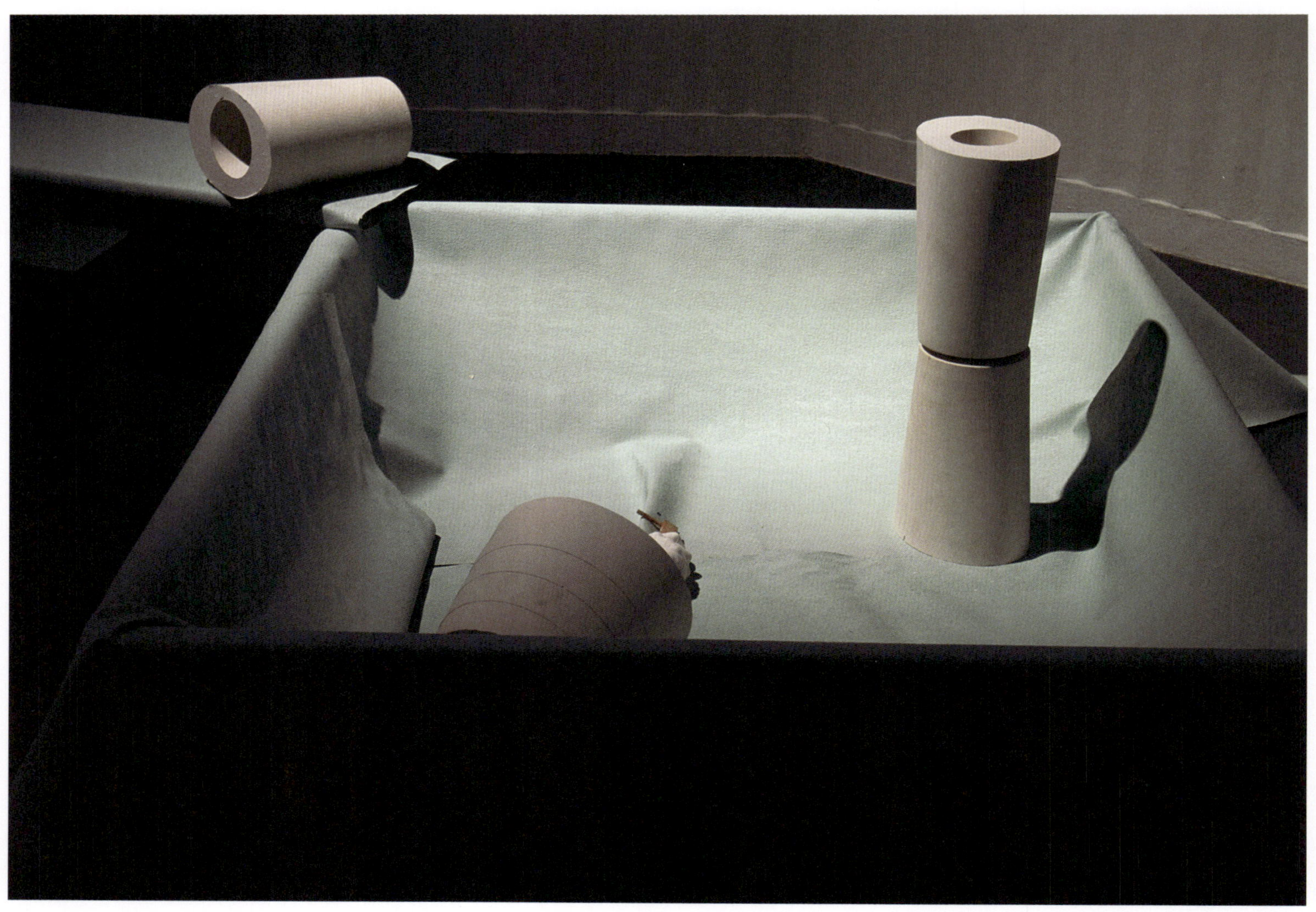

Body Shop, 2003

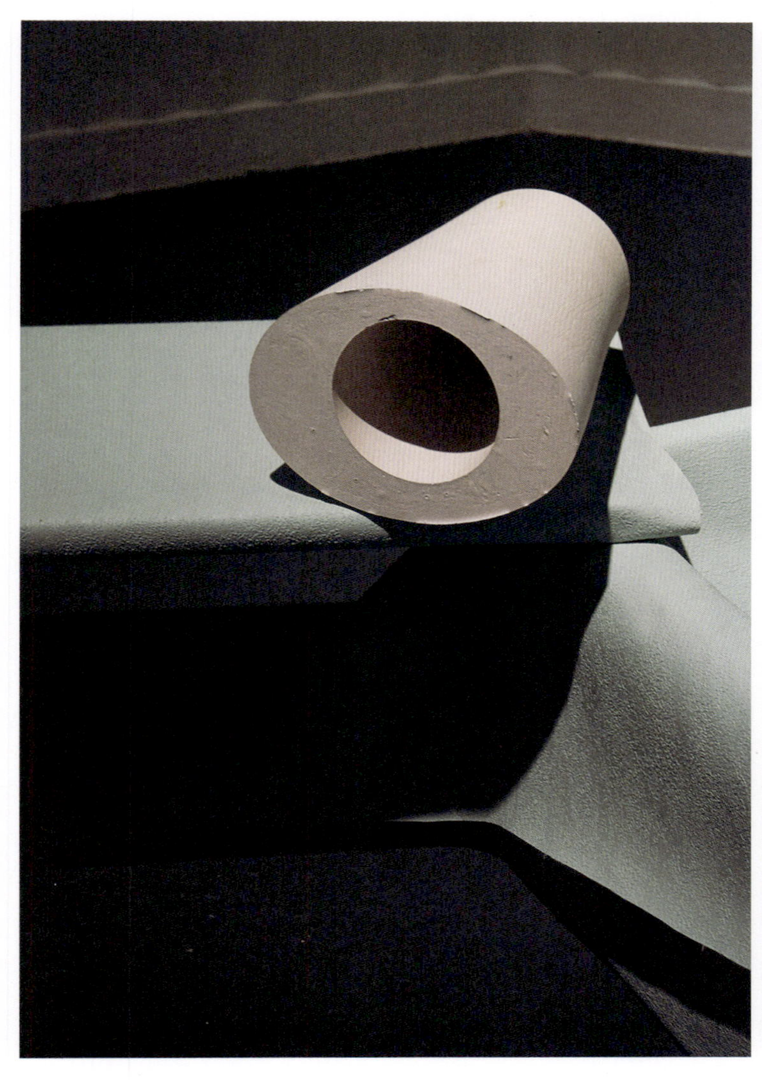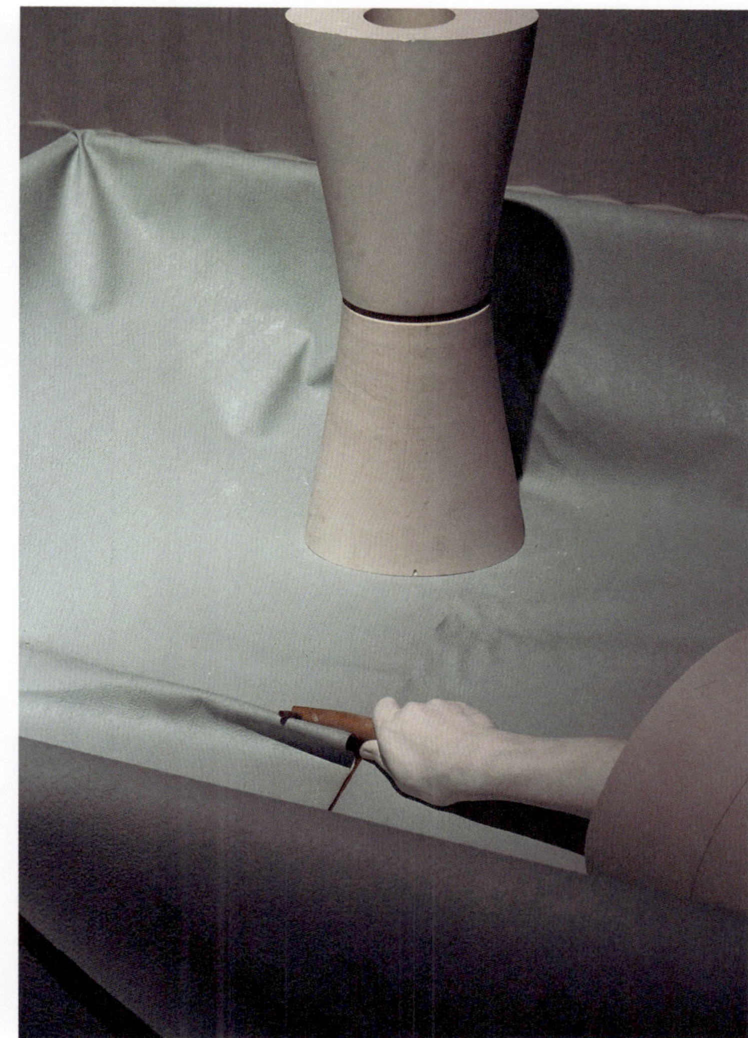

(which could be an installation, a social circumstance or phenomenon, or a performance, as well as a freestanding object). Neither the artistic intent nor the created object stands alone; they form an equation.

Manfred Müller is, for the most part, an object maker; his works are handmade and are almost always complete objects that can be transported from his studio and exhibited in any space—even if they occupy that space obstreperously. But his objects function and declare themselves as having been brought forth in a dynamic world of real events and in minute studio-bound manipulations that are not of mythological significance, nor of historical import, nor of precious material glorification and viewer adulation, but rather of emphatic, deliberate involvement with commonplace materials—paper, paperboard, pigment, machine parts, photographs—that surround us in ordinary situations every day. In the high modern tradition, no illusion, no preciousness, no vanity is deployed. Müller's interventions make viewers take note and heed every considered action that he has taken in the studio. The result is the artist's engagement with us, and ours with him, through the object itself.

And clearly, that encounter takes place through a passage of time; Müller's works are presented not as frozen and perfected objects, as if they had existed that way timelessly in the past and will continue that way in the future, but rather as an expression of how they came into being in the first place. Müller's sculptures openly disclose the process of their formation, and in fact, they are about their genesis as much as they are about their present manifestation. To carefully observe a Müller sculpture or constructed paper sketch is to behold every step of its development as an art object that exists in the world that it and the viewer cohabit. What Müller creates is not an illusory image of a timeless world that we are meant to peer at; we viewers are part of its ongoing history, a history that Müller acknowledges resides as much in himself and in ourselves as it does in the object itself.

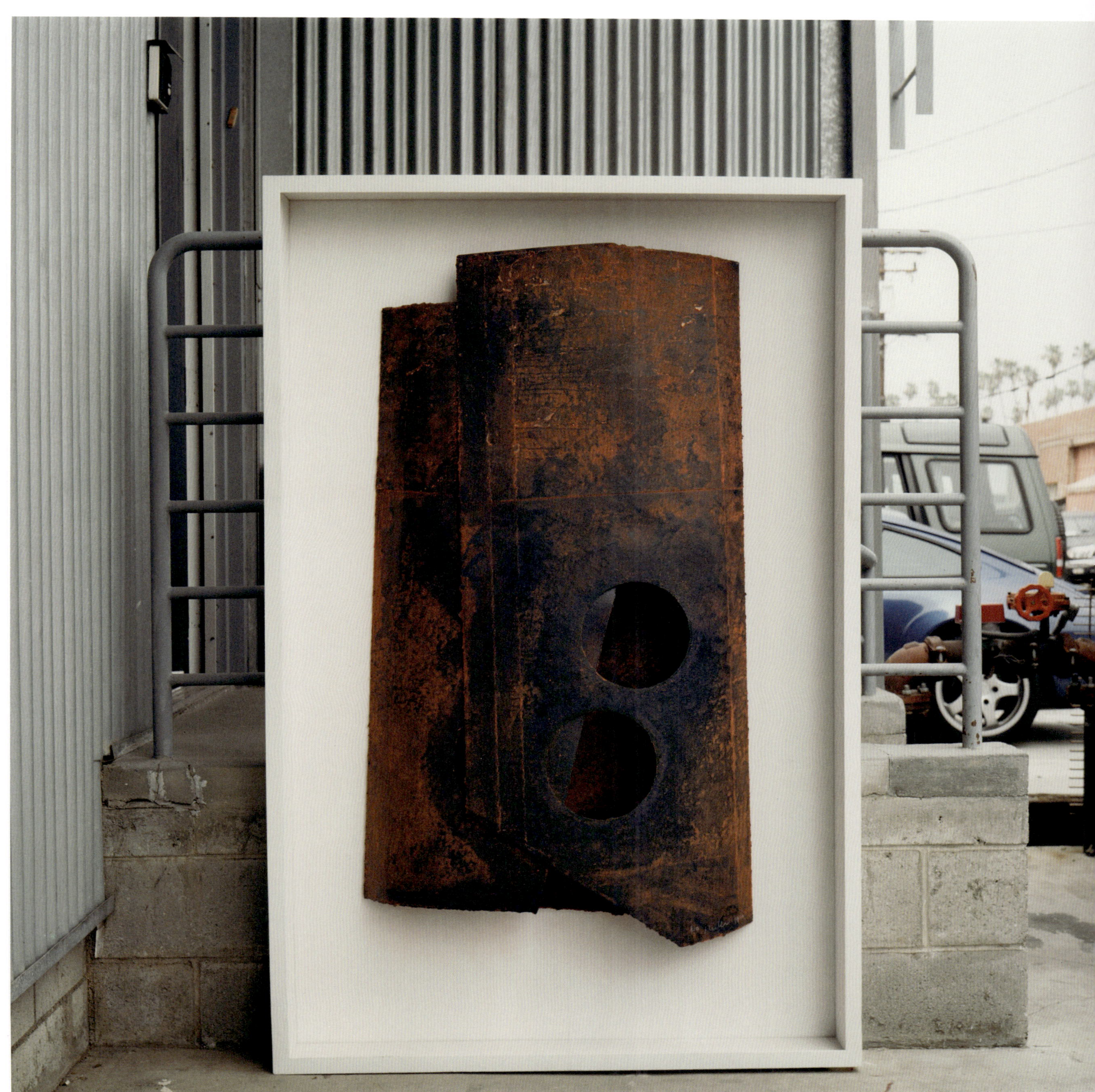

Gray Coat, 2003–4

PLATES

UNITED STATES

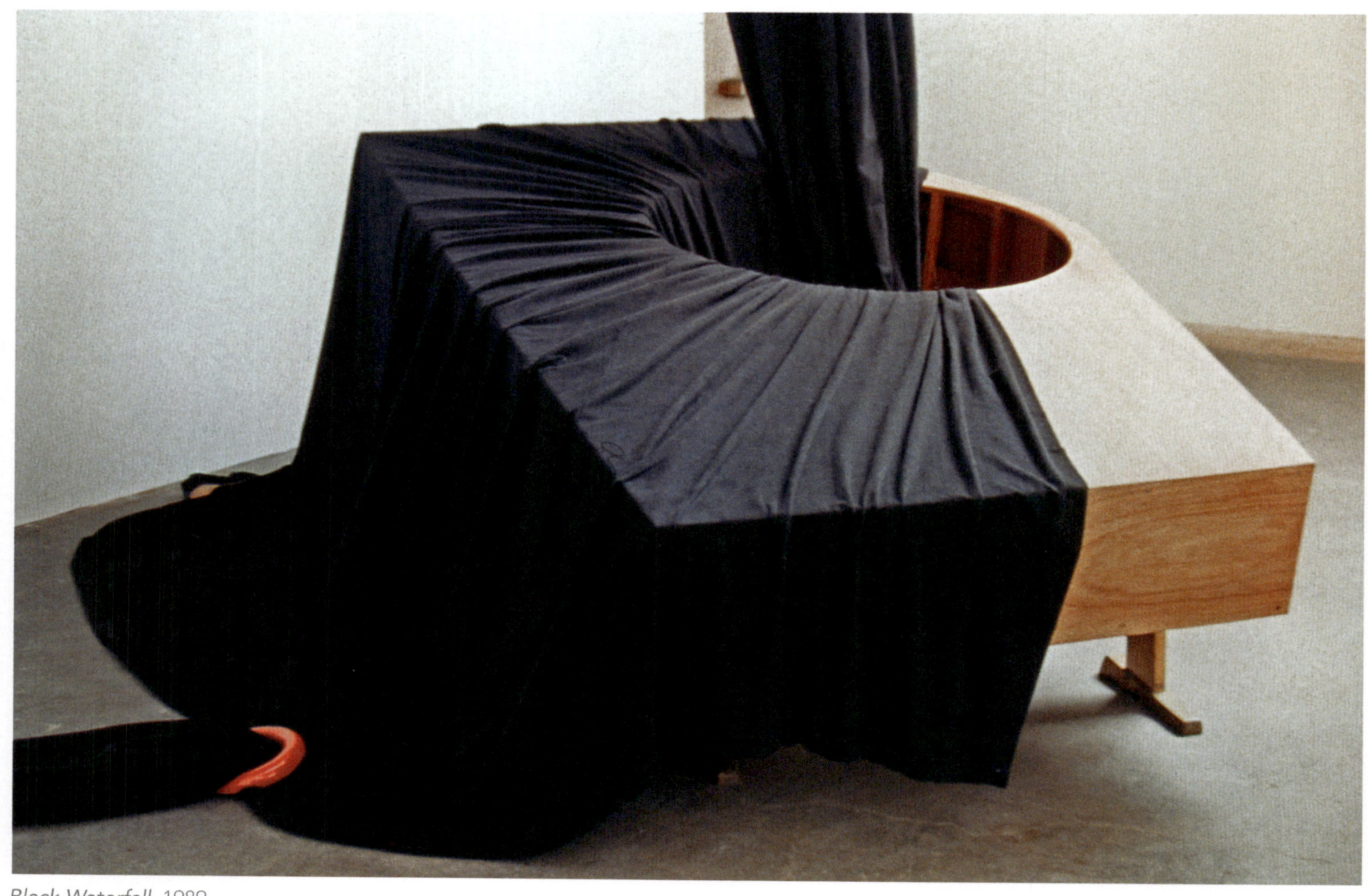

Black Waterfall, 1989

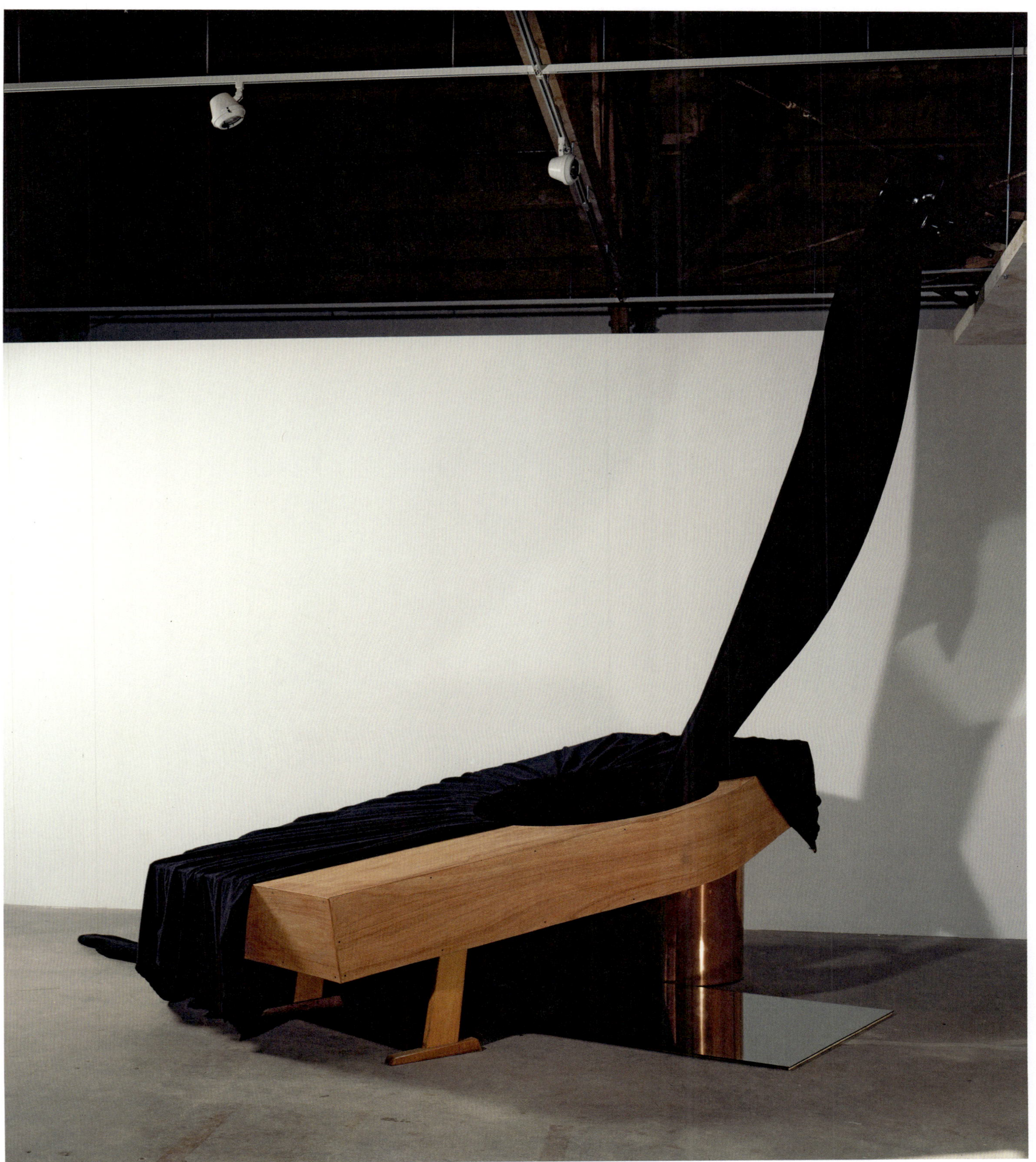

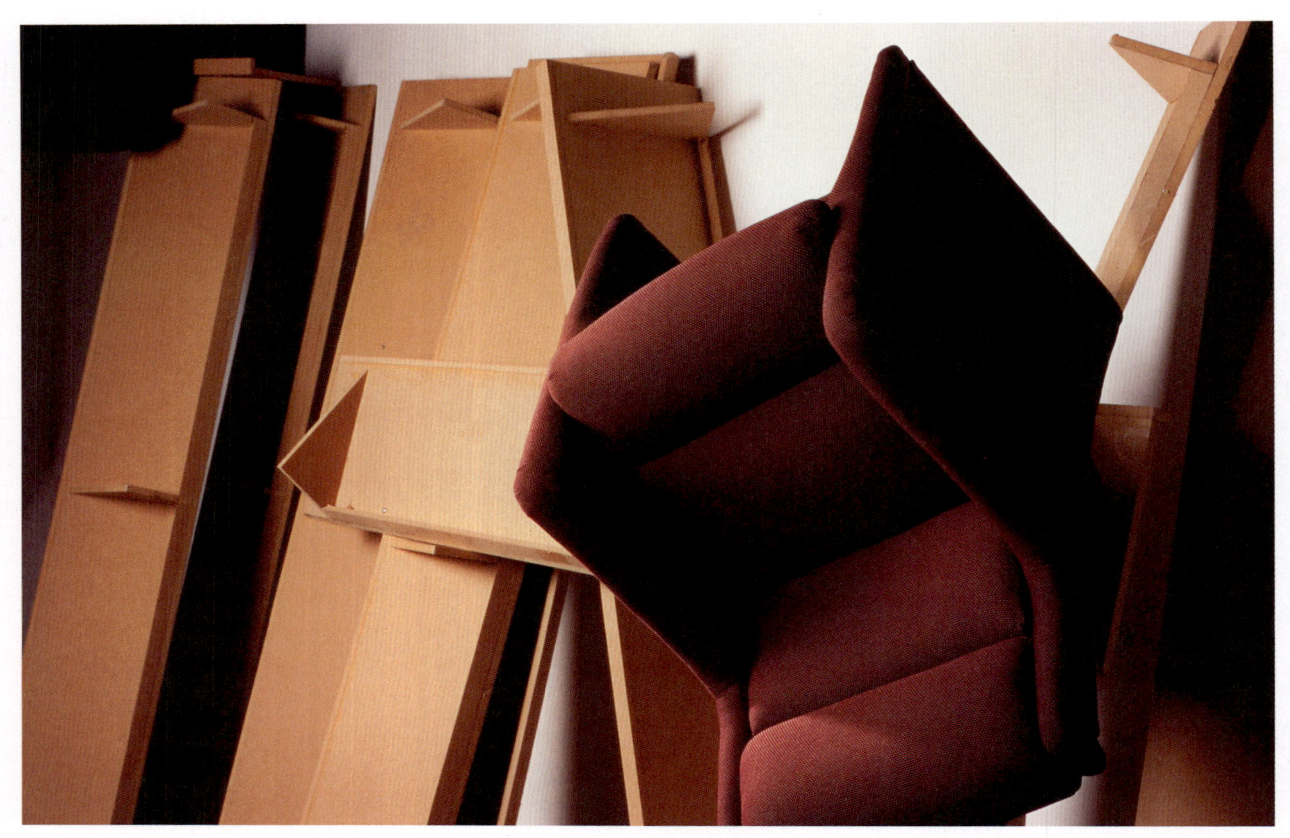

Cave Focused, 1995

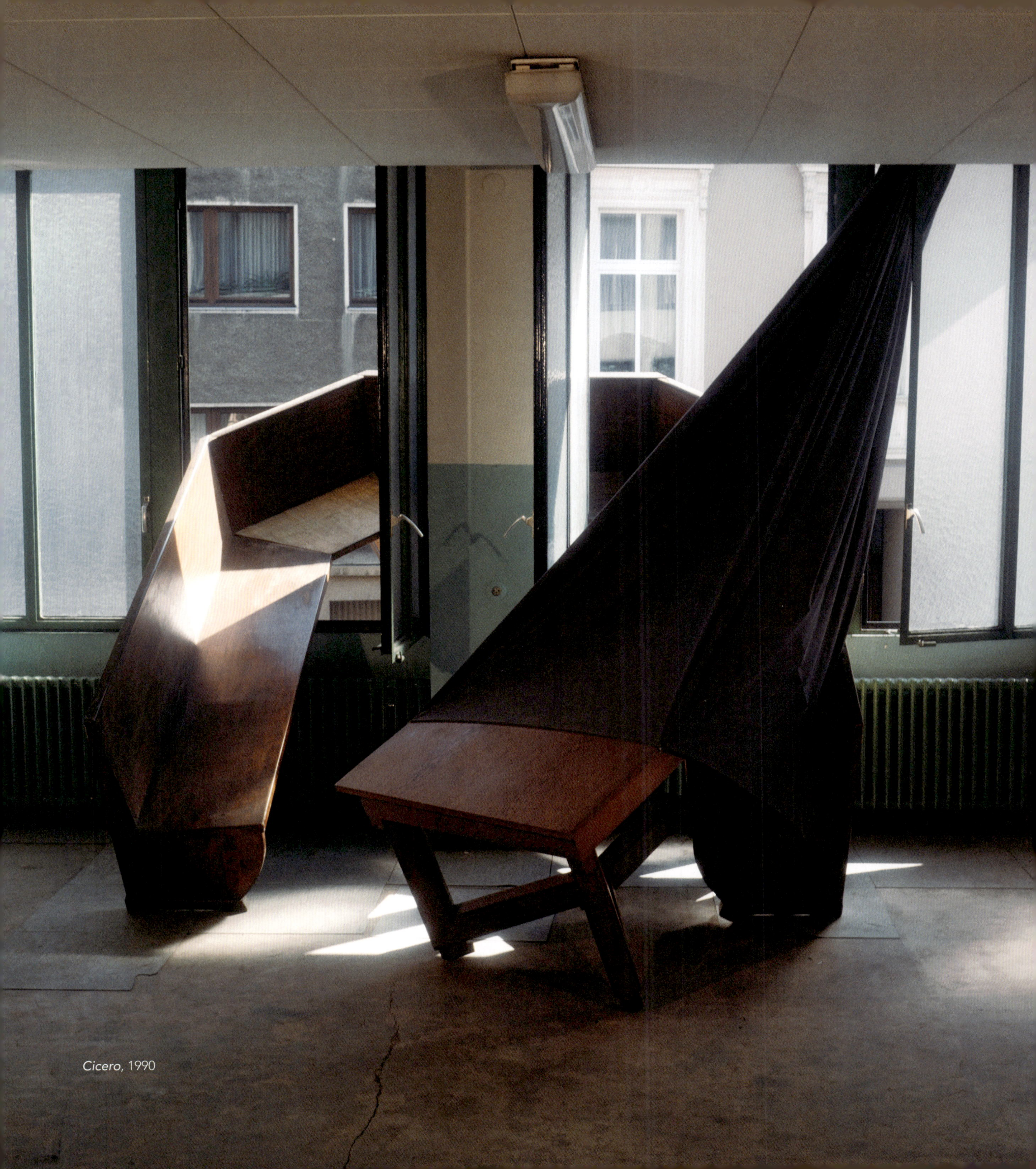

Cicero, 1990

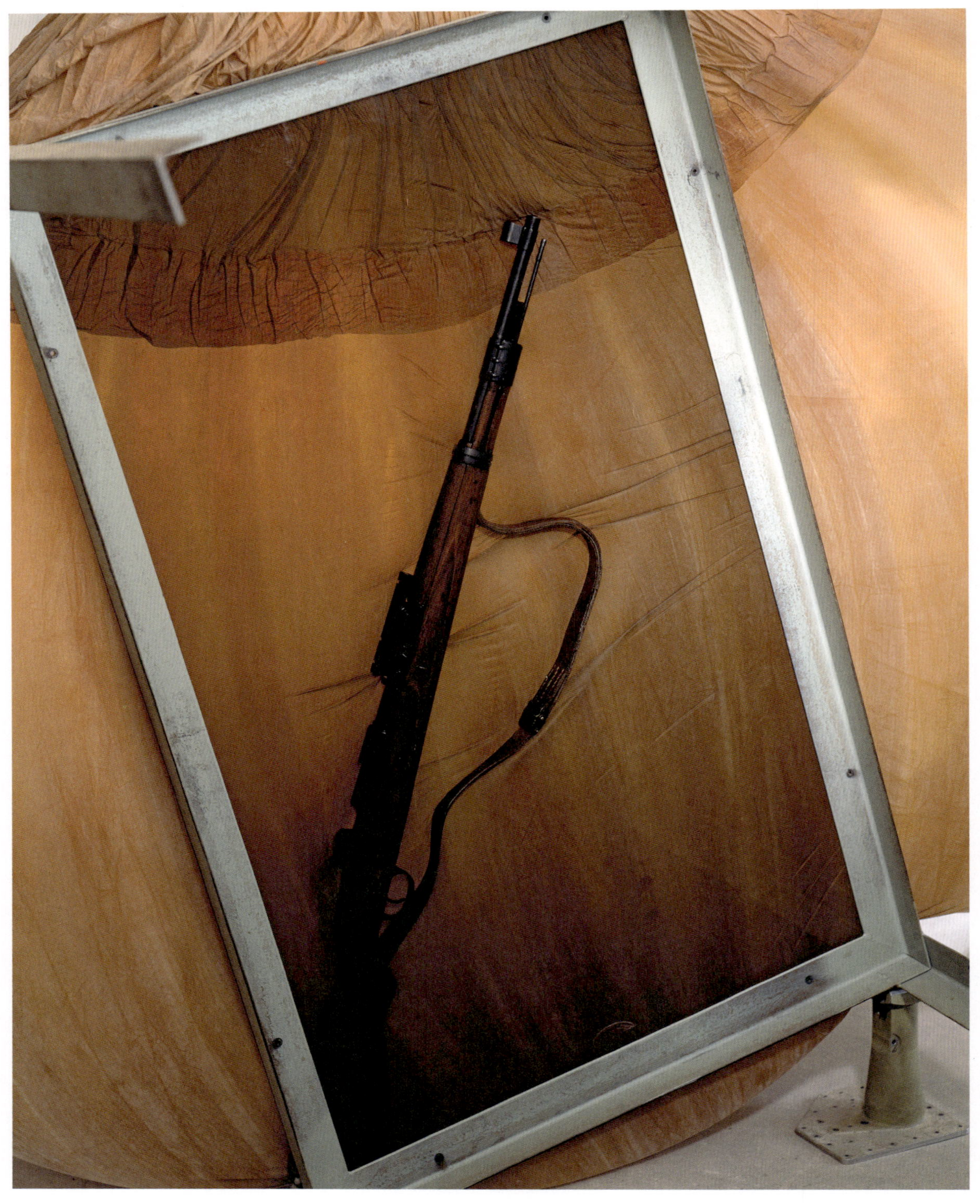

Transformer, 1993

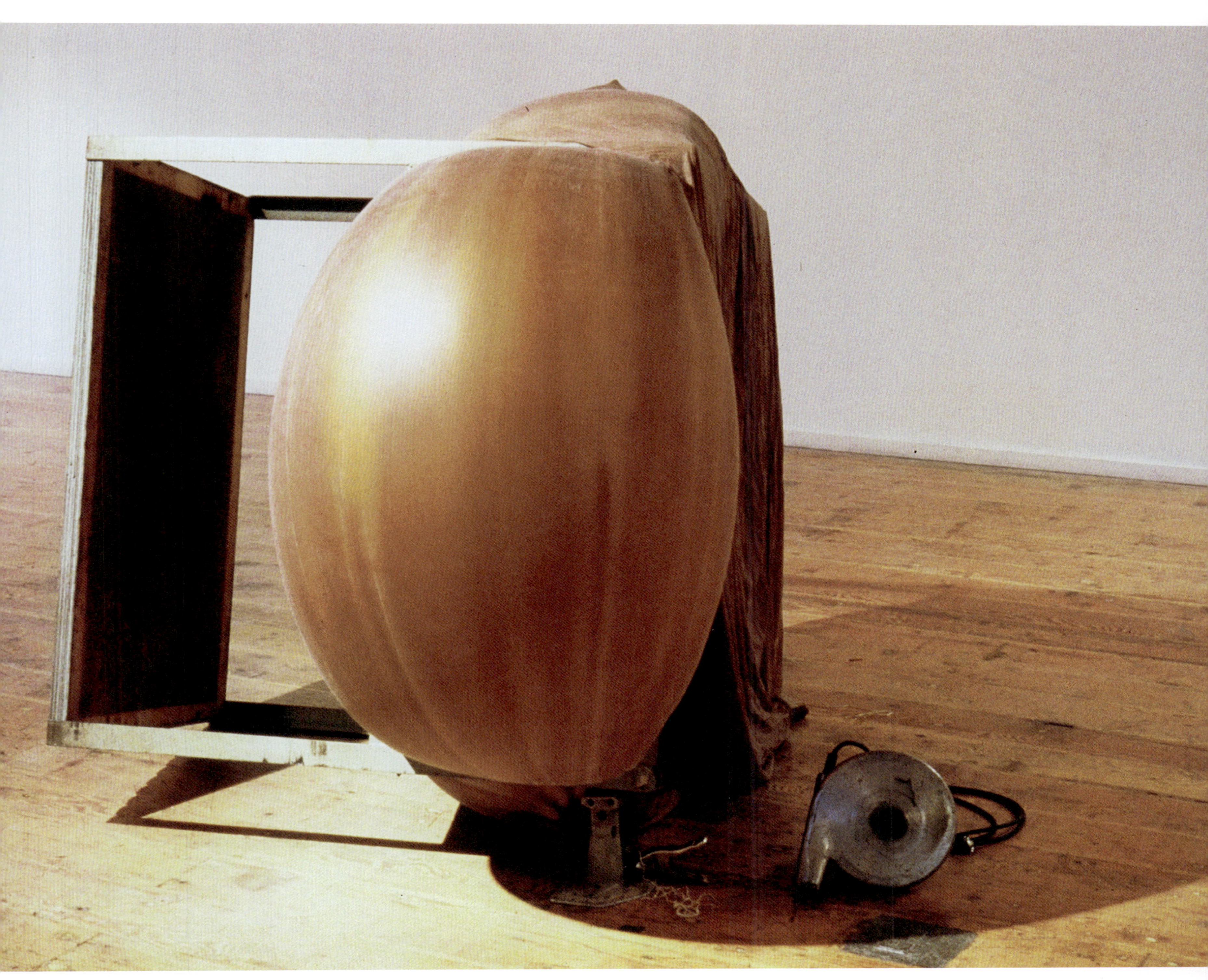

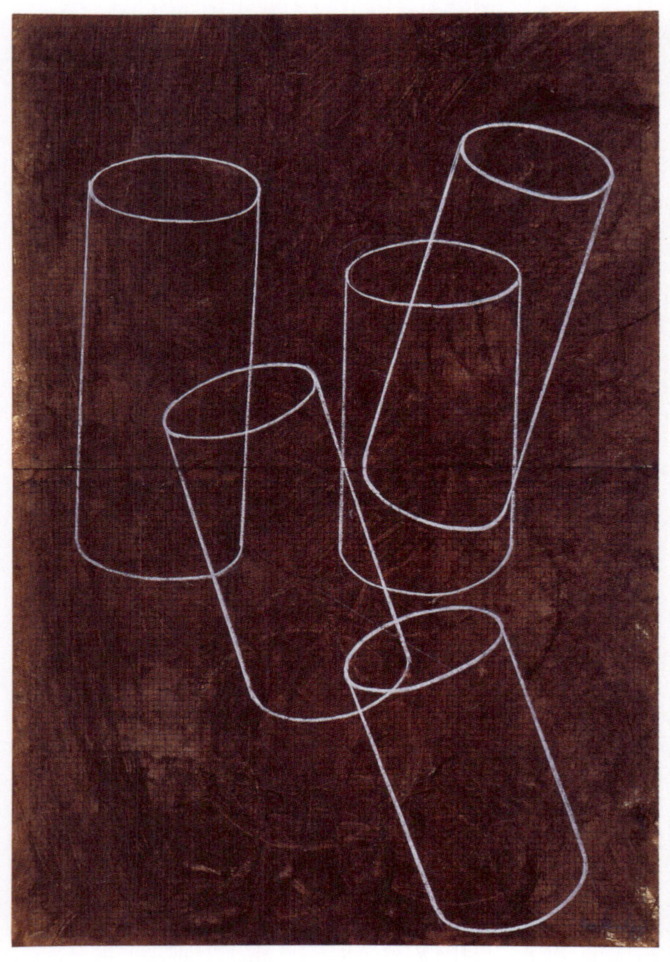

Low Color Intention, 1984–85

Low Color Intention, 1985

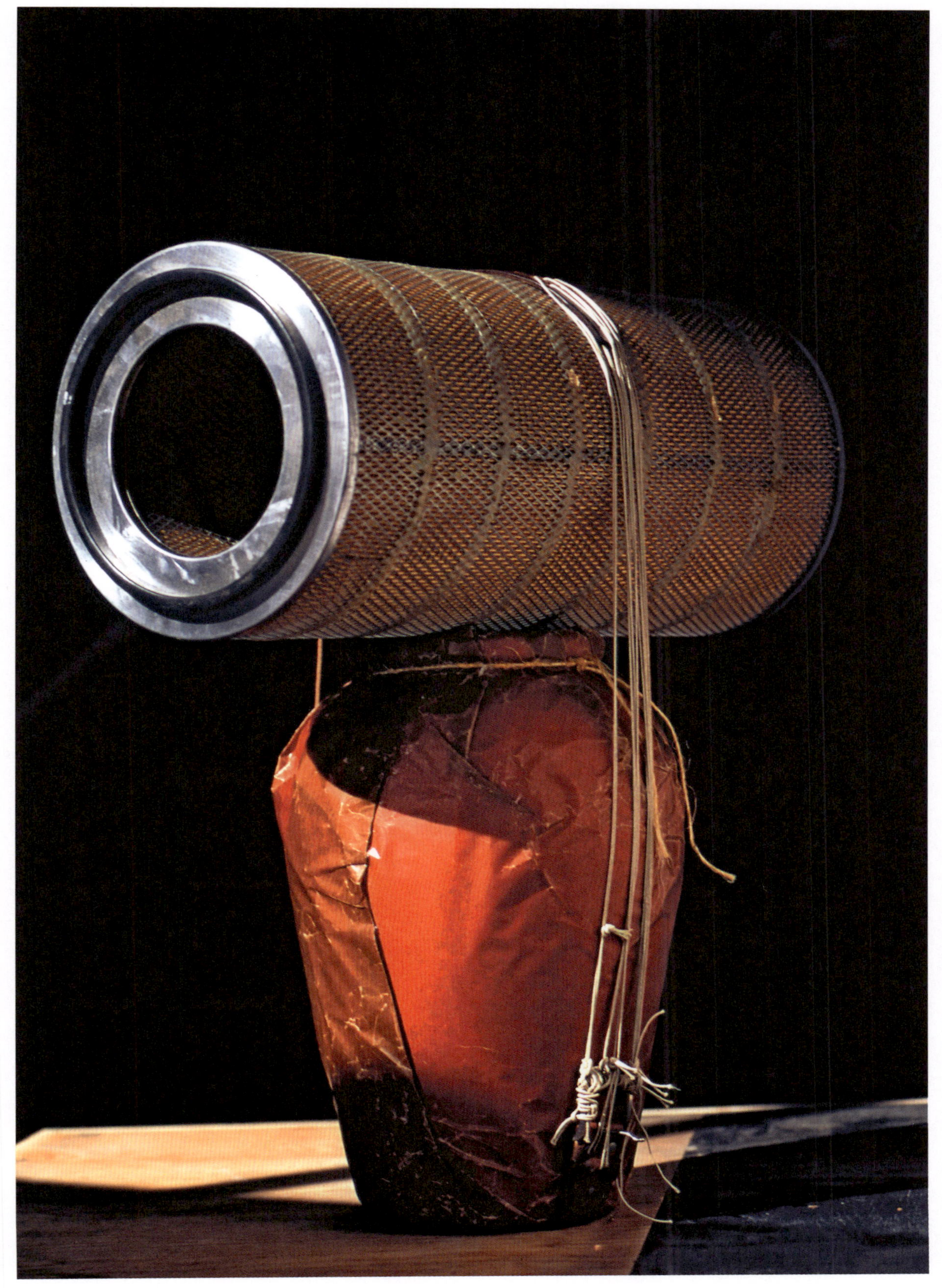

Transformer, 1991

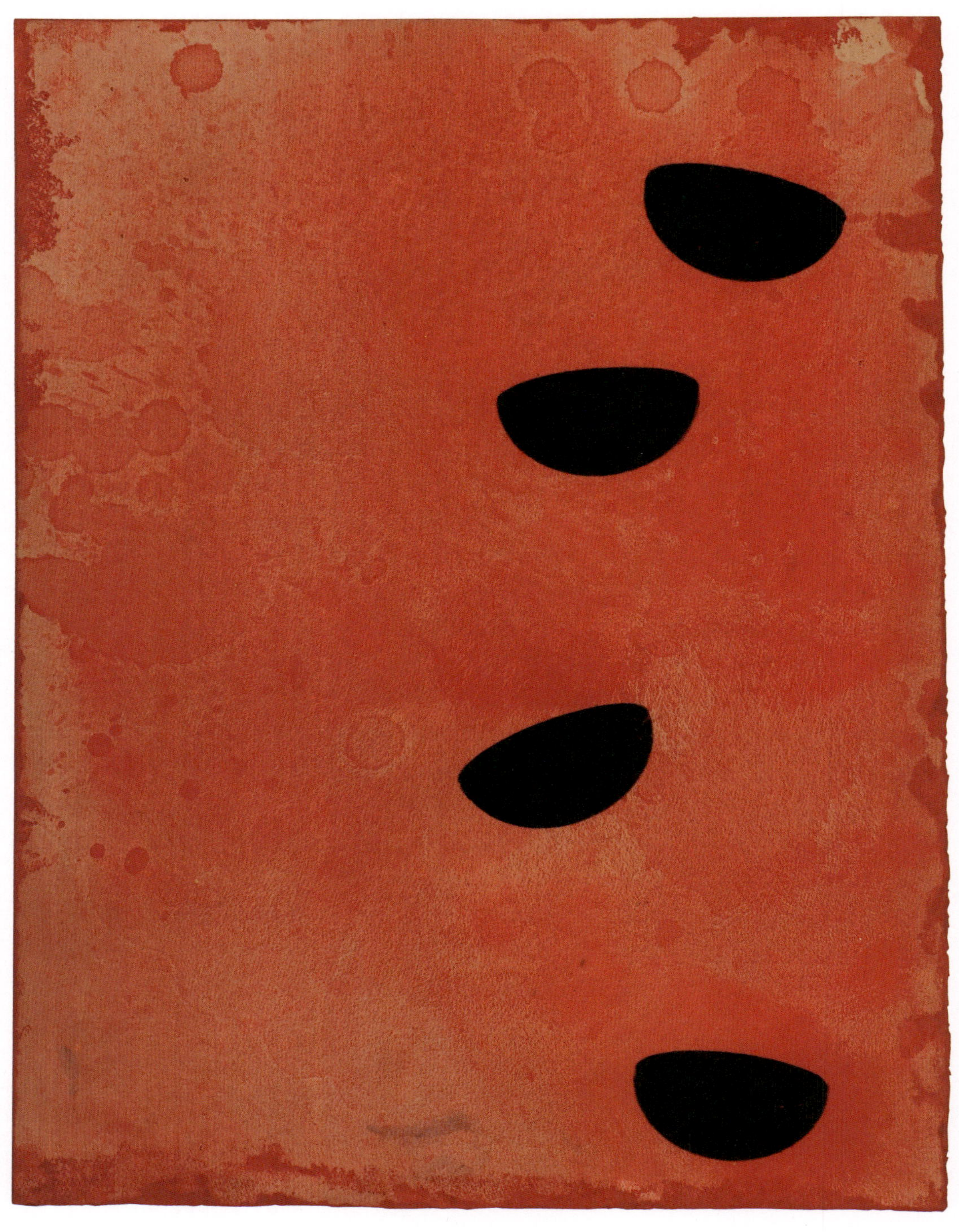

Palacio de Memoria: Four Bowls, 2000

Palacio de Memoria: Five Bowls, 2002

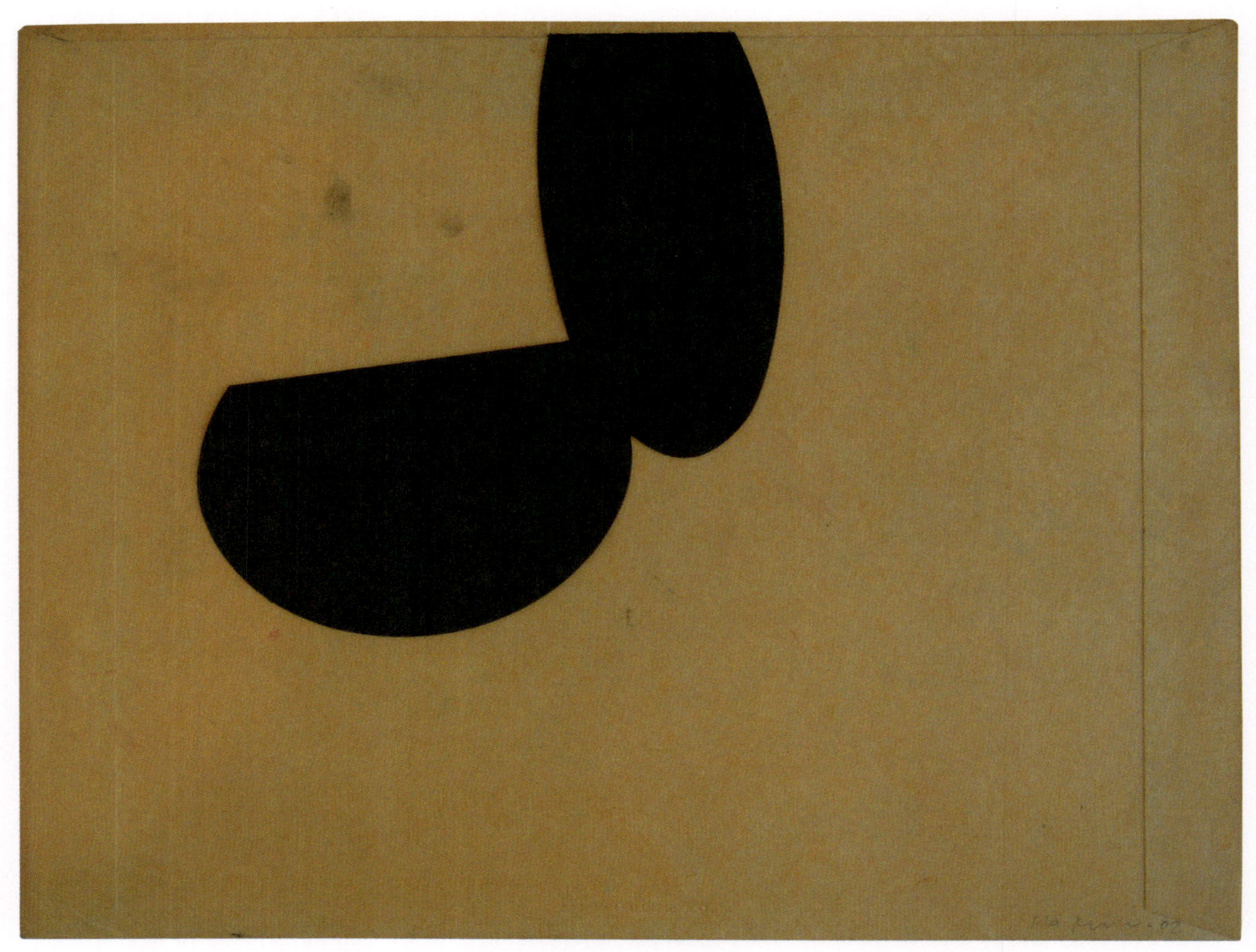

Low Color Intention 41, 1996

Low Color Intention 42, 1996

More Color Intention 1, 2004

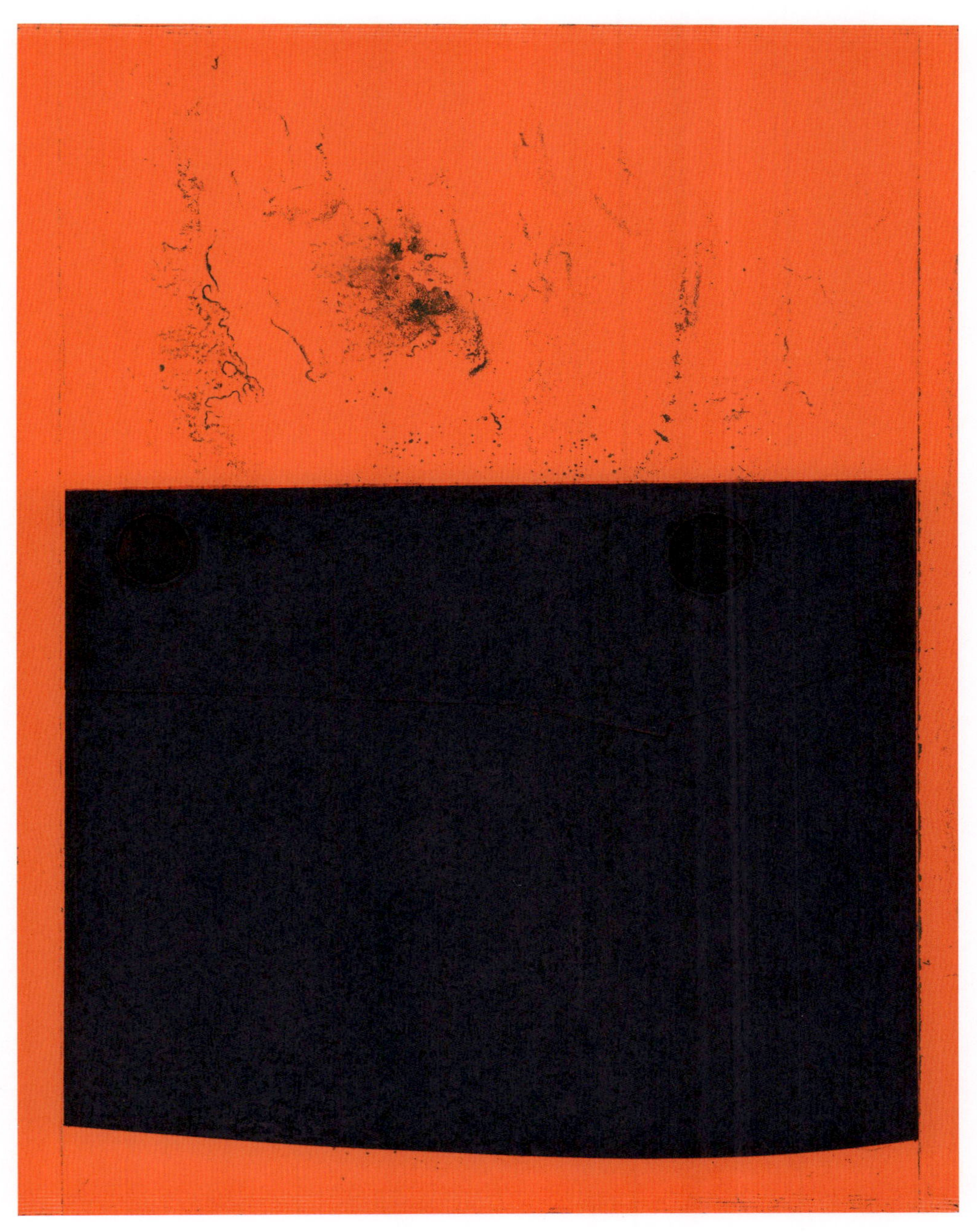

More Color Intention 2, 2013

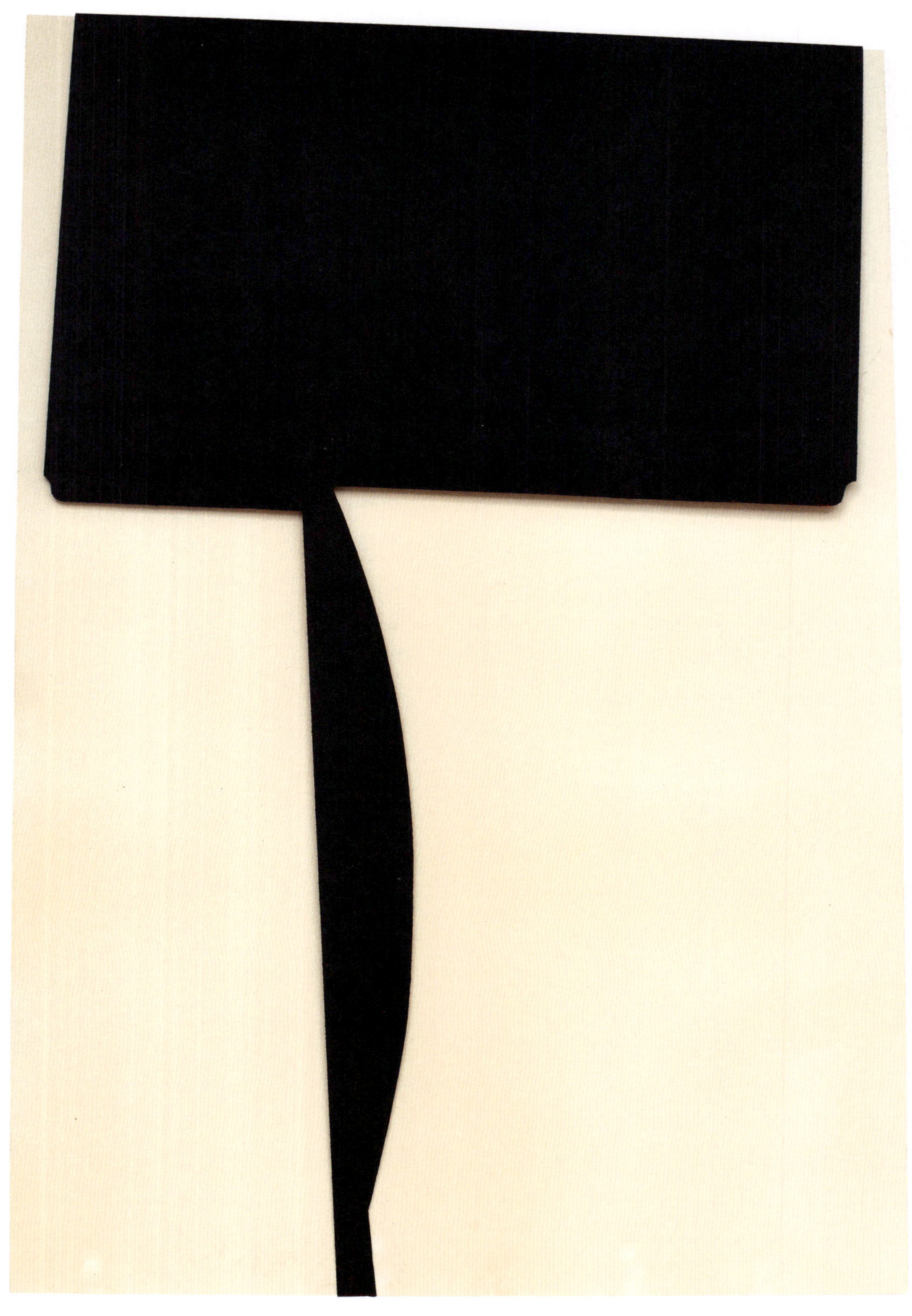

Olympic Boulevard No. 11, 2008

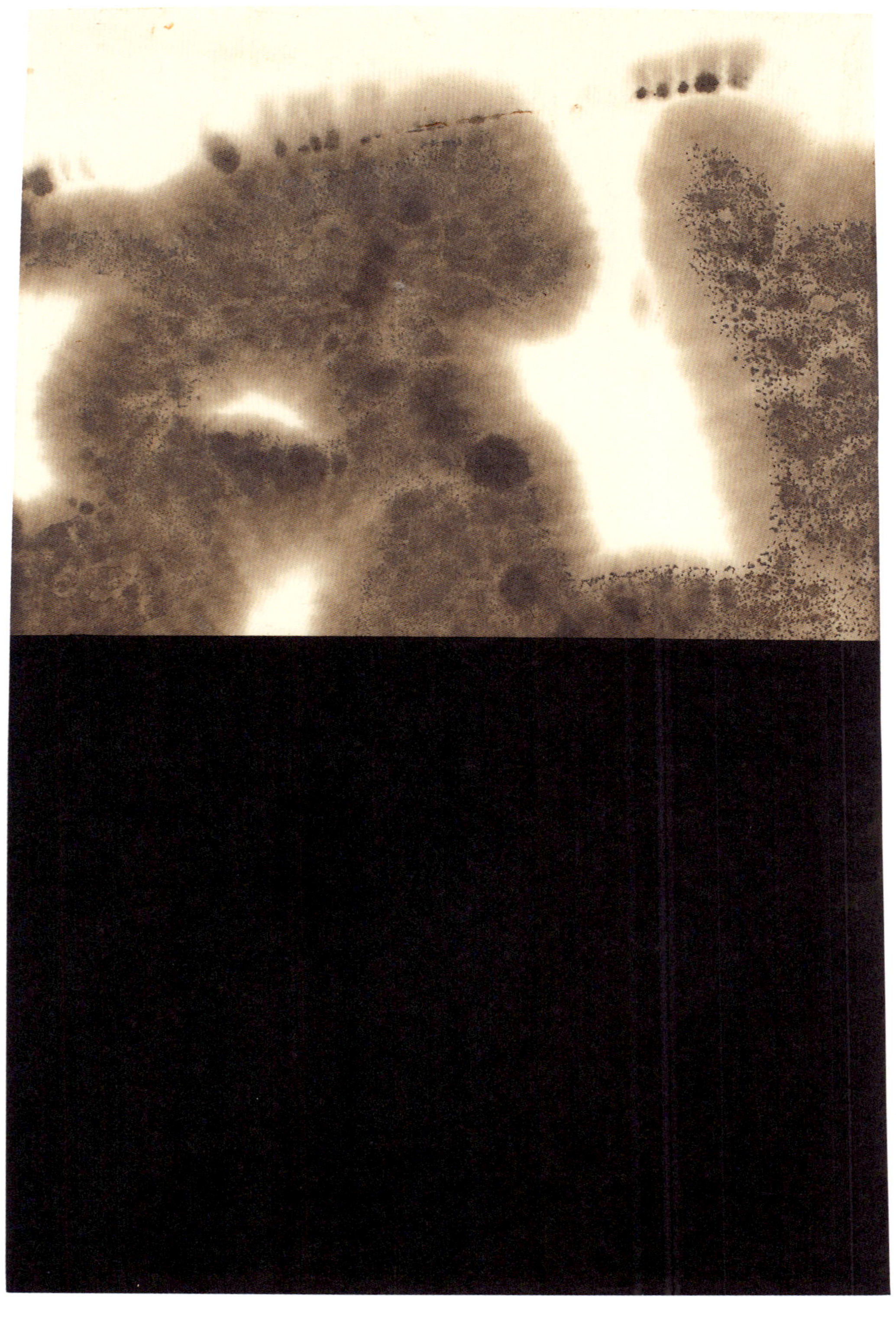

Palacio de Memoria: Echo, 2008

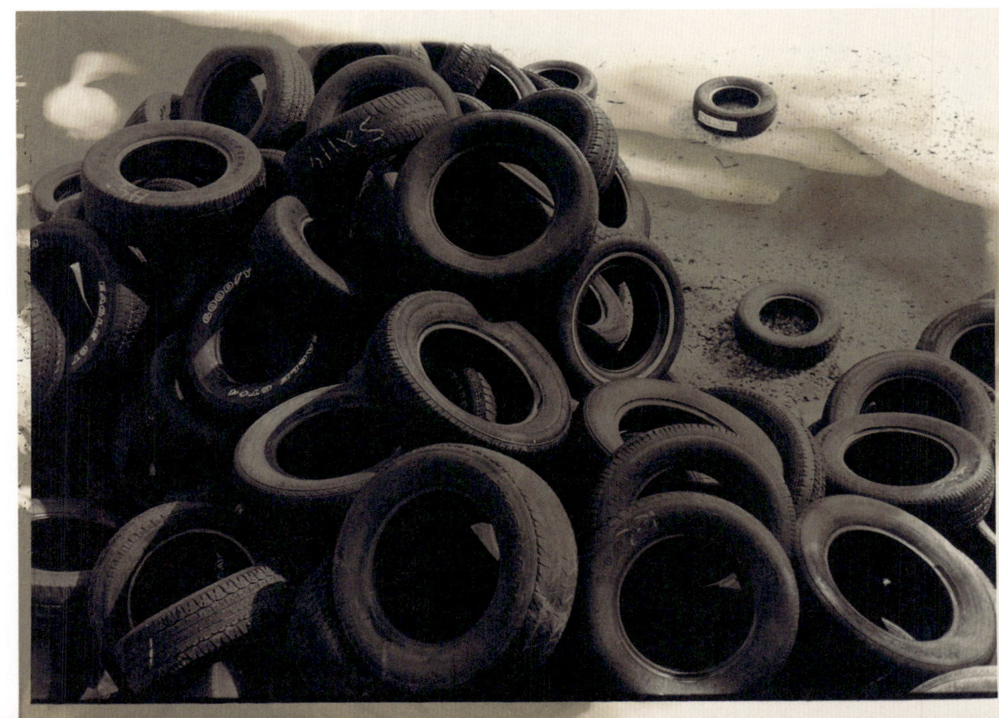

Hidden Cache: Surplus, 2008

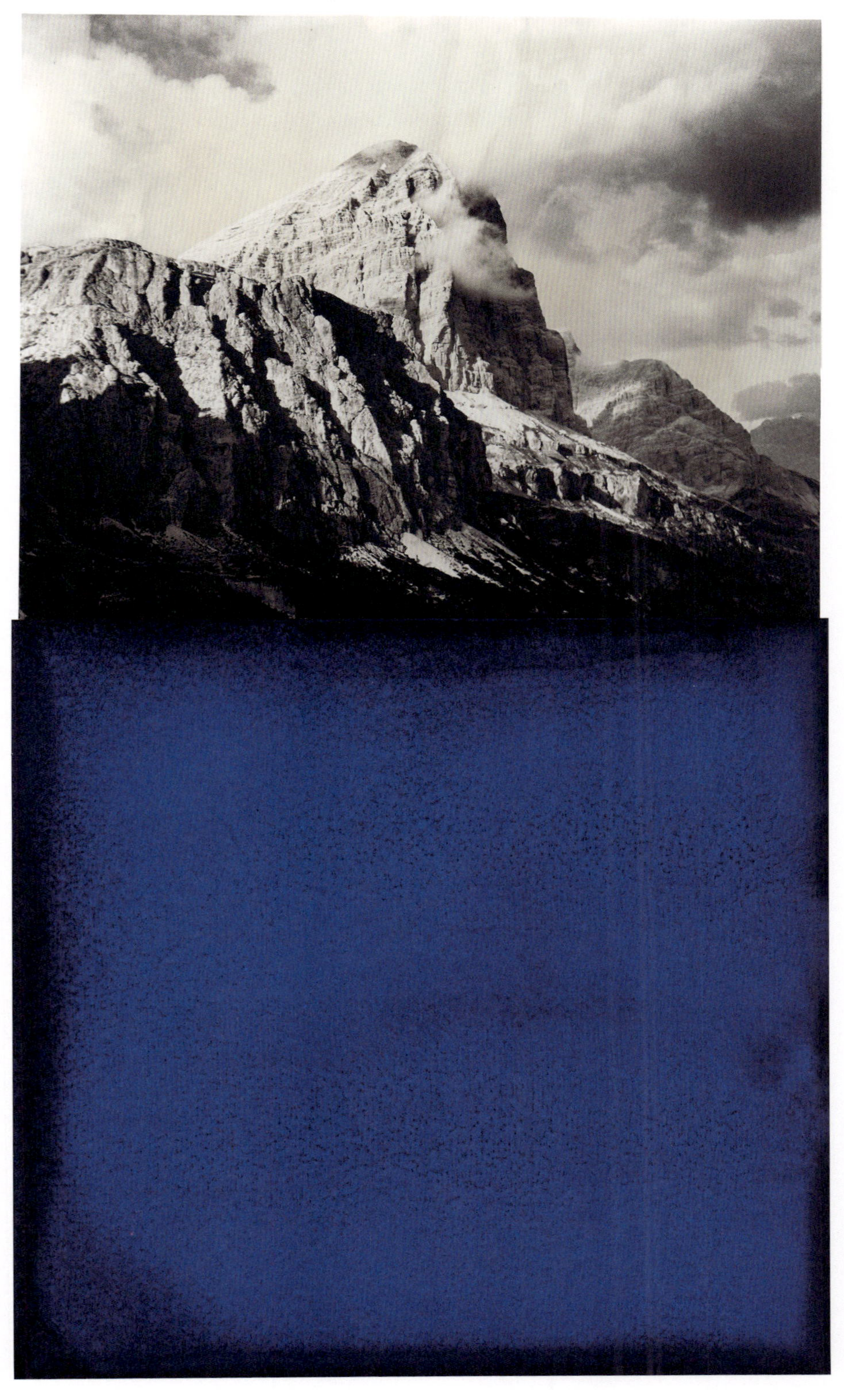

Hidden Cache: Past/Present, 2008

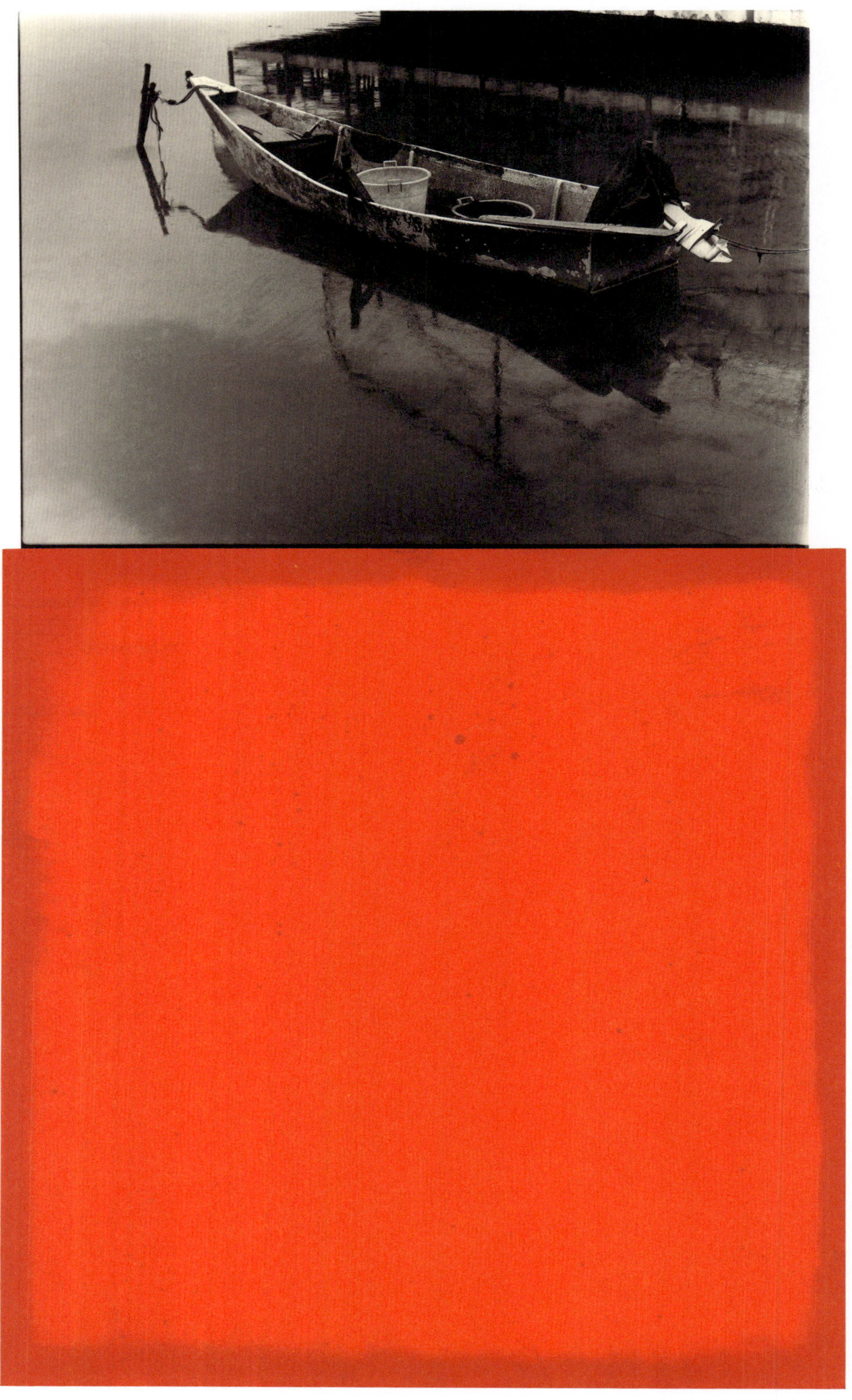

Hidden Cache: Indefinite, 2008

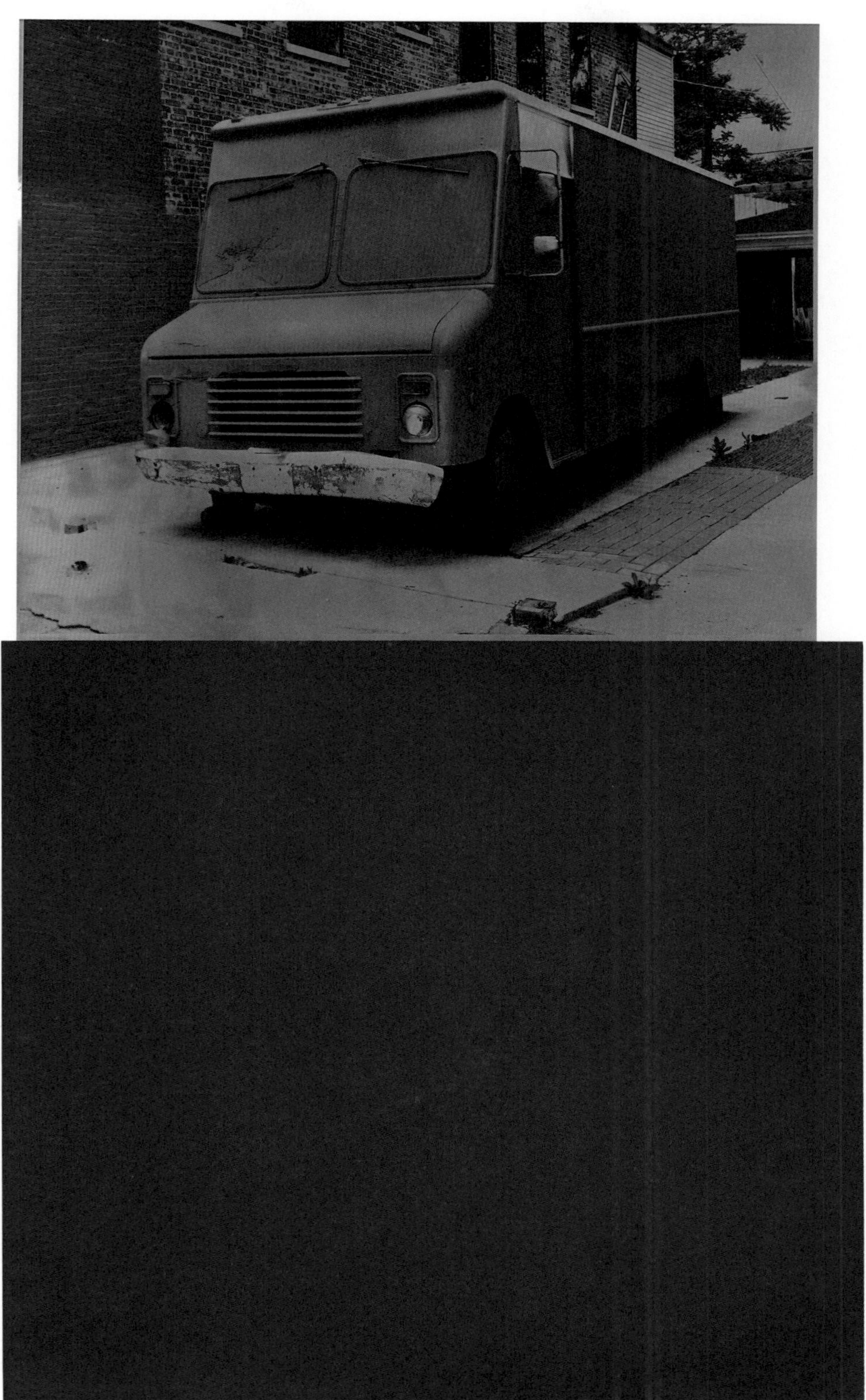

Hidden Cache: Surplus II, 2008

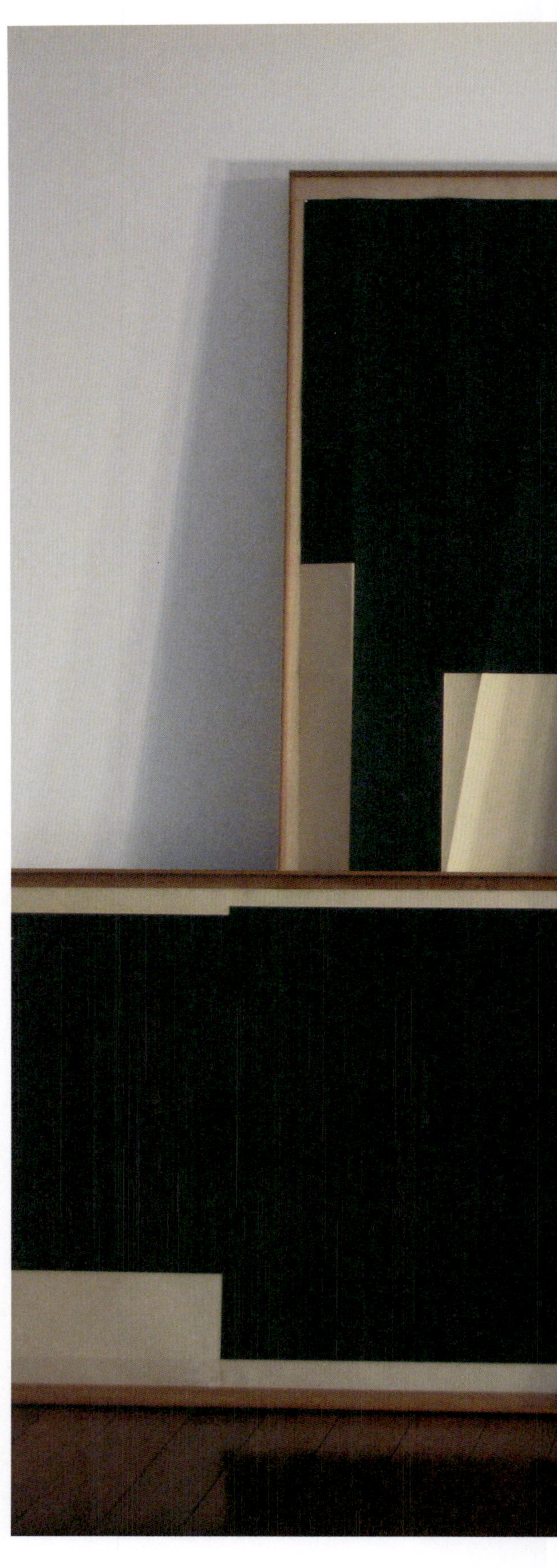

Heliotropos at Federal Avenue studio, Los Angeles, CA

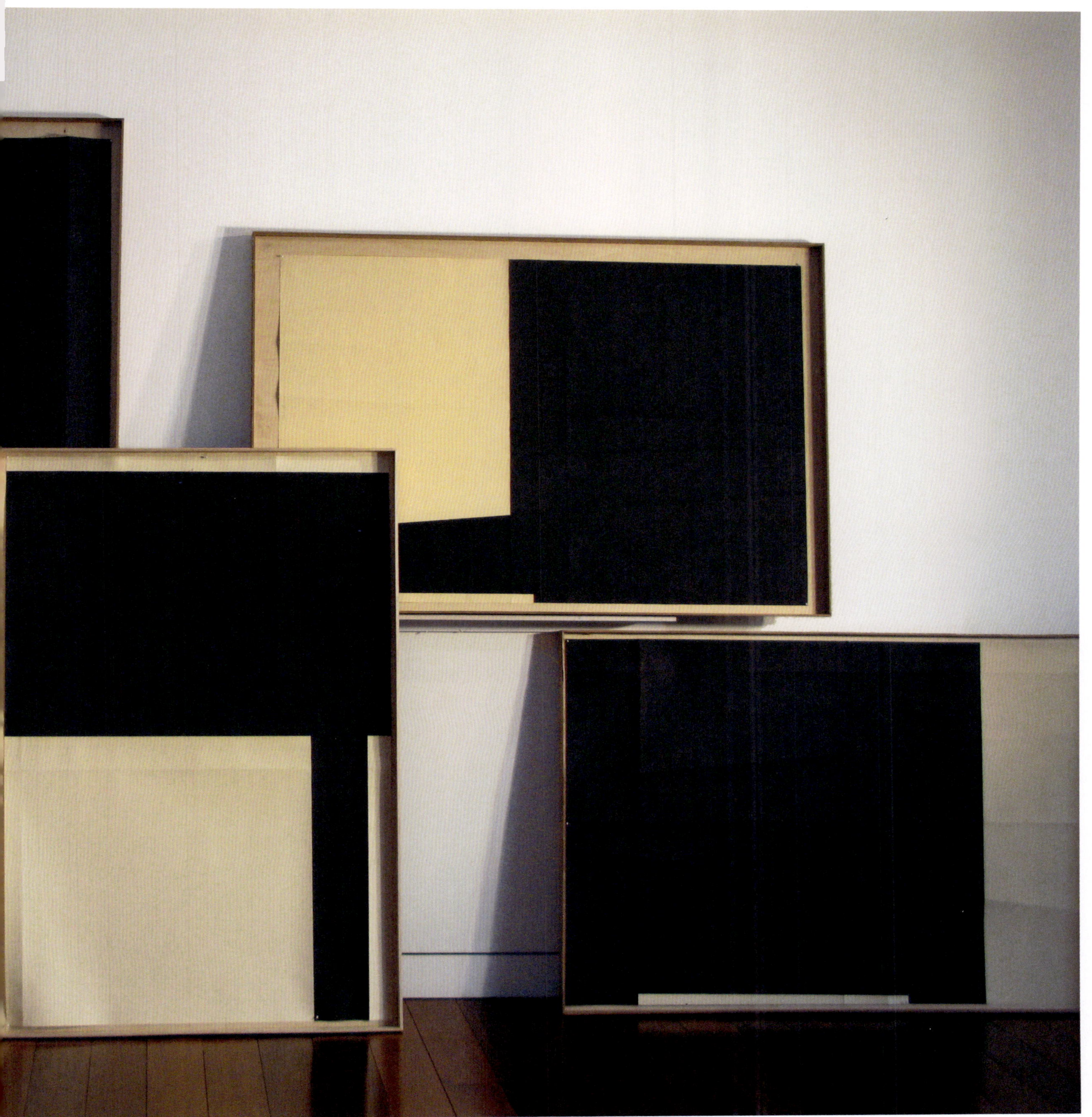

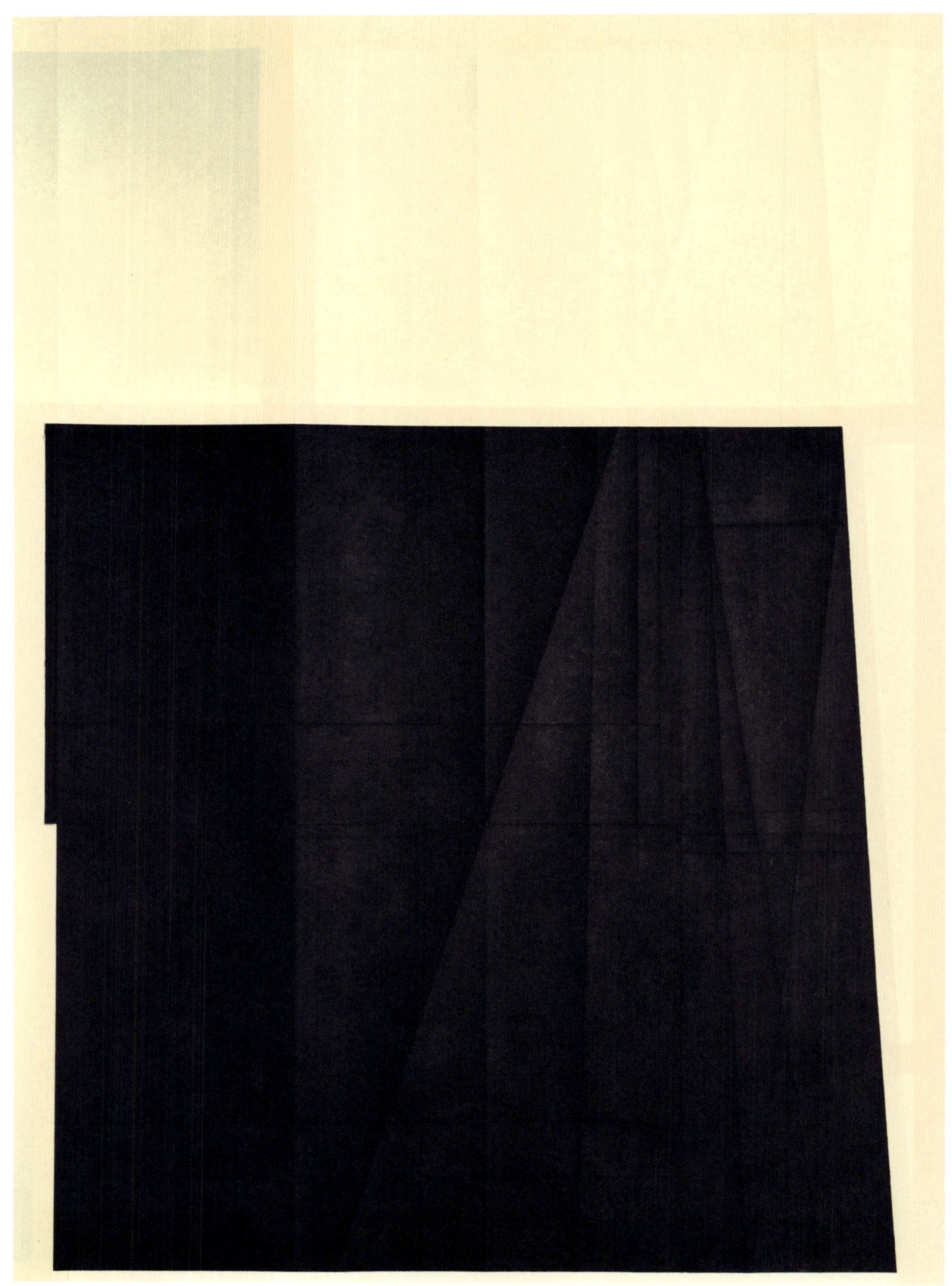

Repercussion 4: Palacio de Memoria, 2011

Repercussion 1: Palacio de Memoria, 2011

Repercussion 2: Palacio de Memoria, 2011

Repercussion 3: Palacio de Memoria, 2011

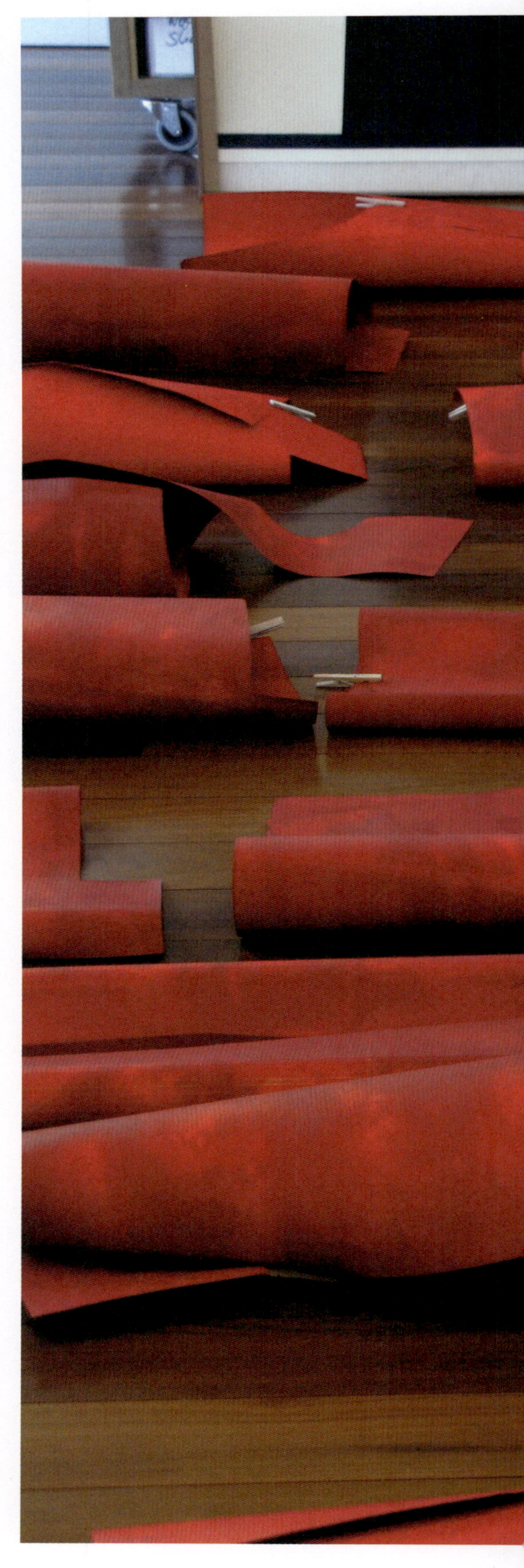

Red Preludes at Federal Avenue studio, Los Angeles, CA

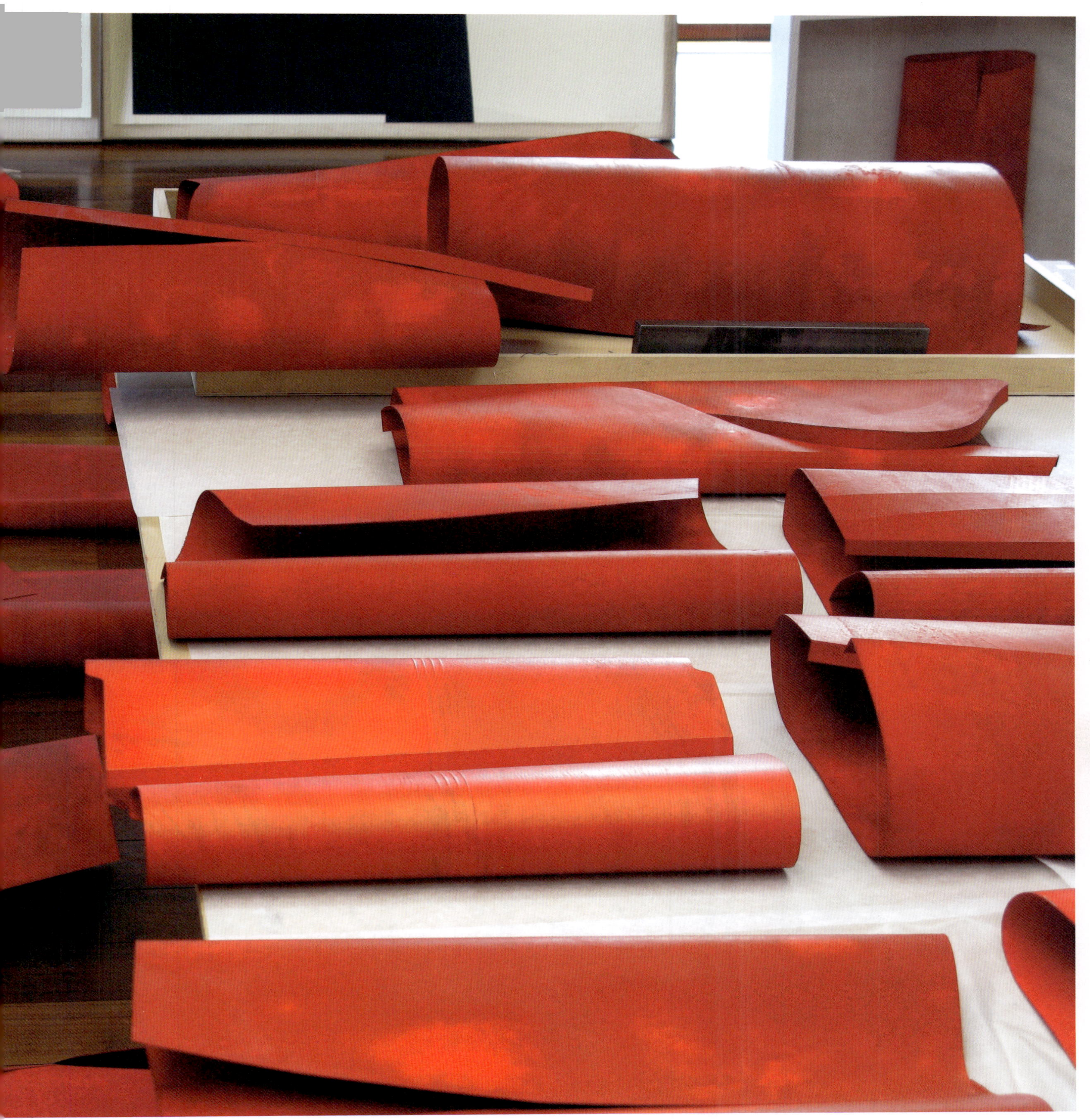

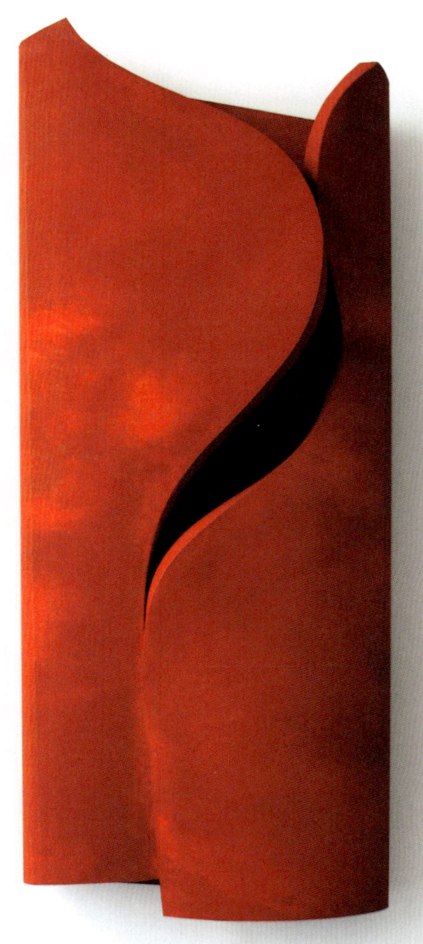

Red Prelude, 2009–11

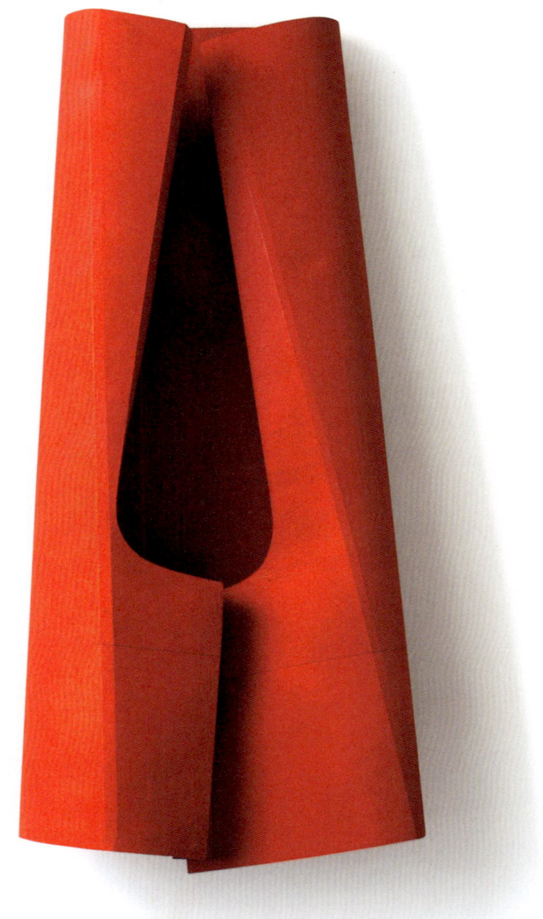

Red Prelude, 2009

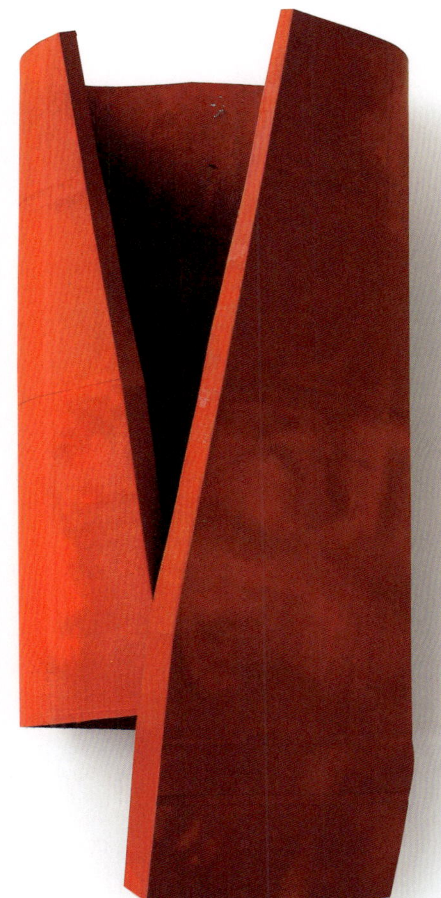

Red Prelude, 2009

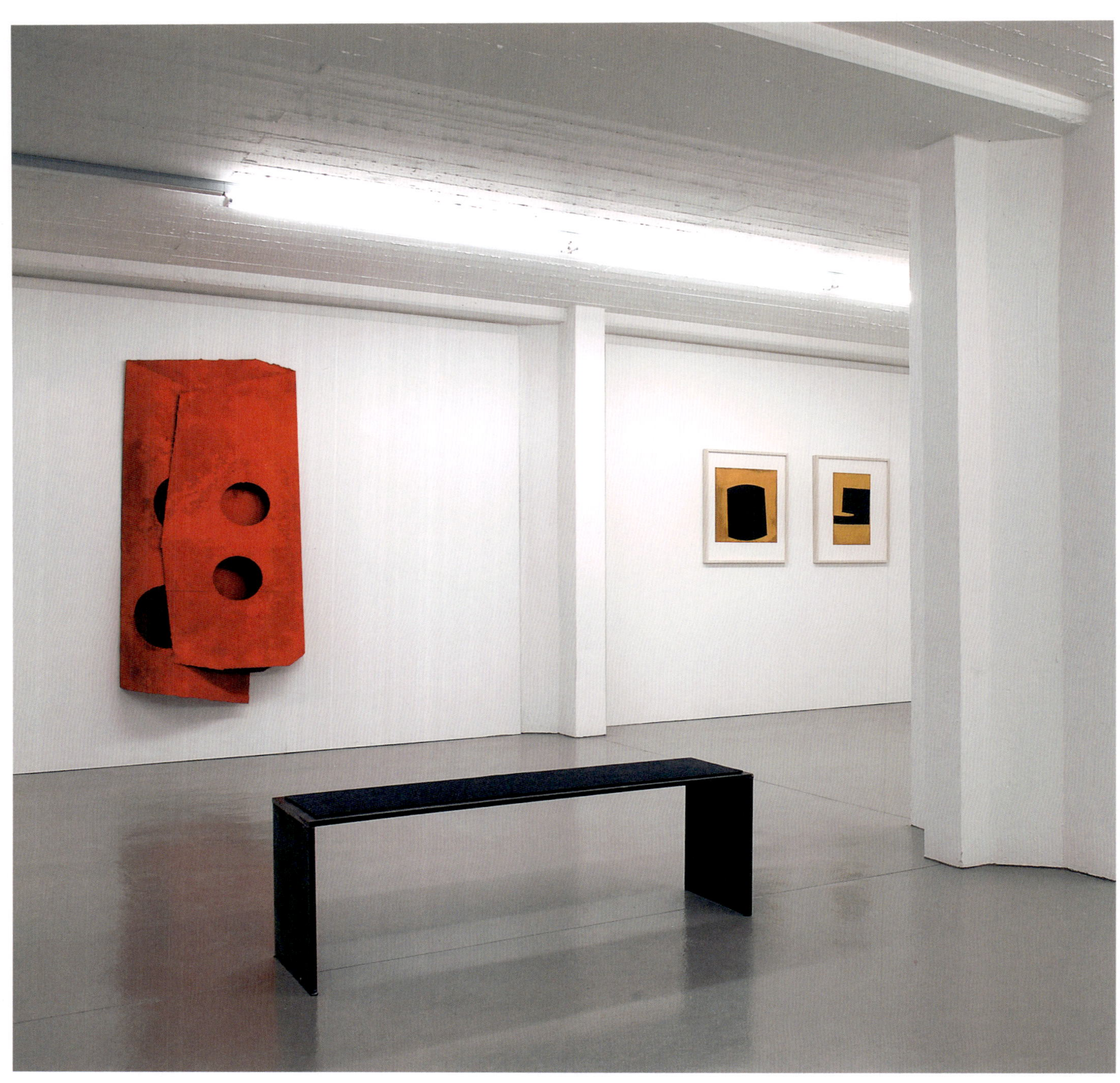

Mike Karstens Galerie, Münster, Germany

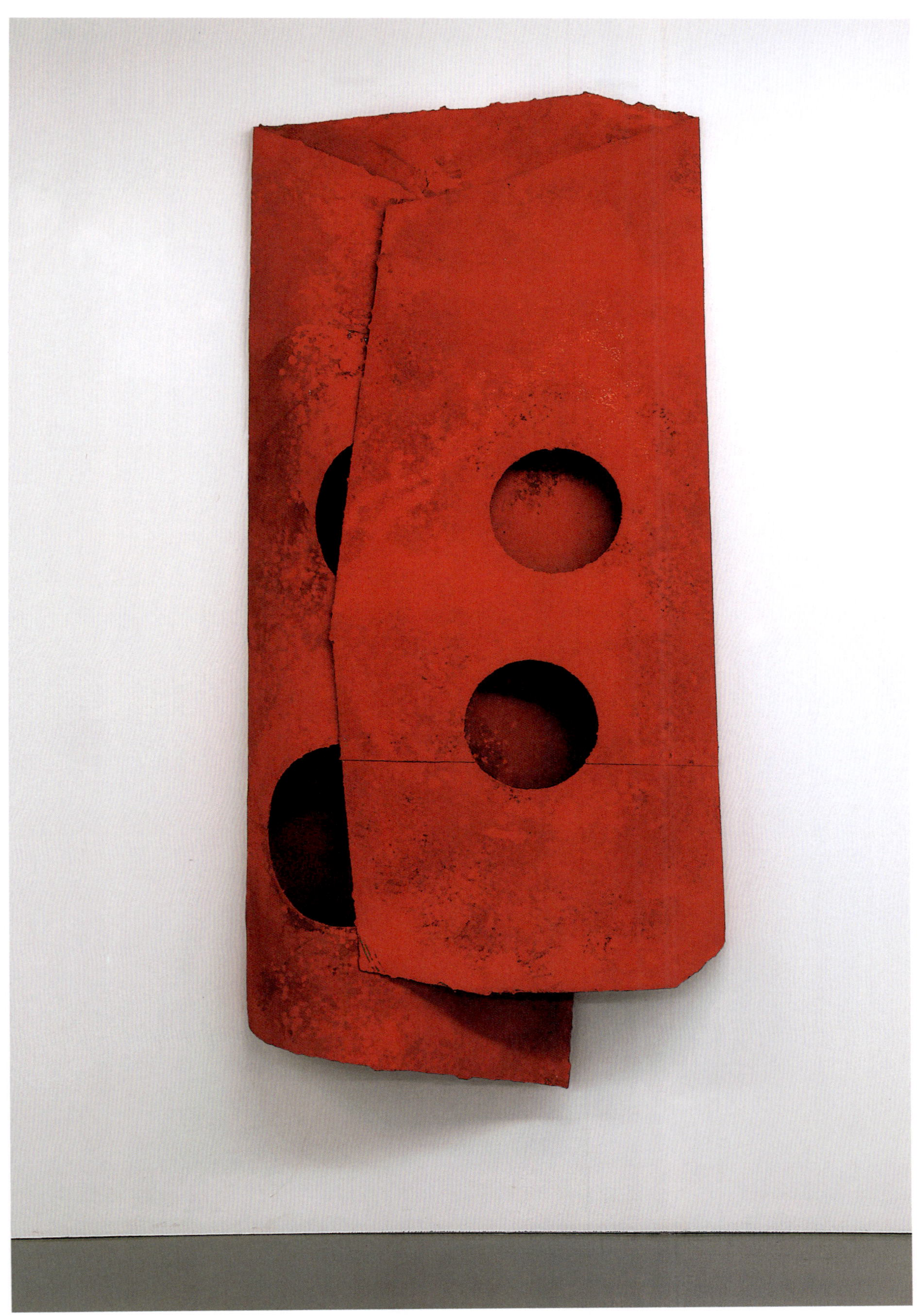

Red Coat, 2006

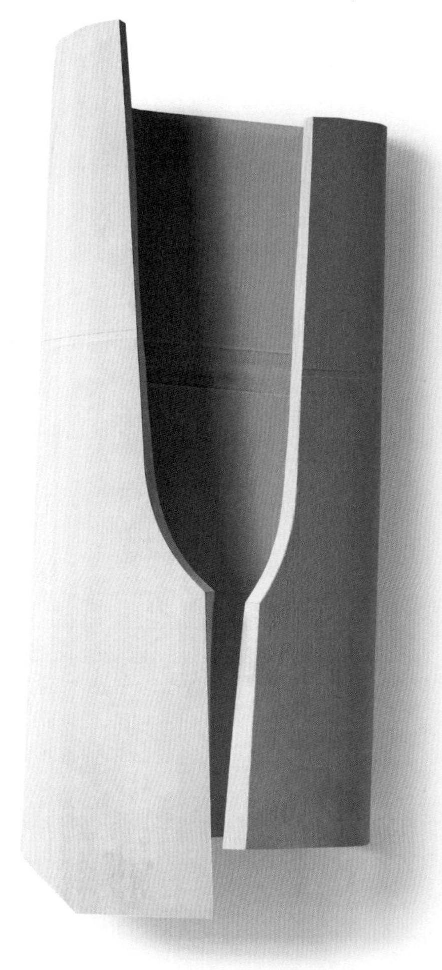

White Prelude No. 614, 2013

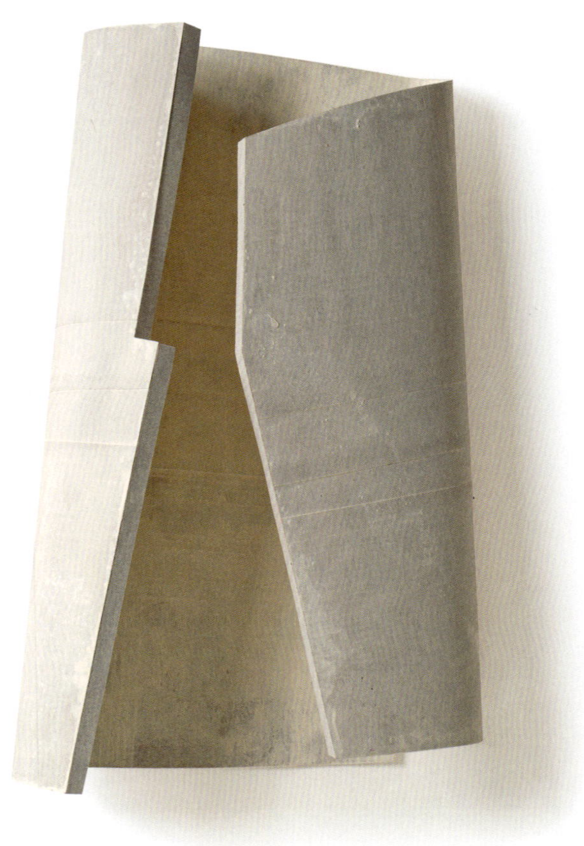

White Prelude No. 608, 2013

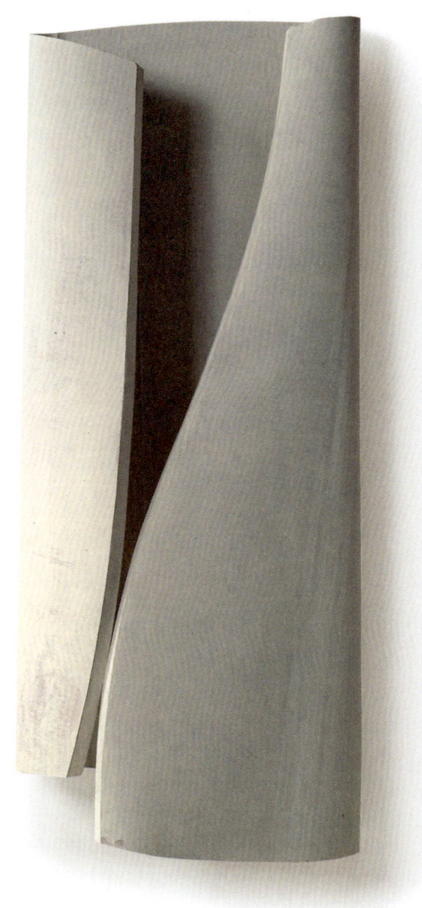

White Prelude No. 617, 2012–13

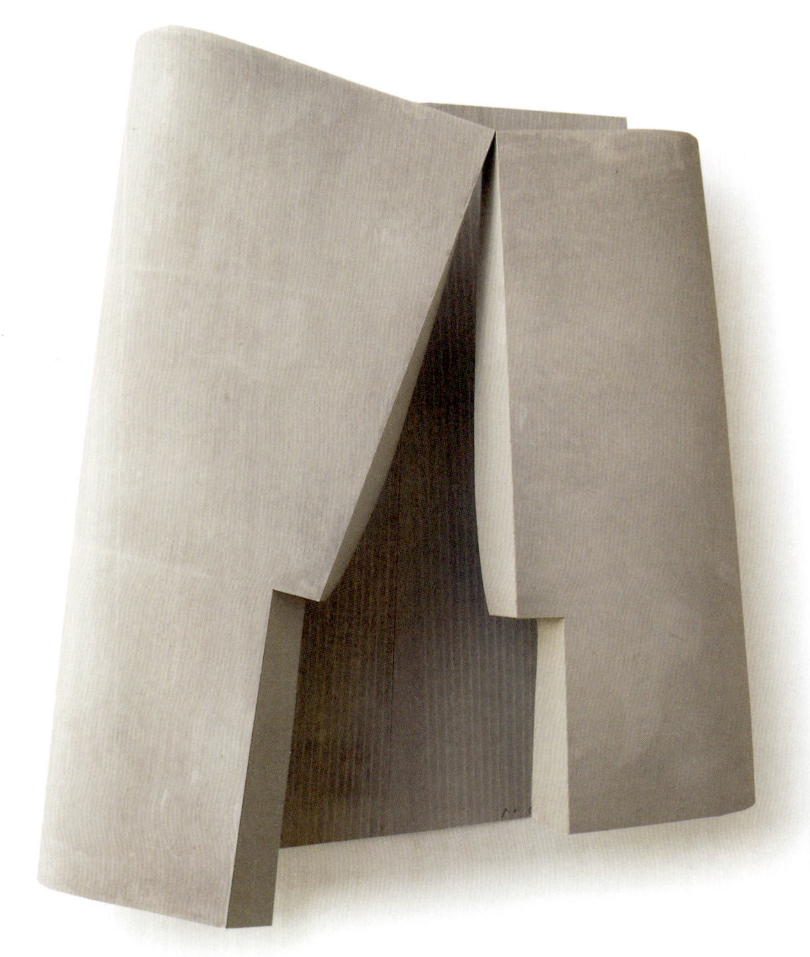

White Prelude No. 373, 2006

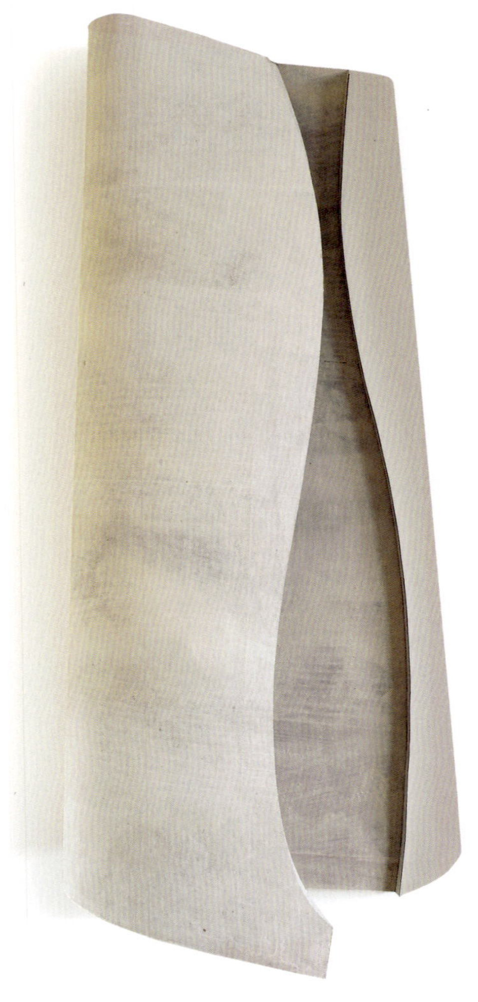

White Prelude No. 803, 2012–13

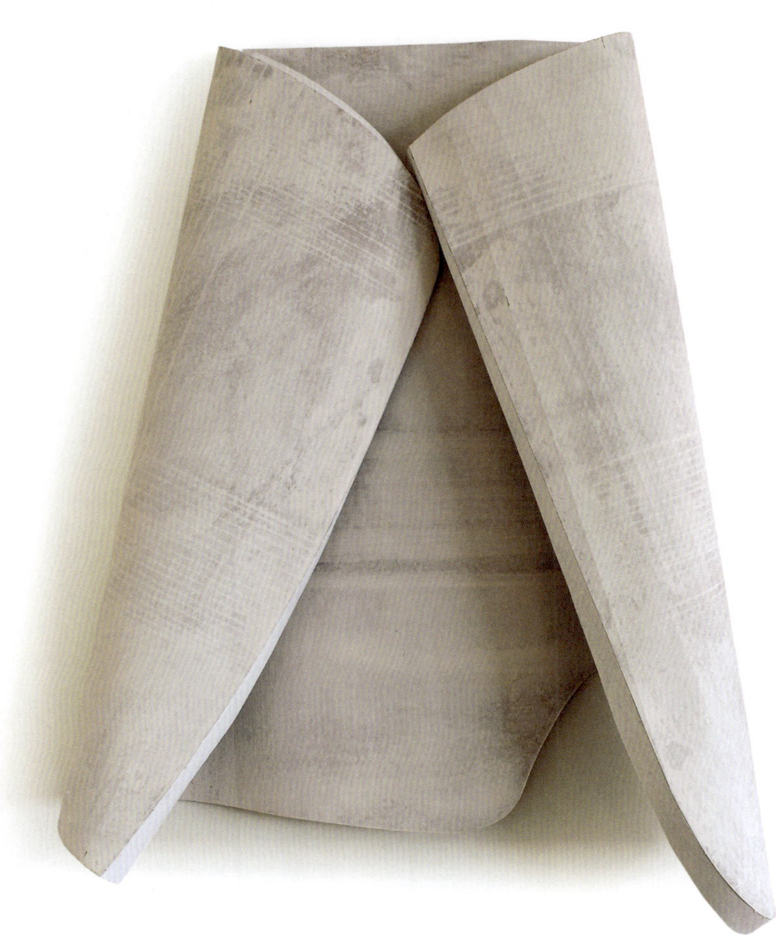

White Prelude No. 505, 2011

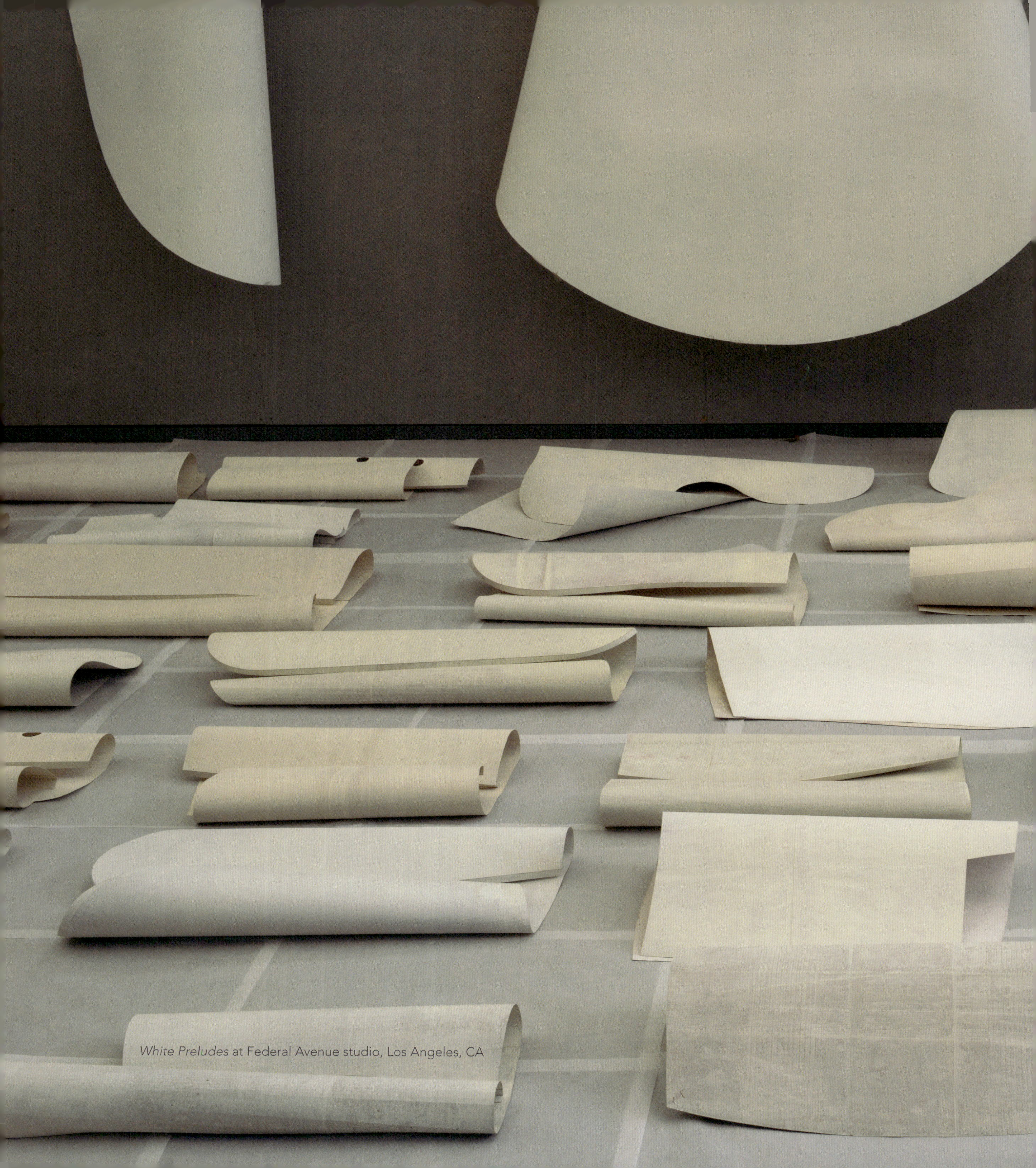

White Preludes at Federal Avenue studio, Los Angeles, CA

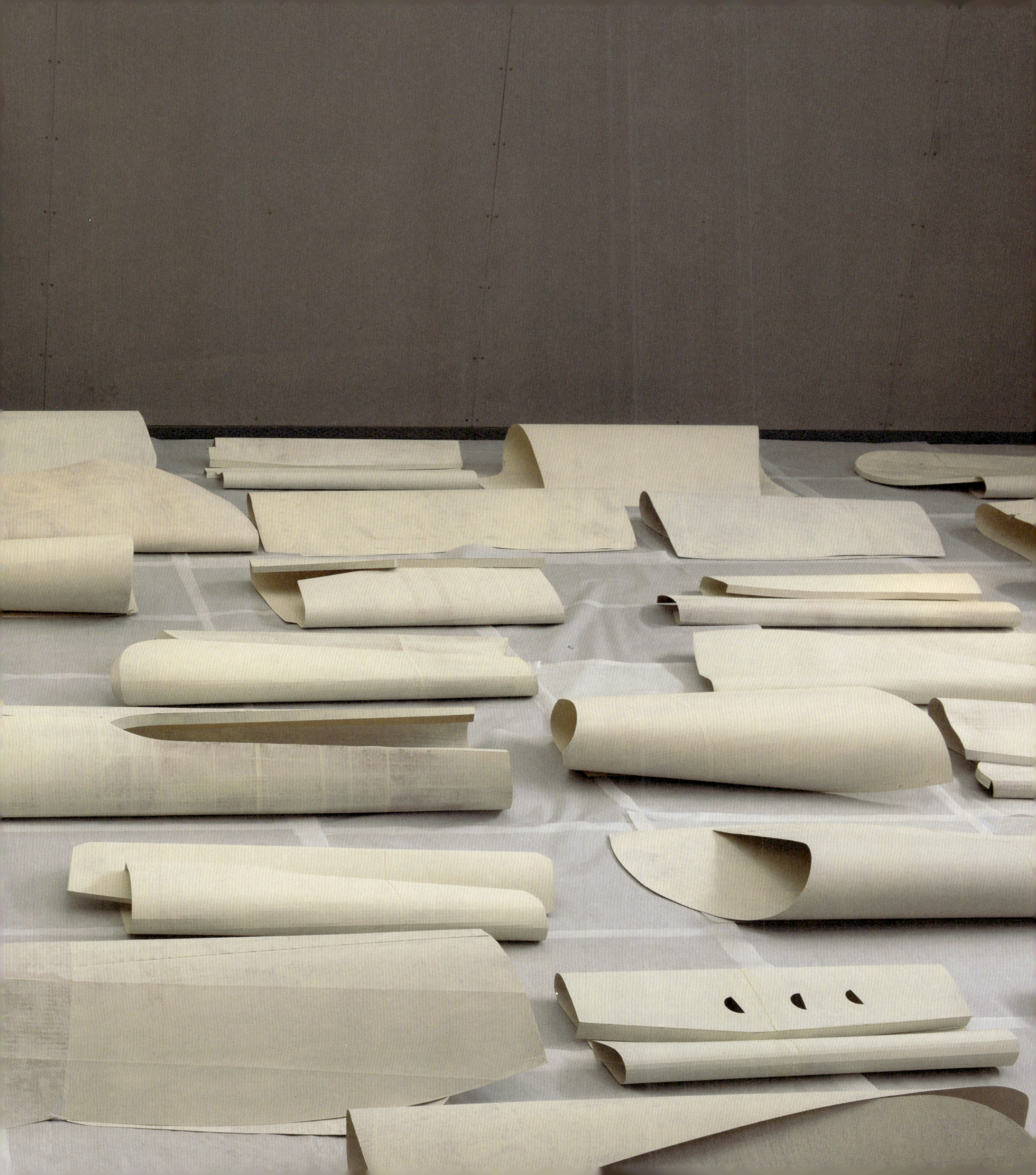

White Overture XL 2, 2013

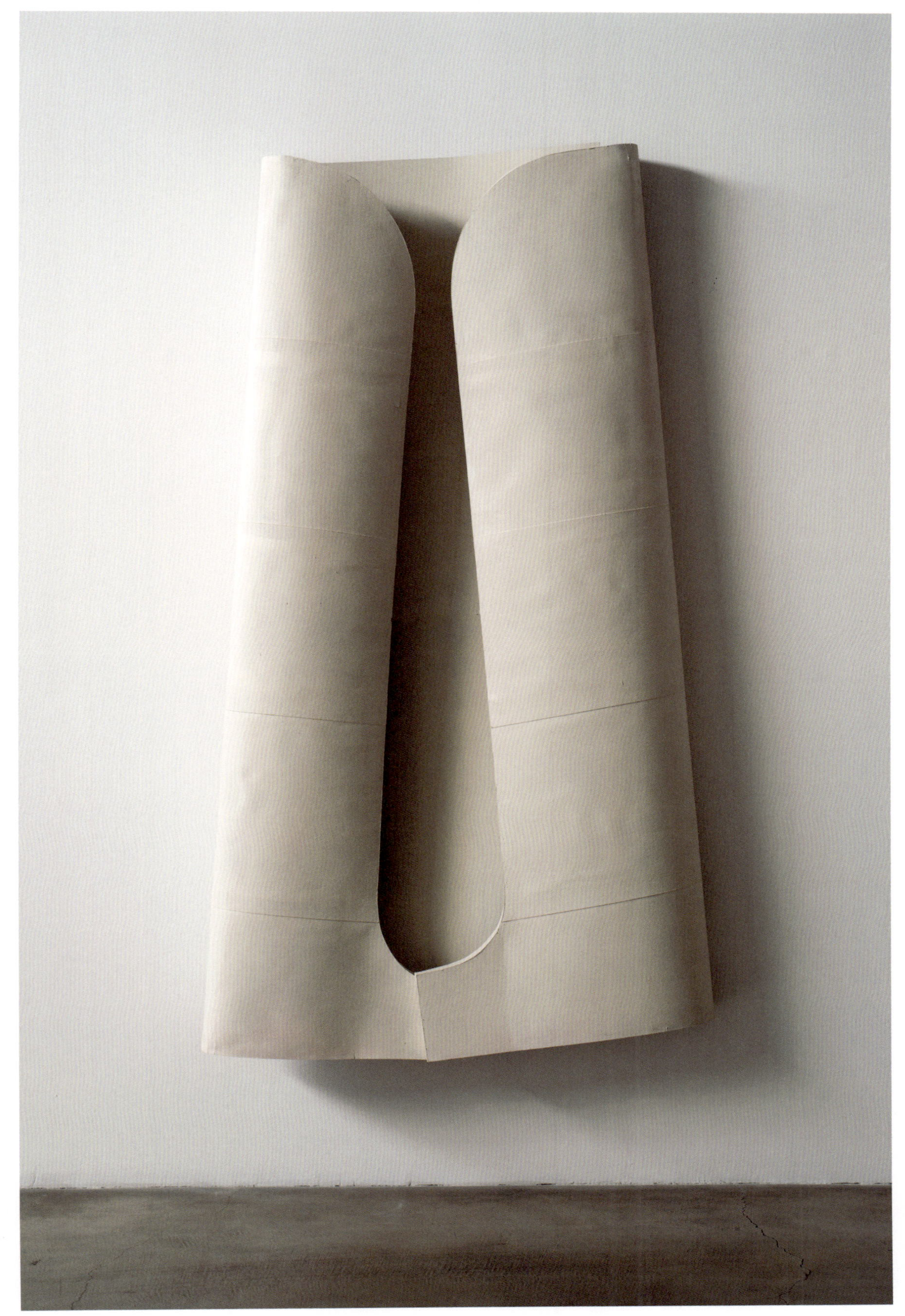

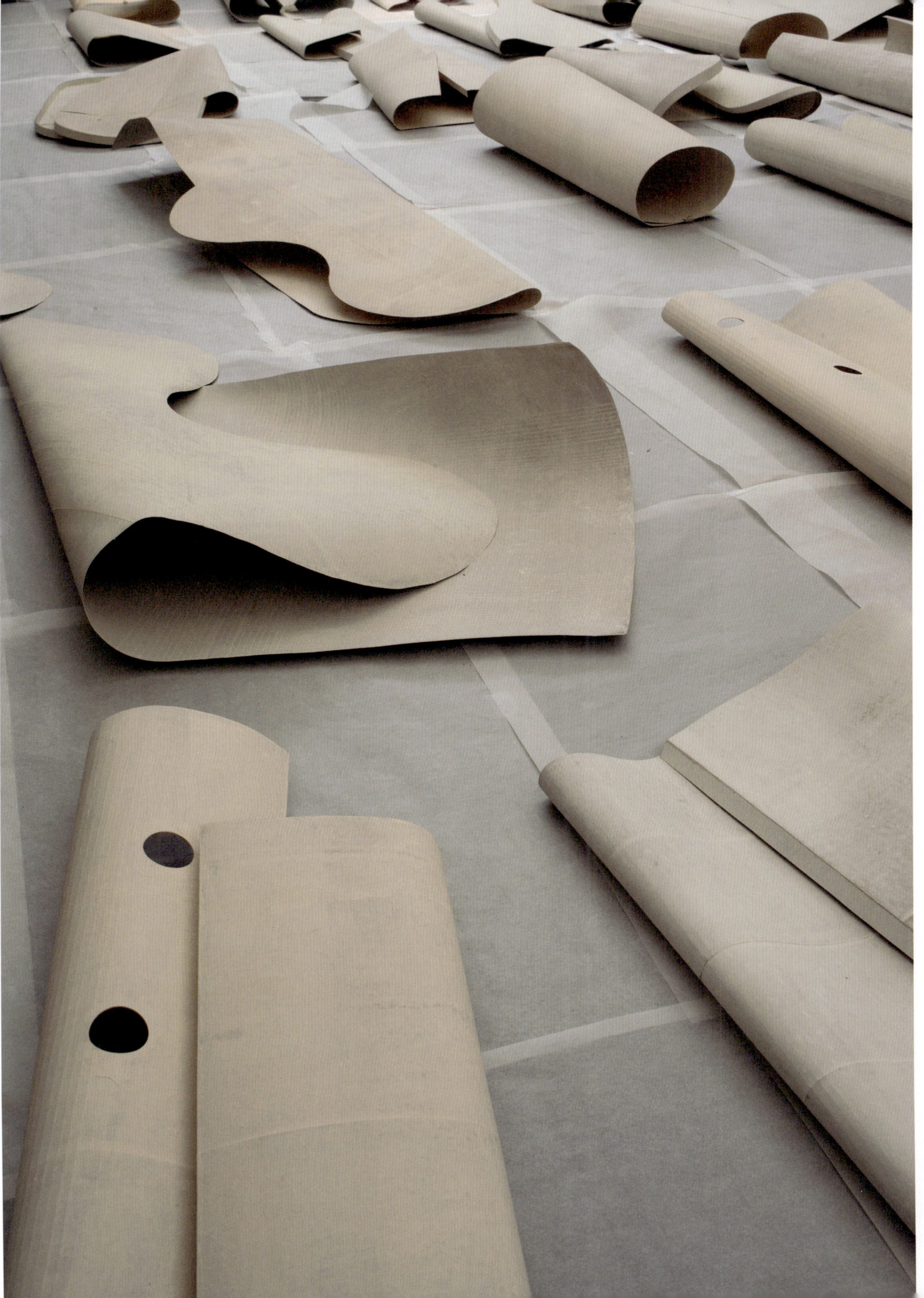

White Overture XL 3, 2013

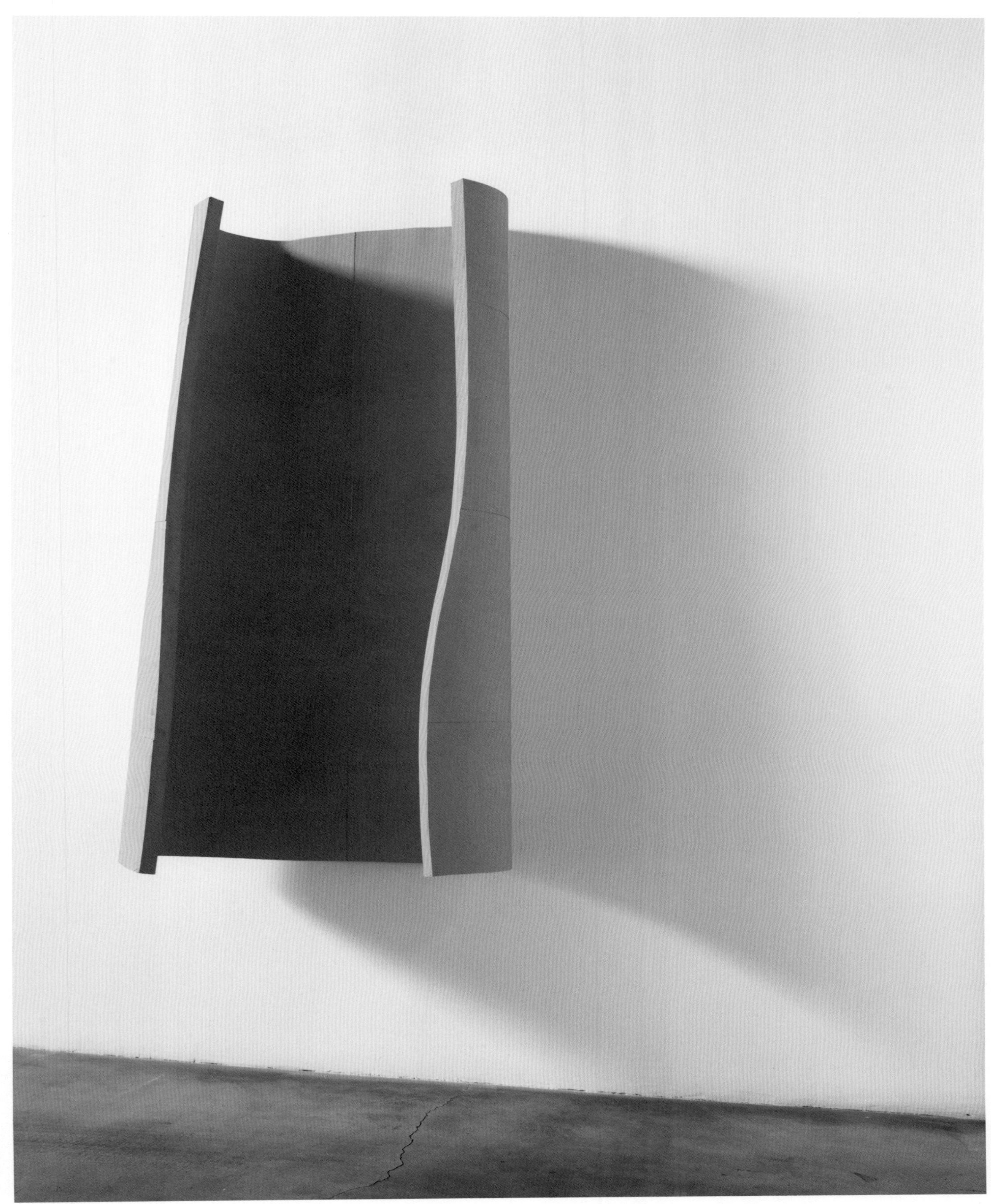

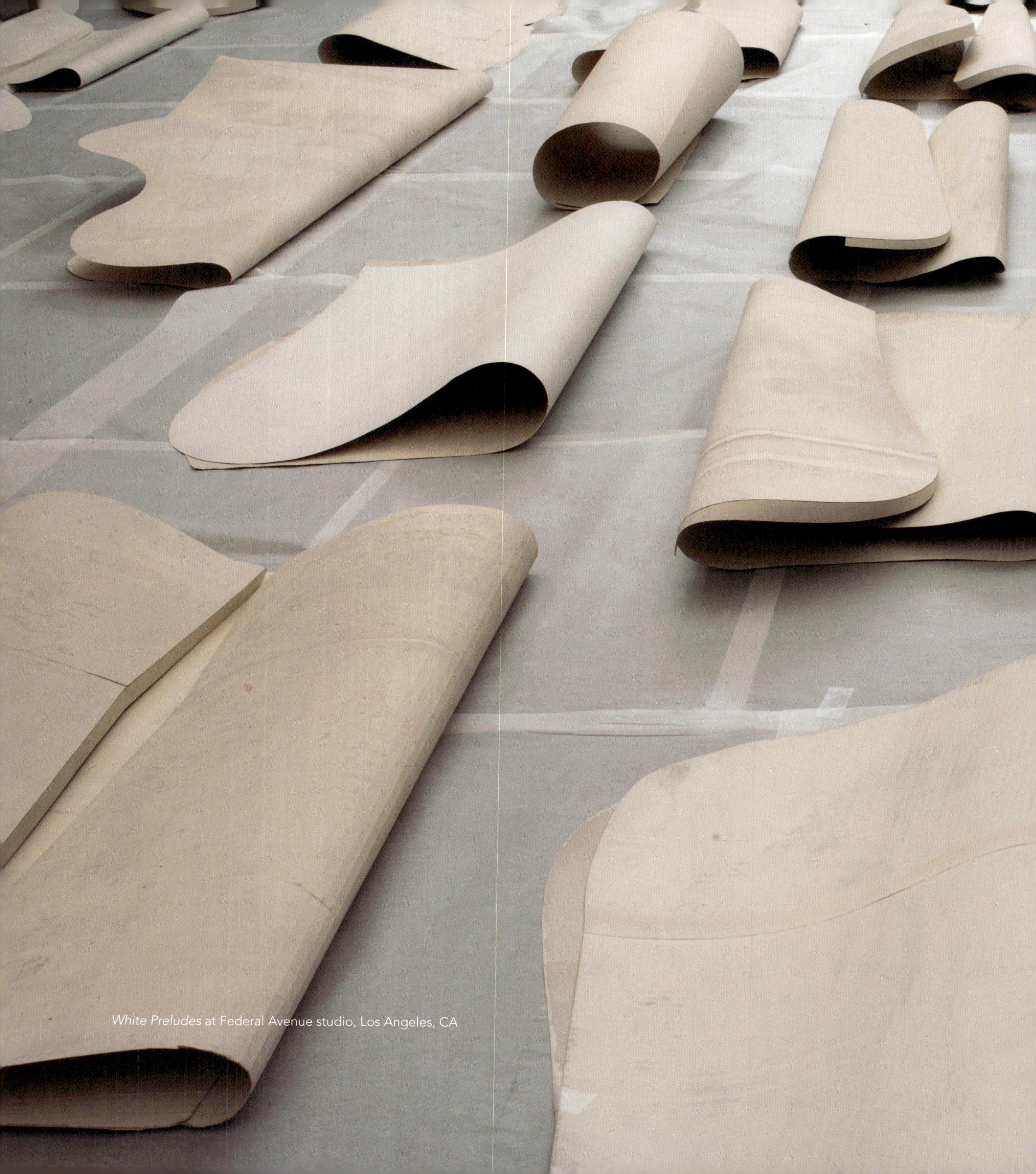

White Preludes at Federal Avenue studio, Los Angeles, CA

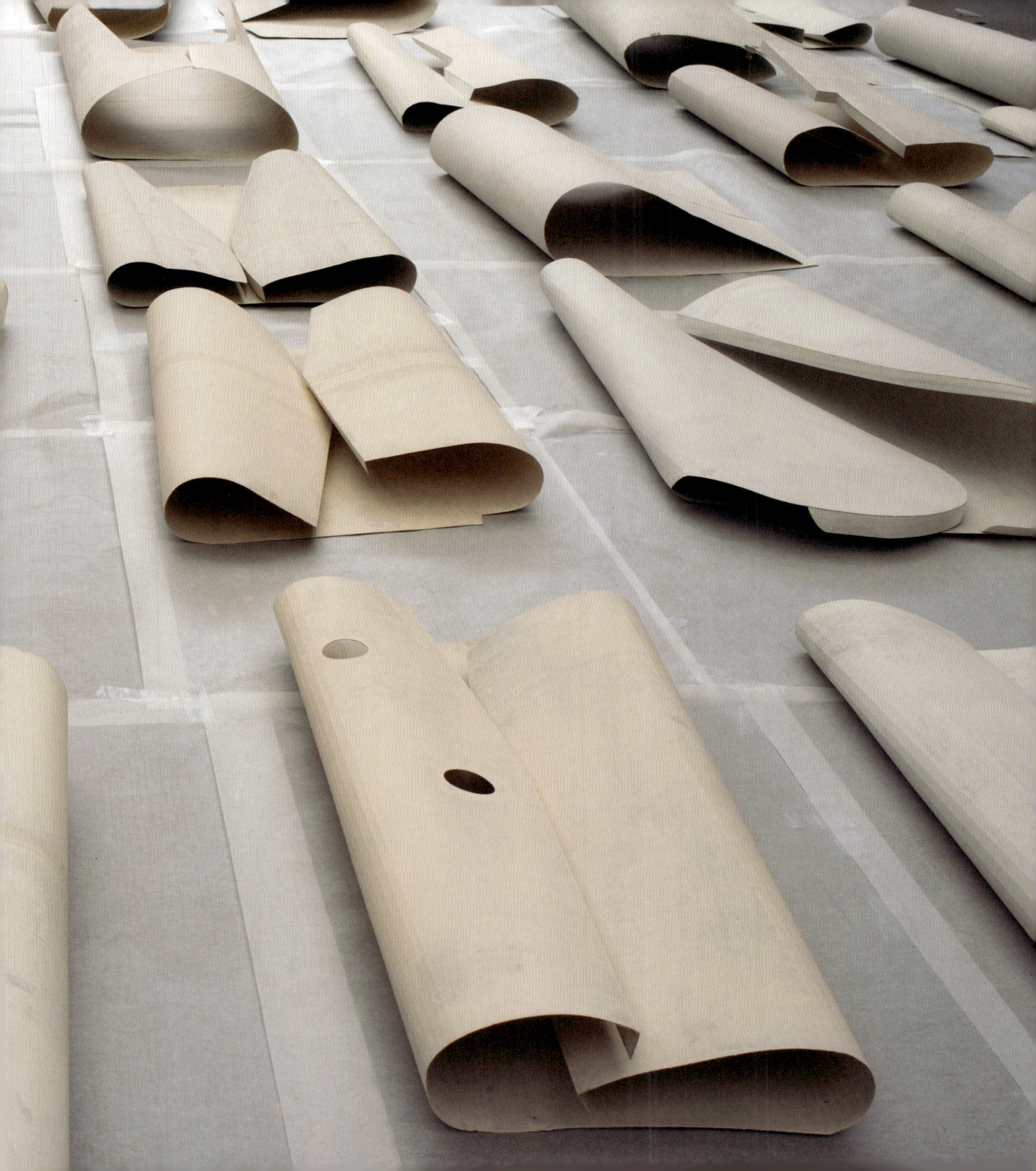

LIST OF ILLUSTRATIONS

Twilight and Yearning, 1998
Installation beneath the Santa Monica Pier, Santa Monica, CA
Wooden rowboats, steel belts
Dimensions variable
(pp. 36–37)

Twilight and Yearning, 1998
Solarized gelatin silver print, oil paint, paper folder
18 × 20 in.
Collection of Annette and Burkhard Richter
(p. 38)

Twilight and Yearning, 1998
Solarized gelatin silver print, oil paint, paper folder
19 × 15 in.
Collection of Annette and Burkhard Richter
(p. 39, left)

Twilight and Yearning, 1998
Solarized gelatin silver print, oil paint, paper folder
22 × 18 in.
Collection of Annette and Burkhard Richter
(p. 39, right)

Palacio de Memoria (Palace of memory), 1999
Installation at Museo Universitario del Chopo, Mexico City,
Mexico
Wood, fabric, paint
Dimensions variable
(p. 41)

Coat Survivor, 1999
Oil color, felt paper
67 × 32 × 12 in.
Collection of Elizabeth and Dennis Kneier
(p. 43)

White Overture XL 1, 2013
Linseed-oil pigment, manila paper
70 × 45 × 6 in.
(p. 45)

Thun Construction, 1983–84
Installation at Studio Ratherstrasse, Düsseldorf, Germany
Wood, primer, concrete, steel
Dimensions variable
(p. 48)

Jöllenbeck Construction, 1985
Installation at Studio Ratherstrasse, Düsseldorf, Germany
Wood, concrete, steel
42 × 96 × 48 in.
(p. 49)

Primavera, 1983–84
Installation at Studio Ratherstrasse, Düsseldorf, Germany
Wood, primer
44 × 96 × 48 in.
(p. 50)

Architektonische Skulptur Studie (Architectural sculpture study),
1984
Primed foam board, plywood
48 × 60 × 60 in.
Public Collection of Museum van Hedendaagse Kunst Antwerpen,
Belgium
(p. 51)

Architektonische Skulptur Studie (Architectural sculpture study),
1982
Paper, wood
24 × 32 × 25 in.
(p. 52)

Architektonische Skulptur Studie (Architectural sculpture study), 1982
Installation at Studio Bilkerstrasse, Düsseldorf, Germany
Paper, wood, primer
30 × 42 × 24 in.
(p. 53)

Tunnel Vision, 1983
Installation at Studio Ratherstrasse, Düsseldorf, Germany
Plywood, concrete, steel
Dimensions variable
(p. 54)

Tunnel Vision: Sculpture Invasion, 1983
Installation at Lehmbruck Museum, Duisburg, Germany
Concrete, wood
Dimensions variable
(p. 55)

Die ewigen Werte von Gestern (The eternal value from yesterday), 1984–85
Installation at Forum Aktueller Kunst Oberhausen, Germany
Red and black earth, concrete, steel, water, found table, found mirror
Dimensions variable
(pp. 56–57)

Seven Bowls (detail), 1984
Installation at Kunsthalle Düsseldorf, Germany
Concrete, wood, water
Dimensions variable
(p. 58)

Studio Ratherstrasse, Düsseldorf, Germany
(p. 59)

Palacio de Memoria: Mi Tierra (Palace of memory: my earth), 1999
Installation at Museo Universitario del Chopo, Mexico City, Mexico
Ceramic, steel, terracotta
84 × 160 × 26 in.
(pp. 60–61)

The Exchange "Two Bowls," 1988
Installation at Hete A. M. Hünerman Galerie, Düsseldorf, Germany
Oil color, felt paper
52 × 66 × 5 in.
(p. 62)

Wall Object, 1984
Installation at Studio Ratherstrasse, Düsseldorf, Germany
Oil color, felt paper
66 × 72 × 5 in.
(p. 63)

Bowl Twist, 1983–84
Installation at Studio Ratherstrasse, Düsseldorf, Germany
Felt paper
Dimensions variable
(p. 64)

Wall Object, 1983
Installation at Studio Bilkerstrasse, Düsseldorf, Germany
Paperboard
60 × 82 in.
(p. 65, top)

Wall Object Reversal, 1983
Installation at Studio Bilkerstrasse, Düsseldorf, Germany
Paperboard
60 × 82 in.
(p. 65, bottom)

Studio Objekte (Studio objects), 1981–84
Installation at Studio Bilkerstrasse, Düsseldorf, Germany
Paperboard
Dimensions variable
(pp. 66–67)

Vintage Prelude Object, 1991–92
Oil color, Fabriano paper
11 × 7 × 2 in.
Courtesy of Roy Boyd Gallery, Chicago, IL
(p. 68)

Vintage Prelude Object, 1991–92
Oil color, Fabriano paper
14 × 5 × 5 in.
Courtesy of Roy Boyd Gallery, Chicago, IL
(p. 69)

Wall Object, 1982
Installation at Studio Bilkerstrasse, Düsseldorf, Germany
Heavy manila paper
60 × 28 × 2 in.
Courtesy of the Rössner Collection
(p. 70)

Wall Object, 1982
Installation at Studio Bilkerstrasse, Düsseldorf, Germany
Heavy manila paper
60 × 24 × 24 in.
(p. 71)

Shield, 1982
Installation at Studio Bilkerstrasse, Düsseldorf, Germany
Oil color, felt paper
Diam.: 30 in.
(p. 73)

Erdzeichen 1 (Earth signs 1) (detail), 1985
Steel plate
48 × 72 × ¾ in.
(p. 74)

Erdzeichen 2 (Earth signs 2), 1985
Steel plate
48 × 72 × ¾ in.
(p. 75)

Black Friday, 1988
Oil paint, paperboard, flexible fabric, rubber belt, wood
82 × 72 × 44 in.
(p. 77)

Concept for a Border Town, 1992
Installation at *Transformer*, Mandeville Annex Gallery, UCSD,
La Jolla, CA
Steel construction, library ladder, ceramic bowls
Diam. 62 in., height 96 in.
(pp. 78–79)

Unique Hidden Cache: River Scene, 2004
Solarized gelatin silver print, museum board, oil color
33 × 21½ in.
(p. 81)

Oxid Yellow, 2007
Oxide pigment, oil pastel, oil color, suede, museum board
16 × 12 in.
(p. 83, top left)

Oxid Yellow, 2007
Oxide pigment, oil pastel, oil color, suede, museum board
16 × 12 in.
(p. 83, top right)

Oxid Yellow, 2007
Oxide pigment oil pastel, oil color, suede, museum board
20 × 16 in.
(p. 83, bottom)

Under My Skin 22/131, 2007
Oil pastel, grid paper
23 × 17½ in.
Collection of the Hillstone Restaurant Group, Los Angeles, CA
(p. 84)

Under My Skin 4, 2007
Oil pastel, grid paper
23 × 17½ in.
Collection of the Hillstone Restaurant Group, Los Angeles, CA
(p. 85, left)

Under My Skin 38/115, 2007
Oil pastel, grid paper
23 × 17½ in.
Collection of the Hillstone Restaurant Group, Los Angeles, CA
(p. 85, right)

White Preludes at Federal Avenue studio, Los Angeles, CA
(p. 87)

Body Shop, 2003
Installation at USC Fisher Museum of Art, Los Angeles, CA
Polyethylene, plaster, wood
Dimensions variable
(pp. 88, 90–91)

Gray Coat, 2003–4
Oil color, felt paper
63 × 35 × 5 in.
Courtesy of Roy Boyd Gallery, Chicago, IL
(p. 93)

Black Waterfall, 1989
Installation at *BoñAngeles*, Santa Monica Museum of Art, Santa
Monica, CA
Wheelbarrow, fabric, wood, copper, mirror
Dimensions variable
(pp. 96–97)

Cave Focused, 1995
Installation on-site, Los Angeles, CA
Ceramic, found wood panels, found armchair
Dimensions variable
(p. 98)

Cicero, 1990
Installation at Kronprinzenstrasse 27, Düsseldorf, Germany
Cafeteria benches, table, existing curtains
96 × 104 × 96 in.
(p. 99)

Transformer, 1993
Installation at *Transformer*, Santa Barbara Contemporary
Arts Forum, Santa Barbara, CA
Weather balloon, steel table, blower, Mauser gun
Dimensions variable
(pp. 100–101)

Low Color Intention, 1984–85
Oil pastel, paper
17 × 14 in.
Collection of Jane and Burt Berman
(p. 102, left)

Low Color Intention, 1985
Dry pastel, oil pastel, paper
17 × 14 in.
(p. 102, right)

Transformer, 1991
Installation at *Transformer,* Mandeville Annex Gallery, UCSD,
La Jolla, CA
B-52 filter, ceramic vase, wax paper, leather belt, string
38 × 32 × 16 in.
(p. 103)

Palacio de Memoria: Four Bowls, 2000
Oil color, oil pastel, paper
17 × 13 in.
(p. 104)

Palacio de Memoria: Five Bowls, 2002
Oil color, oil pastel, paper
29½ × 18½ in.
(p. 105)

Low Color Intention 41, 1996
Oil color, suede, museum board
12 × 13½ in.
(p. 106)

Low Color Intention 42, 1996
Oil color, suede, museum board
15 × 9 in.
(p. 107)

More Color Intention 1, 2004
Oil color, oil pastel, paper
18 × 14 in.
(p. 108)

More Color Intention 2, 2013
Oil color, oil pastel, paper
17 × 16 in.
(p. 109)

Olympic Boulevard No. 11, 2008
Oil pastel, manila paper
24 × 16 in.
Collection of the Frederick R. Weisman Art Foundation
(p. 110)

Palacio de Memoria: Echo, 2008
Oil pastel, manila paper, Fabriano paper
17 × 11 in.
Collection of the Frederick R. Weisman Art Foundation
(p. 111)

Hidden Cache: Surplus, 2008
Solarized gelatin silver print, oil paint, museum board
38 × 21½ in.
(p. 112)

Hidden Cache: Past/Present, 2008
Solarized gelatin silver print, oil paint, museum board
38 × 21½ in.
(p. 113)

Hidden Cache: Indefinite, 2008
Solarized gelatin silver print, oil paint, museum board
38 × 21½ in.
(p. 114)

Hidden Cache: Surplus II, 2008
Solarized gelatin silver print, oil paint, museum board
38 × 21½ in.
(p. 115)

Heliotropos at Federal Avenue studio, Los Angeles, CA
(pp. 116–17)

Repercussion 4: Palacio de Memoria, 2011
Oil pastel, manila paper
72 × 52 in.
(p. 118)

Repercussion 1: Palacio de Memoria, 2011
Oil pastel, manila paper
72 × 52 in.
(p. 119)

Repercussion 2: Palacio de Memoria, 2011
Oil pastel, manila paper
72 × 52 in.
(p. 120)

Repercussion 3: Palacio de Memoria, 2011
Oil pastel, manila paper
72 × 52 in.
(p. 121)

Red Preludes at Federal Avenue studio, Los Angeles, CA
(pp. 122–23)

Red Prelude, 2009–11
Oil color, Fabriano paper
22 × 8 × 4 in.
(p. 124)

Red Prelude, 2009
Oil color, Fabriano paper
20 × 8 × 3 in.
(p. 125, left)

Red Prelude, 2009
Oil color, Fabriano paper
18 × 7 × 3 in.
(p. 125, right)

Mike Karstens Galerie, Münster, Germany
(p. 126)

Red Coat, 2006
Oil color, felt paper
60 × 30 × 6 in.
Collection of Annette and Burkhard Richter
(p. 127)

White Prelude No. 614, 2013
Oil color, Fabriano paper
24 × 10 × 3 in.
Courtesy of ROSEGALLERY, Santa Monica, CA
(p. 128)

White Prelude No. 608, 2013
Oil color, Fabriano paper
22½ × 8 × 4 in.
Courtesy of ROSEGALLERY, Santa Monica, CA
(p. 129, left)

White Prelude No. 617, 2012–13
Oil color, Fabriano paper
31 × 13 × 8 in.
Courtesy of ROSEGALLERY, Santa Monica, CA
(p. 129, right)

White Prelude No. 373, 2006
Oil color, Fabriano paper
18 × 13 × 5 in.
Collection of Jan and Trish de Bont
(p. 130)

White Prelude No. 803, 2012–13
Oil color, Fabriano paper
24½ × 11 × 3 in.
Collection of Claudia Kahn and Anthony Foux
(p. 131, left)

White Prelude No. 505, 2011
Oil color, Fabriano paper
23½ × 18 × 5½ in.
Courtesy of ROSEGALLERY, Santa Monica, CA
(p. 131, right)

White Preludes at Federal Avenue studio, Los Angeles, CA
(pp. 132–33)

White Overture XL 2, 2013
Linseed-oil pigment, Fabriano paper
84 × 38 × 24 in.
Courtesy of ROSEGALLERY, Santa Monica, CA
(p. 135)

White Preludes at Federal Avenue studio, Los Angeles, CA
(p. 137)

White Overture XL 3, 2013
Linseed-oil pigment, Fabriano paper
66 × 35 × 22 in.
Courtesy of ROSEGALLERY, Santa Monica, CA
(p. 139)

White Preludes at Federal Avenue studio, Los Angeles, CA
(pp. 140–41)

White Overture XLs at Federal Avenue studio, Los Angeles, CA
(pp. 156–57)

MANFRED MÜLLER

Born: Düsseldorf, Germany, 1950
Education: Kunstakademie Düsseldorf, Fachhochschule Düsseldorf
Lives and works in Los Angeles, CA

EXHIBITION HISTORY

SOLO EXHIBITIONS

2014 *Objects Are Closer Than They Appear*, Los Angeles Municipal Art Gallery, Barnsdall Art Park, Los Angeles, CA

2011 ML Gallery, Antwerp, Belgium

2010 Heidi Cho Gallery, New York, NY

Heliotropo Galeria López Quiroga, Mexico City, Mexico

2008 *Hidden Cache No. 1*, ROSEGALLERY, Santa Monica, CA

2007 *New Work*, Roy Boyd Gallery, Chicago, IL

Works on Paper, ROSEGALLERY, Santa Monica, CA

2006 *CONTRATO: New Work by Manfred Müller*, Mike Karstens Galerie, Münster, Germany

Roy Boyd Gallery, Chicago, IL

2003 *Human Conditions: Demo: The Body Shop*, USC Fisher Museum of Art, Los Angeles, CA

ROSEGALLERY, Santa Monica, CA

2001 Roy Boyd Gallery, Chicago, IL

1999 *Palacio de Memoria*, Museo Universitario del Chopo, Mexico City, Mexico

1998 Hete A. M. Hünerman Galerie, Düsseldorf, Germany

1997 *Sculpture and Drawing*, Form Zero Architecture Gallery, Los Angeles, CA

1996 *Current Work: Sculpture and Paperworks*, Roy Boyd Gallery, Chicago, IL

1995 *New Objects and Sketches*, Hete A. M. Hünerman Galerie, Düsseldorf, Germany

1994 *Tunnelvision*, Site Gallery, Los Angeles, CA

Transformer: A Change of Past Perceptions, Contemporary Arts Forum, Santa Barbara, CA; traveled to Open Space, Victoria, British Columbia, Canada

1993 *The Exchange*, Hete A. M. Hünerman Galerie, Düsseldorf, Germany

1992 *Sculptural Events*, Mandeville Annex Gallery, UCSD, La Jolla, CA

The Lights at the End of the Tunnel, Heidelberger Kunstverein, Heidelberg, Germany

1991 *New Paperworks*, Galerie Jöllenbeck, Cologne, Germany

Cabinettpiece, Hete A. M. Hünerman Galerie, Düsseldorf, Germany

1989 *Paperobjects*, Galerie Carol Johnssen, Munich, Germany

1988 *Sketches and Paperworks*, Galerie Jöllenbeck, Cologne, Germany

1986 *Wallpiece*, Galerie Christian Fochem, Krefeld, Germany

1985   Galerie Jöllenbeck, Cologne, Germany

Waiting in the Windshade, Lehmbruck Museum, Duisburg, Germany

1984   Stadtmuseum, Düsseldorf, Germany

SELECTED GROUP EXHIBITIONS

2011   *Framing Abstraction: Mark, Symbol, Signifier*, Los Angeles Municipal Art Gallery, Barnsdall Art Park, Los Angeles, CA

2010   *SHOPWEAR*, ROSEGALLERY, Santa Monica, CA

2008   *Reflections from the Artist's Eye: Contemporary Art from the Frederick R. Weisman Art Foundation*, Frederick R. Weisman Museum of Art, Pepperdine University, Malibu, CA

2007   *Made in California: Contemporary California Art from the Frederick R. Weisman Art Foundation*, Frederick R. Weisman Museum of Art, Pepperdine University, Malibu, CA

The Eclectic Eye: Pop and Illusion—Selections from the Frederick R. Weisman Art Foundation, Fine Arts Center Museum, Colorado Springs, CO

2006   *LA Art Scene: Selections of California Artists from the Frederick R. Weisman Art Foundation*, Beverly Hills Municipal Gallery, Beverly Hills, CA

2005   *Group Exhibition for Art Chicago*, Roy Boyd Gallery, Chicago, IL

Art Chicago, Chicago, IL

2004–13 *INCOGNITO*, Santa Monica Museum of Art, Santa Monica, CA

1995–96 *LA Current: Works on Paper*, Armand Hammer Museum, Art Rental and Sales Gallery, Los Angeles, CA

1995   *10 European Artists*, Roy Boyd Gallery, Chicago, IL

1994   *Current Abstractions*, Los Angeles Municipal Art Gallery, Barnsdall Art Park, Los Angeles, CA

In Reference to the Vessel, José Drudis-Biada Art Gallery, Mount St. Mary's College, Los Angeles, CA

1993–97 *Venice Art Walk*, Venice Beach, CA

1993   *Peter's Friends*, Kunsthalle Düsseldorf, Germany

1992   *Für Karl Ernst Jöllenbeck*, Galerie Jöllenbeck, Cologne, Germany

Triennale of Small Sculpture, Lehmbruck Museum, Duisburg, Germany

Triennale Fellbach, Fellbach, Germany

1990   *Fusion*, Sordoni Art Gallery, Wilkes University, Wilkes-Barre, PA

La Jeune Sculpture, Quai d'Austerlitz, Paris, France

Cicero, Kronprinzenstrasse 27, Düsseldorf, Germany

1989   *BoñAngeles*, Santa Monica Museum of Art, Santa Monica, CA

1988   *Figurationen: Der Zusammenhang der Dinge*, Flottmann Hallen, Herne, Germany

Auszugsweise, Galerie Jöllenbeck, Cologne, Germany

Meine Zeit, Mein Raubtier, Museum Kunstpalast, Düsseldorf, Germany

Ucronos, Faux Mouvement, Metz, France

1987   *Paperworks*, T. G. Art Gallery, Los Angeles, CA

Ucronia, Sermig, Piazza Borgo Dora, Turin, Italy

IBM Deutschland, Düsseldorf, Germany

Sub aqua, Peter-Lauten-Strasse, Krefeld, Germany

1985   *Die sich verselbständigenden Möbel*, Wuppertaler Kunstverein, Wuppertal, Germany

Mitten im Werktag, Bonner Kunstverein, Bonn, Germany

Dimensionen V, Kunsthalle, Cologne, Germany

Dimensionen V, Kunsthalle, Berlin, Germany

Dimensionen V, Museum Villa Stuck, Munich, Germany

Thun Naturell, Kunstmuseum, Thun, Switzerland

Kranz ohne König, Südhaus, Frankfurt am Main, Germany

1984   *Dimensionen IV*, Nationalgalerie, Berlin, Germany

Dimensionen IV, Haus der Kunst, Munich, Germany

Dimensionen IV, Kunsthalle, Düsseldorf, Germany

Forum Junger Kunst, Wüttembergischer Kunstverein, Stuttgart, Germany

Forum Junger Kunst, Kunsthalle, Mannheim, Germany

Forum Junger Kunst, Kunsthalle, Baden-Baden, Germany

Vielleicht fiel viel Schatten, Studio Ratherstrasse Collective, Düsseldorf, Germany

Drunter und Drüber, AoRTa Art Galley, Amsterdam, Netherlands

1983   *Standort Düsseldorf*, Kunsthalle, Düsseldorf, Germany

Galerie Jöllenbeck, Cologne, Germany

1982   *Between 9, Bild der Abschreckung*, Kunsthalle, Düsseldorf, Germany

Junge Bildhauer in Düsseldorf, Skulpturenpark Seestern, Düsseldorf, Germany

1981   *Plastische Versuche*, Rheinisches Landesmuseum, Bonn, Germany

Reine Weste, Tote hose, Studio Ratherstrasse Collective, Düsseldorf, Germany

Pflüger auf Grund, Börnestrasse construction site, Düsseldorf, Germany

Perspektiven 2, Kunstverein NRW, Düsseldorf, Germany

1980   *Artistes Allemands à Paris*, Goethe Institut, Paris, France

1979   *Projekt Wupper*, Von der Heydt Museum, Wuppertal,
            Germany

            Weisser Saal Kunstmuseum, Bern, Switzerland

SELECTED PUBLIC ARTWORKS

2002   *When a Person Plants a Tree . . . .*, public installation,
            Civic Center and Library, Agoura Hills, CA

2000   *Ringrotsiebzehngrad* (ringredseventeendegrees),
            Universität Münster, commissioned by the city of
            Münster, Germany

1998   *Twilight and Yearning*, installation beneath the Santa
            Monica Pier, Santa Monica, CA

1997   *Rosso Rotondo*, first-prize sculpture for permanent
            display in the city of Münster, commissioned by the
            County NRW, Germany

1988   *Vom Verteilen der Lasten*, first-prize sculpture for
            permanent display in public place, commissioned by the
            Museum Ludwig, Cologne, Germany

SELECTED BIBLIOGRAPHY

Artner, Alan G. "Artist Conveys Message through Color, Texture." *Chicago Tribune*, August 15, 1996. http://articles.chicagotribune .com/1996-08-15/features/9608150277_1_sculpture-works-color -field.

———. "Evocative Müller Wall Sculptures." *Chicago Tribune*, June 15, 2001. http://articles.chicagotribune.com/2001-06-15/ entertainment/0106150384_1_color-postmodern-eduardo-chillida.

———. "Manfred Müller at Roy Boyd." *Chicago Tribune*, October 27, 2007.

Chattopadhyay, Collette. "Manfred Müller: The Labyrinth of Memory." *Sculpture Magazine*, July/August 2004. http://www .sculpture.org/documents/scmag04/julaug04/webspecials/muller .shtml.

De Backer, Leen. *De Verzameling/The Collection*. Antwerp: Museum van Hedendaagse Kunst, 1988.

Donohue, Marlena. "Manfred Müller at RoseGallery." *Sculpture Magazine*, 2007.

Emphasis Santa Monica. Santa Monica, CA: Pete and Susan Barrett Art Gallery, Santa Monica College, 2008.

Feingold, Danny. "Pier Group—Conceptual Art That's All Wet." *Los Angeles Times Magazine*, October 26, 1997. http://articles.latimes .com/1997/oct/26/magazine/tm-46746.

Frank, Peter. "Art Pick: Plane Speaking." *LA Weekly*, September 2007.

Gercke, Hans. *Foreign Beauty, We Don't Want You*. In *Manfred Müller*. Heidelberg: Heidelberger Kunstverein, 1992.

Hegewisch, Katharina. "Der Philip-Morris-Kunstwettbewerb: DIMENSION." In *Neue Malerei in Deutschland, Dimension IV*. Munich: Prestel Verlag, 1983.

Herbert, Simon. "Artist Profile." *Art Ltd.*, July 2007.

Hofmann, Walter Jürgen. *Leonardo und die neue Kunst*. Münsterschwarzach: Vier-Türme Verlag, 1981.

Illouz, Tiphaine. "Manfred Müller, modeleur d'espaces." *À Vivre*, November/December 2005.

Kohl, Jeanette. "Artwork in Times of Diminishing Distances." In *BoñAngeles*. Santa Monica: Santa Monica Museum of Art; Bonn: Kunstmuseum Bonn, 1989.

"L'atelier de l'artiste Manfred Müller à Los Angeles." *Architectures À Vivre* 58 (January/February 2011).

McKenna, Kristine. Interview with the artist. In *Manfred Müller: Any Given Shape*. Los Angeles: [n.p.], 2001.

Nixon, Christopher. "Art-Home Works." *Los Angeles Magazine*, November 1999.

Pohlen, Annelie. "Mitten im Werktag." In *Bonner Kunstverein*. Bonn: Bonner Kunstverein, 1985.

———. "Wechsel Ströme: Zwischen Forschung und Fiktion, Annäherung an Skulptur heute." In *Skulptur heute, Dimension IV*. Kunsthalle Köln, Kunsthalle Berlin, Villa Stuck München; Philip Morris, 1986.

Pohlen, Annelie, and Manfred Müller. *Manfred Müller: Skulpturen und Rauminszenierungen*. Bonn: Bonner Kunstverein, 1986.

Riquelme, Kathleen. "The Manfred Müller Studio." In *The Studio Book*. New York: Universe, 2004.

Rütz K., Jutta. *Manfred Müller: Scenic Lyricism*. Mexico City: Museo Universitario del Chopo, 1999.

Schneckenburger, Manfred. *Kehraus und Skulptur*. In Hans Henning Hahn, *Cicero: Kronprinzenstrasse 27*. Düsseldorf: [n.p.], 1990.

————. *The Purity Laws No Longer Hold True*. In *Manfred Müller*. Heidelberg: Heidelberger Kunstverein, 1992.

Schrenk, Klaus. "Schöne Fremde." In *BoñAngeles*. Santa Monica: Santa Monica Museum of Art; Bonn: Kunstmuseum Bonn, 1989.

Schulz, Max F. "A Bi-Focal Aperçu: The German-American Art of Manfred Müller." In *Human Conditions: Three Solo Installations* (Manfred Müller, Laurie Litowitz, Marta Palau). Los Angeles: Fisher Gallery, University of Southern California, 2003.

"Spooky, Unsettling, Mad." *Art Talk*, hosted by Edward Goldman, KCRW, Santa Monica, CA. September 16, 2008. http://www.kcrw.com/etc/programs/at/at080916spooky_unsettling_ma.

Stempel, Karin. "Figurationen: Der Zusammenhang der Dinge." In *Figurationen*. Flottmann Halle: Heine Verlag, 1988.

Syring, Marie Luise. *Rohre bluten Kohle*. Cologne: Galerie Jöllenbeck, 1988.

Weinberg, Lauren. "Manfred Müller." *Art News*, February 2008.

"West Coast Special." *Art das Kunstmagazin*, December 1997.

Wiese, Stephan von. "Die Verwandlung des Gewöhnlichen: unzeitgemäss." In *Ucronia*. Turin: [n.p.], 1987.

"Zwischen Rhein und Weser." Text from WDR radio program hosted by Enno Hungerland, Cologne, July 6, 1979. In *Projekt Wupper*. Düsseldorf: Kunst und Museumsverein Wuppertal, 1979.

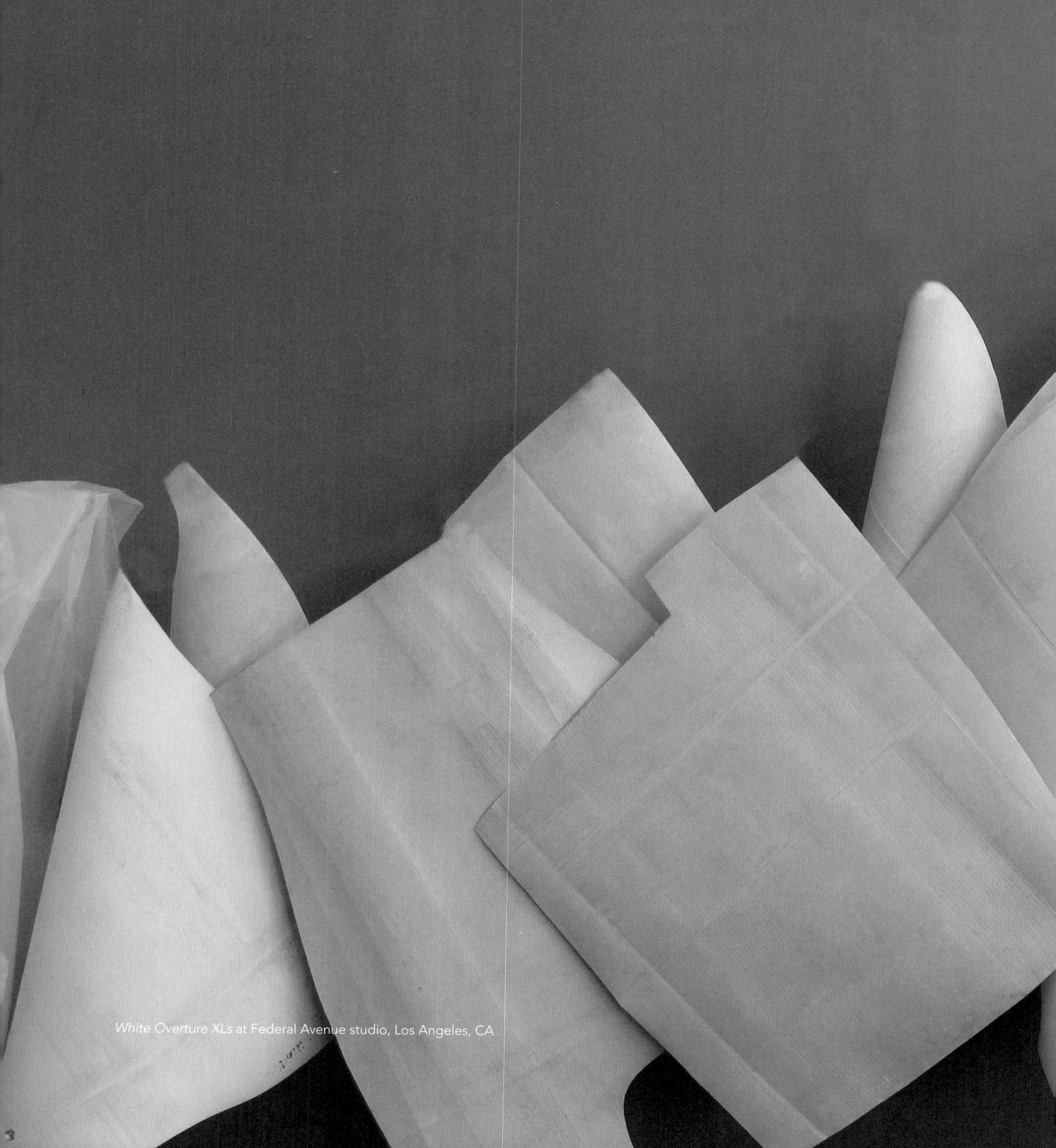

White Overture XLs at Federal Avenue studio, Los Angeles, CA

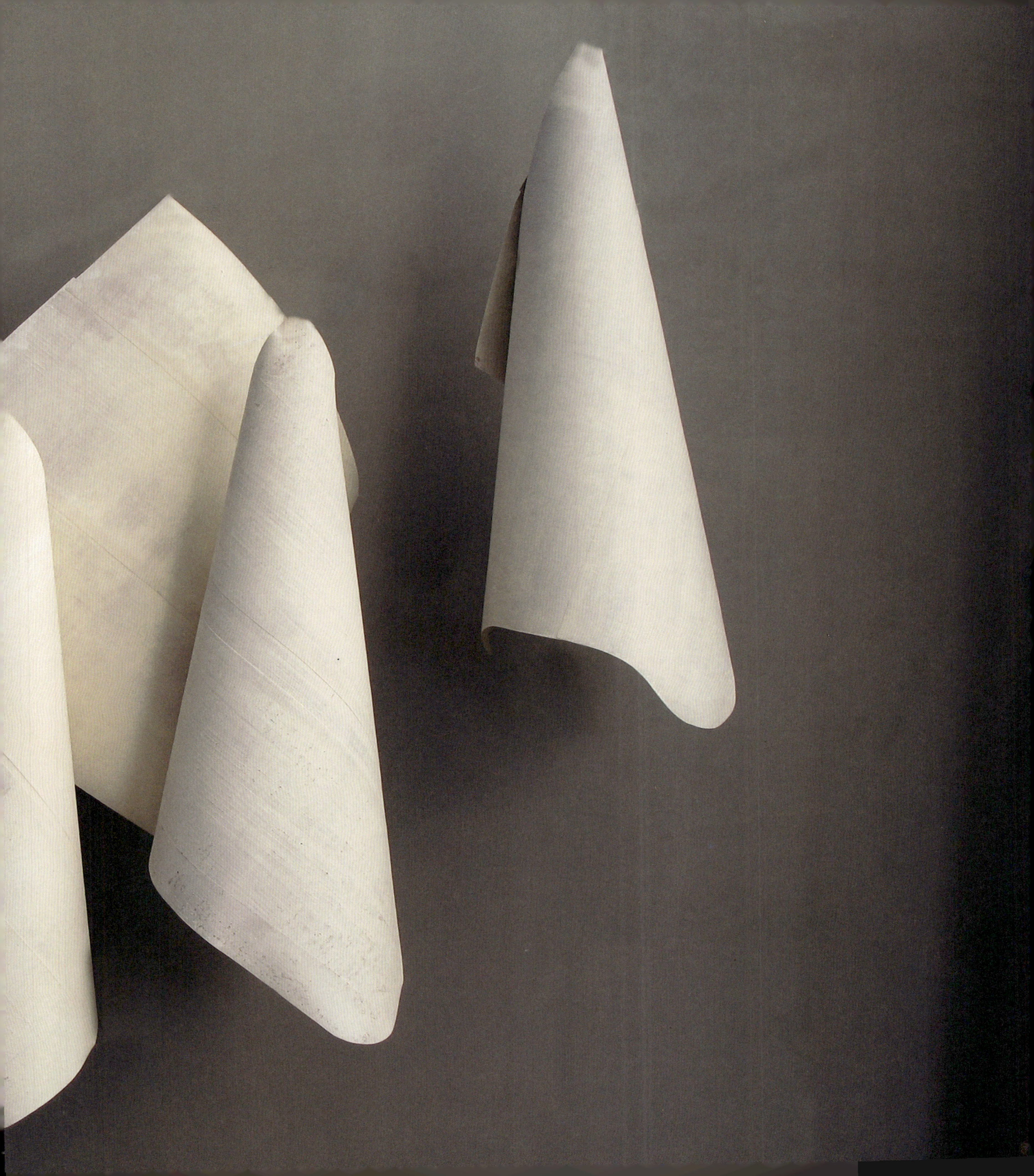

ARTIST'S ACKNOWLEDGMENTS

A special thanks to ROSEGALLERY
  (Rose Shoshana, Mark Giorgione,
  Shaun McCracken, Kelsey Shell,
  Hannah Sloan, Molly Toberer,
  Rudolfo Canseco, Dave Crotwell,
  Carina Ramirez, Sofia Bernstein)
The Frederick R. Weisman Art Foundation
Ray and Wyn Ritchie Evans Foundation
Ann and Roy Boyd, Roy Boyd Gallery
Mike Karstens Galerie
Nada Alavanja
Colette, Aurelia, and Genoveva
  Álvarez Urbajtel
Ulrike Arnold
Lea and Bruce Berman
Julie and Brian Biel
Shoshana and Wayne Blank
Sabine Bonhoff
Martin Brest
Jeff Bridges
Jo Ann Callis and David Pann
Gricelda Canales
Scott Canty
Gianna Carotenuto
Diane and William Cobert
Trish, Jan, Alexander, and Anneke
  de Bont
Godeleine de Rosamel and Ira Ziering
Alice and Bernd Dieckmann
Erla and Tryggvi Dögg Ingjaldsdóttir
Marlena Donohue
Lutz Driessen
Susanne and Nils Dubbick
Bill Eggleston

William Eggleston III and family
Vladan Elakovic
Martje and Elger Esser
Hanna and Yosef Finkelstein
Scott Flax and David Wauch
Eddie and Leigh Fortson
Peter Frank
Mercedes Gertz
Angie and Gerd Glatzel
Edward Goldman
Nancy Goliger
Daniel Greenberg and Susan Steinhauser
Eva and Klaus Greulich
Jürgen Harten
Virginia Heckert
Erwin Heerich
Karl Heinz and Dorothe Moosecker
Beatrix and Ernst Hesse
Thilo and Bärbel Hiersig
Elizabeth and Chris Hogan
Selma and Fred Holo
Hete Hünerman
Gloria Katz and Willard Huyck
Graciela Iturbide
Manuel Rocha Iturbide
Mathias and Diego Rocha Iturbide
Mauricio Rocha Iturbide
Ann Janss
Claudia Kahn and Anthony Foux
Pamela Kaplan
Judy Keller and Ken Breisch
Elizabeth and Dennis Kneier
Erika Koch
Ulrich Krempel
Gerd Krüger
Sarah Lee
Inge Lichtenberg
Rosalba and Ramón López Quiroga
Richard Lovett
Tahir Lušić
Alia Malley and Robin Hurley
Summer and Michael Mann
Ute Margis
Inge and John Markarian
Brigitte Marx
Kristine McKenna
Beatrice McKenzie

Lesley Meyer
Lee Miller and Kai Loebach
Susan Morse
Annemarie and Valentin Müller
Regine Müller
Christoph Münstermann
LeAnn Miller Nealz and Grahame Fowler
Fred Nicholas
Mona and Anthony Nicholas
Marjorie Ornston
Marie-Luise Otten
Marie-Louise and Willem Overdyk
Laura Peterson
Gwynne Pugh
Kathy and John Quisenberry
Marlise Rademacher
Renate and Werner Raeune
Rosvita Rauch
Bettina Rhode
Annette and Burkhard Richter
Klaus Rinke
Lena and Sam Romano
Hannes Rössner
Peter Royen Sr.
Alma Ruiz
Edith Sauvageot
Wolfgang and Sontka Schickert
Klaus Schrenk
Ursula Schulz-Dornburg
Topey Schwarzenbach
Ruth Seymour
Jacqueline, Greg, Sophie,
  and Daniel Stern
Janet Sternberg and Steven Lavine
Kathy Suder and Timothy Potts
Marie Luise Syring
Dr. Regine Angela Thompson
Thomas von Lintel
Bruce Wagner
Shonda Warner
Billie Milam Weisman
Meridee Williams
Jane and Michael Wilson
Axel Zitzmann
Thomas Zöller

CONTRIBUTORS

The preparation of a catalogue is always a collaborative effort, and I am grateful to the following people for contributing their extraordinary expertise and experience. This project has been greatly enriched because of their involvement.

Claudia Bohn-Spector is an independent scholar and curator with a doctorate in art history from the University of Munich, Germany. She has worked in various roles for such institutions as the J. Paul Getty Trust, Los Angeles; the National Gallery of Art, Washington, DC; and the International Center of Photography and the Museum of Modern Art in New York. Her most recent projects include the exhibitions *Speaking in Tongues: Wallace Berman and Robert Heinecken* at the Armory Center for the Arts in Pasadena, CA, and *This Side of Paradise: Body and Landscape in Los Angeles Photographs* at the Huntington Library in San Marino, CA. She is also the founding publisher of Thistle & Weed Press, a small independent press specializing in limited edition art books.

Independent curator **Howard N. Fox** was curator of contemporary art from 1985 through 2008 at the Los Angeles County Museum of Art (LACMA), where he organized numerous major exhibitions and authored their catalogues, including *Avant-Garde in the Eighties, A Primal Spirit: Ten Contemporary Japanese Sculptors, Lari Pittman,* and *Eleanor Antin.* Often focusing on issues of content and meaning in contemporary art, Fox has published widely, and he authored a principal essay for the catalogue accompanying the 2006 exhibition *Los Angeles 1955–1985: Birth of an Art Capital*, organized by the Centre Georges Pompidou, Paris. He is currently serving as guest curator for *Playing with Fire: The Art of Carlos Almaraz*, a major survey scheduled to open at LACMA in 2017.

Nora Suárez, an independent graphic designer from Monterrey, Mexico, currently lives and works in Los Angeles, California. Throughout her career, Suárez has been immersed in the field of arts and culture. Some of her initial design projects were art catalogues for Sylvia Ordoñez, Segundo Planes, and Alberto Vargas. In Los Angeles, one of her major clients is ROSEGALLERY. For almost a decade, Suárez has designed a vast array of printed matter for artists like Manuel Álvarez Bravo, Bruce Davidson, William Eggleston, Elger Esser, Todd Hido, Graciela Iturbide, Abelardo Morell, and Martin Parr, among many others. She holds a BFA in graphic design and has received further training in printing techniques and bookbinding.

Nola Butler has spent her entire career in books. Most recently, she was head of publications at the Los Angeles County Museum of Art, overseeing major publications such as *John Baldessari: Pure Beauty* and *California Design, 1930–1965: "Living in a Modern Way."* Previously, she worked as an editor at the art book publisher Harry N. Abrams in New York. Before that, shortly after graduating from college, she owned and operated a bookstore for many years in Westwood, near the University of California, Los Angeles. She is currently working as an independent art book editor.

This book is published in conjunction with the exhibition *Objects Are Closer Than They Appear* at the Los Angeles Municipal Art Gallery, Barnsdall Art Park, February 2 to March 16, 2014.

Supported by ROSEGALLERY

Library of Congress Cataloging-in-Publication Data
Manfred Müller : objects are closer than they appear / essays by Claudia Bohn-Spector, Howard N. Fox.
    pages cm
 "This book is published in conjunction with the exhibition Objects Are Closer Than They Appear at the Los Angeles Municipal Art Gallery, Barnsdall Art Park, February 2 to March 16, 2014."
 Includes bibliographical references.
 ISBN 978-0-615-86454-9 (alk. paper)
 1. Müller, Manfred, 1950---Exhibitions. I. Bohn-Spector, Claudia. II. Fox, Howard N. III. Los Angeles Municipal Art Gallery.
 N6888.M797A4 2014
 709.2--dc23
                                2013048042

Published by Marquand Books
www.marquand.com

Available through D.A.P./Distributed Art Publishers
155 Sixth Avenue, 2nd Floor, New York, NY 10013
Tel: (212) 627-1999; fax: (212) 627-9484
www.artbook.com

Edited by Nola Butler
Designed by Nora Suárez
Typeset in Avenir and Kelson Sans by Brielyn Flones
Proofread by Carrie Wicks
Color management by iocolor, Seattle
Printed and bound in China by Artron Color Printing, Co., Ltd.

Photography credits: pp. 6--13, 36–39, 43, 81, 83–85, 88, 90–91, 102, 104–7, 115: Vladan Elakovic; pp. 19, 21, 22 (left), 25–31, 48–55, 58–59, 64–67, 70–71, 73–75, 93, 98–101, 116–17, 122–23: Manfred Müller; pp. 22–23: Christoph Rihs; pp. 35, 96–97: David Familian; pp. 45, 110–11, 156–57: Kelsey Shell; pp. 78–79: Rose Shoshana; pp. 87, 108–9, 118–21, 124–25, 128–29, 131–33, 135, 137, 139–41: Shaun McCracken; pp. 126–27: Christoph Münstermann

Cover:
Coat Survivor, 1999